THE EDUCATION OF MAN

THE
EDUCATION
OF MAN

BY

FRIEDRICH FROEBEL

AUGUSTUS M. KELLEY • PUBLISHERS
CLIFTON 1974

First Published in English 1887
Revised Edition 1900
(*New York*: D. Appleton, 1900)

Reprinted 1974 by

Augustus M. Kelley Publishers

Clifton New Jersey 07012

Library of Congress Cataloging in Publication Data

Froebel, Friedrich Wilhelm August, 1782-1852.
    The education of man.

    Reprint of the 1900 ed. published by Appleton,
New York, in series: International education series.
    1. Education. I. Title.
LB1153.H15 1974   370   73-21967
ISBN 0-678-00764-0

PRINTED IN THE UNITED STATES OF AMERICA
by SENTRY PRESS, NEW YORK, N. Y. 10013
Bound by A. HOROWITZ & SON, CLIFTON, N. J.

EDITOR'S PREFACE.

THIS work of Froebel admits us into his philosophy, and shows us the fundamental principles upon which he based the kindergarten system. His great word is *inner connection*. There must be an inner connection between the pupil's mind and the objects which he studies, and this shall determine what to study. There must be an inner connection in those objects among themselves which determines their succession and the order in which they are to be taken up in the course of instruction. Finally, there is an inner connection within the soul that unites the faculties of feeling, perception, phantasy, thought, and volition, and determines the law of their unfolding. Inner connection is in fact the law of development, the principle of evolution, and Froebel is the Educational Reformer who has done more than all the rest to make valid in education what the Germans call the "developing method."

Unlike Pestalozzi, Froebel was a philosopher. The great word of the former is *immediate perception* (*anschauen*). Pestalozzi struggled to make all education begin with immediate perception and abide with it for a long period. Because, say his followers, sense-

perception is the source of all our knowledge. Froebel
and his disciples would defend the great educational reformer by saying that by beginning with immediate
perception education is sure of arousing the self-activity
of the pupil. Froebel's aim is to educate the pupil
through his self-activity. This, we see at once, goes
much further than the cultivation of perception. The
pupil unfolds his will-power quite as much as his sense-
perception, and by this arrives in the surest way at thinking reason, which is the culmination of self-activity.
The child is to begin with what he can easily grasp.
That is well. But he must also begin with that which
is attractive to him. The best of all is to begin with
that activity which, while easy and attractive, leads him
forward, develops all his powers, and makes him
master of himself.

Froebel goes down into the genesis of objects of
study in order to discover the relation of such objects
to the nourishment of mind. The chemists and physi-
ologists have ascertained the relation of bread and meat
to the sustenance of human life. Froebel has investi-
gated the relation of the child's activities in play to the
growth of his mind. The mind grows by self-revelation.
In play the child ascertains what he can do, and discovers his possibilities of will and thought by exerting
his power spontaneously. In work he follows a task
prescribed for him by another, and does not reveal his
own proclivities and inclinations, but another's. In
play he reveals his own original power. But there are
two selves in the child—one is peculiar, arbitrary, capricious, different from all others, and hostile to them,
and is founded on short-sighted egotism. The other

self is reason, common to all humanity, unselfish and universal, feeding on truth and beauty and holiness. Both of these selves are manifested in play. There is revelation of bad as well as of good. Froebel, accordingly, attempts to organize a system of education that will unfold the rational self and chain down the irrational. He wishes to cultivate selfhood and repress selfishness. This must be done, if done effectively, by the pupil himself. If he does not chain the demon within him, external constraint will do it, but at the same time place its chains on the human being who has permitted his demon to go loose. Self-conquest is the only basis of true freedom.

The insights of Froebel into the unfolding of rational selfhood have enabled him to organize the method of infant education to which he, in 1840, gave the name of "Kindergarten." In the work here presented to the public, which was published fourteen years before that date, we have a discussion of the essential ideas which moved him in his subsequent experiments to discover the methods and more especially the *appliances* to be employed in early education.

Pestalozzi uttered the noble sentiment that all should be educated. All children of men are children of the same God, and all are born for an infinite career. This Christian doctrine he construed to mean that all should receive alike a school education, developing the intellect, and giving it possession of the power to master the treasures of science—the wisdom of the race. This intellectual education it should have, as well as religious and moral education and training in a special industrial calling (education in religion, morality, and industry had long been conceded). Froebel shares Pestalozzi's enlightened sentiments, but goes further in the matter of method. He invents an efficient means for securing the development of the child between the ages of three and six years—a period when the child is not yet ready for the conventional studies of the school—a period when he is not mature enough for work, and when there is no temptation on the part of the parent to employ him at any labor. The child has, by the beginning of his fourth year, begun to outgrow the merely family life, and to look at the outside world with interest. He endeavors to symbolize life as it appears to him by plays and games. The parents are unable to give the child within the house all the education that he needs at this period. He needs association with other children and with teachers from beyond the family circle. Froebel's invention is the happiest educational means for this symbolic epoch of infancy.

Froebel sees better than other educators the true means of educating the feelings, and especially the religious feelings. He reaches those feelings that are the germs of the intellect and will. It must be always borne in mind that clear ideas and useful deeds exist in the heart as undefined sentiments before they are born in the intellect and will.

Froebel is, in a peculiar sense, a religious teacher. All who read this book on the Education of Man will see that he is not only full of faith in God, but that his intellect is likewise illumined by theology. He sees the worlds of physical nature and human history as firmly established on a divine unity which to him is no abstraction but a creative might and a living Providence.

God to him is infinite reason. Pestalozzi has the piety of the heart, while Froebel has also the piety of the in. tellect, which sees God as the principle of truth.

The work before us is divided substantially into two parts: The first deals with general principles and considers the development of man during infancy and boy. hood. The second part (beginning with § 60) discusses the chief subjects of instruction, grouping them under (1) religion, (2) natural science and mathematics, (3) language, (4) art.

Especial attention is called to §§ 68–73, wherein the author deduces the forms of the crystal exhaustively from the nature of force and space, and makes some application of it to botany and human development. This deduction is worthy of the fertile and suggestive mind of Schelling or Oken. In subsequent sections he asserts (to our no small surprise) that even mathematics is the expression of life as such.

But Parts I and II (§§ 1–44) contain the most important doctrines of the work, and deserve a thorough annual study by every teacher's reading club in the land. A good plan for study is to form small classes of three to eight members, and meet weekly for two hours' discussion of the text, sentence by sentence. The slower one goes over the book, the faster grows his original power of thinking, and his ability to read profound and difficult writings.

Perhaps the greatest merit of Froebel's system is to be found in the fact that it furnishes a deep philosophy for the teachers. Most pedagogic works furnish only a code of management for the school-room. Froebel gives a view of the world in substantial agreement with the spiritual systems of philosophy that have prevailed in the world. A view of the world is a perpetual stimulant to thought—always prompting one to reflect on the immediate fact or event before him, and to discover its relation to the ultimate principle of the universe. It is the only antidote for the constant tendency of the teacher to sink into a dead formalism, the effect of too much iteration and of the practice of adjusting knowledge to the needs of the feeble-minded by perpetual explanation of what is already simple *ad nauseam* for the mature intelligence of the teacher. It produces a sort of pedagogical cramp in the soul for which there is no remedy like a philosophical view of the world, unless, perhaps, it be the study of the greatest poets, Shakespeare, Dante, or Homer. It is, I am persuaded, this fact—that Froebel refers his principles to a philosophic view of the world—that explains the almost fanatical zeal of his followers, and, what is far more significant, the fact that those who persistently read his works are always growing in insight and in power of higher achievement.

W. T. HARRIS.

CONCORD, MASS.

TRANSLATOR'S PREFACE.

"The Education of Man" appeared in 1826, under the title: *Die Menschenerziehung, die Erziehungs-Unterrichts- und Lehrkunst, angestrebt in der allgemeinen deutschen Erziehungsanstalt zu Keilhau, dargestellt von dem Vorsteher derselben, F. W. A. Froebel. 1. Band bis zum begonnenen Knabenalter. Keilhau, 1826. Verlag der Anstalt. Leipzig in Commission bei C. F. Doerffling. 497 S.**

The very title-page reveals the history of the growth and development of this remarkable book. Similarly we read in the expressive countenance of a mature man or woman the life history of its possessor.

Froebel established the *Educational Institute* at Keilhau, a small village of about one hundred inhabitants, in 1817. It was not a business enterprise in any sense of the word. Yielding to the entreaties of his widowed sister-in-law, he had given up excellent exter-

---

* The Education of Man, the Art of Education, Instruction, and Training, aimed at in the Educational Institute at Keilhau, written by its Principal, F. W. A. Froebel. Volume I ; to the beginning of Boyhood. Keilhau, 1826. Published by the Institute. Sold in Commission at Leipzig by C. F. Doerffling. 497 pp.

nal prospects in Berlin in order to undertake the education of her three boys. To these, two other nephews
were added, and Middendorff had brought a younger
brother of Langethal, who himself joined the little band
a few months later. Thus the six boys and the three
high-souled men—Froebel, Middendorff, and Langethal—constituted the nucleus of this remarkable enterprise, established wholly in the interest of the new
educational ideas of Froebel.

In spite of many difficulties and vicissitudes that
would have discouraged less faithful men, however, the
institute grew even beyond the dimensions originally
planned for it. Froebel had intended to limit it to
twenty-four pupils and the three teachers mentioned,
but circumstances seemed to render it desirable or necessary to admit a greater number of pupils. Possibly
this very success aroused the hostility of low-minded
men, which led to persecution by the Prussian Govern-
ment on political and religious grounds, and the scattering of the three friends; and would have submerged
the institute itself had it not been saved by the tact of
Barop, who joined the enterprise in 1823, and assumed
its control in 1833. Froebel himself had left it in
1831.

The persecutions on the part of the Prussian Gov-
ernment induced the local duke to send Superintendent
Zech to inspect the institution. The report of this visit
throws so much light upon the character of Froebel's
work and aims that I translate its essential portions in
this place. He says, among other things :

" Both days which I passed in the institute, almost
as one of its members, as it were, were in every way

pleasant to me, highly interesting, and instructive. They increased and strengthened my respect for the institute as a whole, as well as for its director, who upheld and maintained it amid the storms of care and want with rare persistence and with the purest and most unselfish zeal. It is most pleasing to feel the influence which goes out from the buoyant, vigorous, free, and yet orderly spirit that pervades this institution, both in the lessons and at other times.

"I found here what is never seen in actual practical life, a thoroughly and intimately united family of at least sixty members, living in quiet harmony, all showing that they gladly perform the duties of their very different positions; a family held together by the strong ties of mutual confidence, and in which, consequently, every member seeks the interest of the whole, where all things thrive in joy and love, apparently without effort.

"With great respect and real affection all turn to the principal; the little five-year-old children hang about his knees, while his friends and assistants hear and honor his advice with the confidence due to his insight and experience, and to his indefatigable zeal in the interest of the institution; and he himself seems to love in brotherliness and friendship his fellow-workers, as the props and pillars of his life-work, which to him is truly a holy work.

"It is evident that a feeling of such perfect harmony and unity among the teachers must in every way exert the most salutary influence on the discipline and instruction, and on the pupils themselves. The love and respect in which the latter hold all their teachers is

shown in a degree of attention and obedience that renders needless almost all disciplinary severity. During
the two days I heard no reproving word from the lips
of the teachers, neither in the joyous tumult of intermission nor during the time of instruction; the merri-
est confusion with which, after instruction, all sought
the play-ground, was free from every indication of ill-
breeding, of rude and unmannerly, and, most of all, of
immoral conduct. Perfectly free and equal among
themselves, reminded of their privileges of rank and
birth neither by their attire nor by their names—for
each pupil is called only by his Christian name—the
pupils, great and small, live in joyousness and serenity,
freely intermingling, as if each obeyed only his own
law, like the sons of one father; and while all seem unrestrained, and use their powers and carry on their plays
in freedom, they are under the constant supervision of
their teachers, who either observe them or take part in
their plays, equally subject with them to the laws of
the game.

"Every latent power is aroused in so large and
united a family, and finds a place where it can exert itself; every inclination finds an equal or similar inclination, more clearly pronounced than itself, by which it
can strengthen itself; but no impropriety can thrive, for
whoever would commit some excess punishes himself,
the others no longer need him, he is simply left out of
the circle. If he would return, he must learn to adapt
himself, he must become a better boy. Thus the boys
guide, reprove, punish, educate, cultivate one another
unconsciously, by the most varied incitements to activity and by mutual restriction.

"The agreeable impression of the institution as a whole is increased by the domestic order which is everywhere manifest, and which alone can give coherence to so large a family by a punctuality free from all pedantry, and by a cleanliness which is rarely met in so high a degree in educational institutions.

"This vigorous and free, yet well-ordered, outer life, has its perfect counterpart in the inner life of heart and mind that is here aroused and established. Instruction leads the five-year-old child simply to find himself, to differentiate himself from external things, and to distinguish these among themselves, to know clearly what he sees in his nearest surroundings, and, at the same time, to designate it with the right words, to enjoy his first knowledge as the first contribution toward his future intellectual treasure. Self-activity of the mind is the first law of instruction ; . . . slowly, continuously, and in logical succession it proceeds . . . from the simple to the complex, from the concrete to the abstract, so well adapted to the child and his needs, that he learns as eagerly as he plays ; nay, I noticed how the little children, whose lesson had been somewhat delayed by my arrival, came in tears to the principal of the institution and asked ' should they to-day always play and never learn, and were only the big boys to be taught to-day ? '

"In the last winter semester the pupils of the highest grade of the classical course read Horace, Plato, Phaedrus, and Demosthenes, and translated Cornelius Nepos into Greek. On the day of my first visit, when I looked more closely into the elementary instruction, I could not suppress the wish that the instruction might

be such in all elementary schools. Now, when I inspected the classical instruction, which has been in
operation fully only since 1820, I was compelled to ad-
mire the progress and the intense thoroughness of the
school in this short time; . . . and I was as thoroughly
gratified by the instruction as I was by the discipline.

"My experience was the same as that of all impar-
tial examiners of the institution. Of all strangers who
had visited and inspected the institution, and whose
opinion I heard, none left without being pleased, and
many whom I deem specially competent came away
full of enthusiasm, and fully appreciated the high aim
of the institution, and the perfectly natural method it
follows in order to attain its object as surely and completely as possible. This object is by no means mere
knowledge, but the free, self-active development of the
mind from within. Nothing is added from without
except to enlighten the mind, to strengthen the pupil's
power, and to add to his joy by enhancing his consciousness of growing power. The principal of the institution beholds with enthusiasm the nobility that
adorns the mind and heart of the all-sidedly developed
human being; in the high destiny of such a man he has
found the aim of his work, which is to develop the
whole man, whose inner being is established between
true *insight* and true *religiousness* as its poles. Every
pupil is to unfold this from his own inner life, and is to
become in the serene consciousness of his own power
what this power may enable him to become.

"What the pupils know is not a shapeless mass, but
has form and life, and is, if at all possible, immediately
applied in life. Each one is, as it were, familiar with

himself; there is not a trace of thoughtless repetition of the words of others, nor of vague knowledge among any of the pupils. What they express they have inwardly seen, and is enounced as from inner necessity with clearness and decision. Even the objections of the teachers can not change their opinion until they have clearly seen their error. Whatever they take up they must be able *to think;* what they can not think they do not take up. Even dull grammar, with its host of rules, begins to live with them, inasmuch as they are taught to study each language with reference to the history, habits, and character of the respective people. Thus seen, the institution is a gymnasium in the fullest sense, for all that is done becomes mental gymnastics.

"Happy the children who can be taught here from earliest school-life (six years)! If all schools could be transformed into such educational institutions, they would send out in a few generations a people intellectually stronger, and, in spite of original depravity, purer, nobler."

I have reproduced this documentary evidence because I desired to show that Froebel was not a dreamer nor an empty enthusiast, but that his "Education of Man," like all his other writings of this and subsequent periods, flowed from the fullness of an earnest, practical life, that struggled in every way to utter itself productively, creatively, in full, teeming deeds.

Again, I desired to show once for all that his educational principles and methods, like his practical educational activity, were not confined to the earliest years of childhood, but embraced the entire impressionable period of human life. It is true, the succeeding vol

umes of the "Education of Man" were never written;
not, however, because they were not clear and complete
in Froebel's mind when he gave us his first volume, but
rather because he was too much taken up with efforts to
live them out practically against untold hindrances.

The report of Commissioner Zeh averted, indeed,
the immediate and forcible dissolution of the Keilhau
Institute, but it could not undo the indirect evil effects
of the Prussian persecution. By this the little colony
was reduced to straits that placed book-publishing and
even book-writing beyond the power of its members.
It is true, in the very next year after Commissioner
Zeh's report (in 1826), the first volume appeared. Yet
the institute had not enough popularity left to induce a
publisher to assume the risk of the work, although there
was still enough substance and faith in the little band
to enable it to do this independently.

Immediately after the publication, however, affairs
rapidly grew worse. In 1829 the number of pupils had
been reduced from sixty to five, and in 1831 Froebel
was driven from his post, although the enterprise was
still kept up in the hands of friends.

The greatness of Froebel's soul appears at no time
in a brighter light than it does in these days of trouble.
On the first day of April, 1829, he wrote: "I look upon
my work as *unique* in our time, as *necessary* for it, and
as *salutary* for all time. In its action and reaction, it
will give to mankind all that it needs and seeks in
every direction of its tendencies and being. I have no
complaint whatever that others should think differently;
I can endure them; I even can—as I have proved—live
with them; but I can not have with them the same

aim, the same purpose in life. However, this is not
my fault, but theirs; I do not cut them off, they do it
themselves."

What high and perfect faith speaks from these
words! No wonder if his contemporaries, still groping
in the darker depths of the valley, failed to see him on
his height, and, still more, to appreciate his higher aspirations. No wonder if even now many, who have
laboriously climbed half way up the eminence, sit down
in weariness and despondency, turn their backs upon
his light, and gaze longingly down upon the rank weeds
that gave them sustenance below. Poor creatures! the
light that holds blessedness they contemn because of
their weakness, and the few imperishable rays that
have entered their souls have irretrievably lifted them
out of the darkness they cherish.

It would be a most grateful task to present in this
preface a succinct review of Froebel's great plan of
education; to show it in its complete unity and perfect
harmony; to sketch how he receives the almost uncon-
scious child from the hands of the Eternal and leads him
surely and persistently to eager, conscious unity with the
infinite source of life and being—how in earliest childhood he kindles the religious sense—the sense of complete, all-sided, responsible kinship with all created
things—and gently fans it into a mighty blaze of universal good-will—how skillfully he enables the child to
gather golden harvests of knowledge and skill from the
burdened fields of experience and life, and again to sow
these in an intensely creative life of unwearied, vigorous well-doing for the sustenance and uplifting of generations to come—how completely he blends in the

bosom of a holy family the interests of the individual,
of fellowmen, of mankind, and leads all to an ever-
creative worship of an ever-creative God—how he imparts to his pupils a thorough knowledge of the inner
connection and oneness of all things, and enables them
to control and handle in life and for life all they know of
life—how, thus, he fills them with an eager thirst for ever
wider and higher knowledge and with a holy hunger
for ever broader and deeper efficiency in whatever
practical calling may be theirs—and how, by showing
the intrinsic importance and indispensableness of every
calling and occupation, he plants in every human being
the feeling that on his efficiency depends the welfare of
the whole, a sense of inner, responsible manhood which
is the measure of true worth in every station of life, a
practical, real Christianity that holds every human being, as a beloved manifestation of The Man, equally in
the bosom of the Father. To the reader, however, who
will thoughtfully and reverentially peruse the book,
such a review would bring little help, inasmuch as the
book shows all these things more clearly and powerfully
than such a review could do.

    In 1836, Froebel, in a remarkable essay on " The Re-
newal of Life," pointed to the United States of America
as the country best fitted, by virtue of its spirit of freedom, true Christianity, and pure family life, to receive his
educational message and to profit thereby. To a large
extent, his prophecy has already been realized. May this
translation help to hasten and strengthen its still further
and fuller realization !

                                    W. N. HAILMANN.

    La Porte, Ind.

ANALYTICAL INDEX.

I. GROUNDWORK OF THE WHOLE.—§ 1. Universal law; unity; God. § 2. Destiny and life-work of man; education defined. § 3. Science of education; theory and practice. § 4. Value of wisdom; need of education. § 5. Object of education. § 6. Method of education; law of inverse inference; misunderstandings. § 7. Originally passive character of education. § 8. Development needs freedom; dangers of mandatory education; proper time for mandatory education. § 9. Free self-activity, a requirement of the divine origin of man. § 10. Human perfection can serve as a model only in spirit. § 11. Jesus, as an exemplar, calls for free, self-active development. § 12. Faith and insight render the ideal mandatory; law of opposites in good education; education itself must obey law and banish despotism. § 13. Teacher and pupil equally subject to the law of right. § 14. Law of spiritual development. § 15. Man as a child of God; as a child of humanity. § 16. Humanity developed in successive individual human beings. § 17. Duty of parents; destiny of child. § 18. Trinity of relations—*unity, individuality, diversity.* § 19. Need of early education; self-activity. § 20. Force, the child's first utterance; joy and sorrow; willfulness; value of small suffering; stage of infancy; need of adjustment of surroundings; the first smile. § 21. Sense of community, as first germ of religious spirit; the mother's prayer; value of religious spirit. § 22. Continuity of development in the child's life. § 23. Creativeness; productive work; singleness of purpose; relentlessness of law; need of industrial work in education; temperance.

II. MAN IN THE PERIOD OF EARLIEST CHILDHOOD.—§ 24. The child finding his individuality; agreement between the child's de-

home-industry; love of the past; love of tales and stories; love of song; symbolism of play. § 50. Actual boy-life very different from this; causes of difference. § 51. Man essentially good. § 52. Nature and origin of falsehood; how to overcome evil with good. § 53. Influence of common sympathy; faults of ignorance; the boy and the wig; the boy and the bowl; the broken window; the boy and the pigeon; how boys are *made* bad; false conversion; the boy and the beetle; ravages of harsh words. § 54. Sins against childhood. § 55. Seeking unity.

IV. MAN AS A SCHOLAR OR PUPIL.—§ 56. Aim of the school; aim of instruction; the schoolmaster; the faith of boyhood; spirit of the school; inner power of boyhood; playing with this inner power; the spirit makes the school. § 57. Need of schools. § 58. What shall schools teach? § 59. Mind; nature; language.

V. CHIEF GROUPS OF SUBJECTS OF INSTRUCTION.—*A. Religion and Religious Instruction.*—§ 60. Religion defined; religious instruction; assumption of some degree of religion; difficulty of understanding original unity; the thinker and the thought; father and son; spiritual unity. § 61. Essence of Christianity; parental and filial relations, the key; Sonship of Jesus; Christian religion; threefold manifestation of God—unity, individuality, diversity.

B. Natural Science and Mathematics.—§ 62. Nature and religion. § 63. Nature and art; immortality of the spirit; nature as God's work; nature a revelation of God. § 64. Importance of nature-study to boyhood; excursions; loss of sensitiveness. § 65. Nature in inner and outer contemplation. § 66. External view unconnected. § 67. The boy's desire to find unity; character of force; the source of all things. § 68. Definition of force; force and matter; spherical tendency of force. § 69. The sphere; origin of diversity in form and structure. § 70. Crystallization; the crystal the first result of simply active force. § 71. Analogies between human and crystalline development. § 72. Laws of crystallogenic force; the cube; the octahedron; the tetrahedron; the "fall" of the octahedron; forms derived from the cube, etc.; the rhombohedron and derivative forms; compound and cumulative forms; organized material. § 73. Living force; vegetable and animal forms; binary plants; quinary relations; relation of animals to plants; law of opposition; law of equipoise. § 74. Man, the first step of spiritual development; evil effects of studying nature fragmentarily. § 75. Nature, a living organism; the sun; technical terms not essential;

technical knowledge not essential; mission of colleges; God every-where; natural objects, a Jacob's ladder; number, as guide; cor-rectness of the boy's instinct; honest seeking. § 76. Mathematics, the fixed point for nature-study; mathematics, a Christian science; mathematics, the expression of life, as such; all forms proceed from the sphere; number, form, extent; mathematics and mind.

C. Language.—§ 77. Relation to religion and nature; their unity. § 78. Language defined. § 79. Language, a product of the human mind; born in consciousness; its mediatory character; significance of word-elements; roots not adventitious; illustrations of the mean-ing of letters and sounds. § 80. Rhythmic law of language; evil effects of its neglect; elocutionary tricks. § 81. Historical develop-ment of writing; pictorial and symbolic writing; presupposes a rich life; satisfies an inner want. § 82. Forms of letters not arbi-trary; O and S. § 83. Reading naturally follows; value of the alphabet; the use of letters presupposes knowledge.

D. Art and Objects of Art.—§ 84. Art, the representation of inner life. § 85. Its relation to religion, nature, and language; its materials; art, a universal talent; mediatory character of drawing and poetry; Christian art.

VI. Connection between School and Family, and the Sub-jects of Instruction it implies.—*A.* General Considerations.—§ 86. Union of family and school; mere extraneous knowledge per-nicious; value of the family; need of soul-training. § 87. Subjects of study enumerated; domestic duties and industrial work.

B. Particular Considerations.—*a. Cultivation of Religious Sense.*—§ 88. Religious instruction, based on sense of community; spiritual union of father and son; religious intuition of boyhood; need of religious experience; errors of dogmatism; contemplation of the tree; renunciation; pernicious effect of promising rewards; consciousness of duty well done. § 89. Memorizing of religious maxims; prayer.

b. Knowledge and Cultivation of the Body.—§ 90. Respect for the body; physiology.

c. Nature and Surroundings.—§ 91. To be studied in natural connection; from the near to the remote; method and course illus-trated; necessary ramifications; additional illustrations; natural history; physics; sociology; objections met.

d. Memorizing Poems.—§ 92. Memory-gems; song; illustration of singing-lessons.

THE EDUCATION OF MAN.

I.

GROUNDWORK OF THE WHOLE.

§ 1. In all things there lives and reigns an eternal law. To him whose mind, through disposition and faith, is filled, penetrated, and quickened with the necessity that this can not possibly be otherwise, as well as to him whose clear, calm mental vision beholds the inner in the outer and through the outer, and sees the outer proceeding with logical necessity from the essence of the inner, this law has been and is enounced with equal clearness and distinctness in nature (the external), in the spirit (the internal), and in life which unites the two. This all-controlling law is necessarily based on an all-pervading, energetic, living, self-conscious, and hence eternal Unity. This fact, as well as the Unity itself, is again vividly recognized, either through faith or through insight, with equal clearness and comprehensiveness; therefore, a quietly observant human mind, a thoughtful, clear human intellect, has never failed, and will never fail, to recognize this Unity.

This Unity is God. All things have come from the Divine Unity, from God, and have their origin in the

Divine Unity, in God alone.   God is the sole source of all things.   In all things there lives and reigns the Divine Unity, God.   All things live and have their being in and through the Divine Unity, in and through God.   All things are only through the divine effluence that lives in them.   The divine effluence that lives in each thing is the essence of each thing.

§ 2. It is the destiny and life-work of all things to unfold their essence, hence their divine being, and, therefore, the Divine Unity itself—to reveal God in their external and transient being.   It is the special destiny and life-work of man, as an intelligent and rational being, to become fully, vividly, and clearly conscious of his essence, of the divine effluence in him, and, therefore, of God; to become fully, vividly, and clearly conscious of his destiny and life-work; and to accomplish this, to render it (his essence) active, to reveal it in his own life with self-determination and freedom.

Education consists in leading man, as a thinking, intelligent being, growing into self-consciousness, to a pure and unsullied, conscious and free representation of the inner law of Divine Unity, and in teaching him ways and means thereto.

[In his educational work this principle of life-unity was ever uppermost in Froebel's mind.   The full, clear, consistent translation of this principle into life, and into the work of education, constitutes the chief characteristic, as well as the chief merit, of his work. Viewed in its light, education becomes a process of unification; therefore, Froebel frequently called his educational method " developing, or human culture for all-sided unification of life."   In his letter to the Duke of Meiningen he characterizes his tendency in these words: " I would educate human beings who with their feet stand rooted in God's earth, in nature, whose heads reach even into heaven and there behold truth, in whose hearts are united both earth and heaven, the varied life of earth and nature, and the glory and peace of heaven, God's earth and God's heaven." Still later he said, in the same vein : " There is no other power but that of the idea; the identity of the cosmic laws with the laws of our mind must be recognized, all things must be seen as the embodiments of *one* idea." With reference to the individual human being, this *unification of life* means to Froebel harmony in feeling, thinking, willing, and doing; with reference to humanity, it means subordination of self to the common welfare and to the progressive development of mankind; with reference to nature, it means a thoughtful subordination to her laws of development; with reference to God, it means perfect faith as Froebel finds it realized in Christianity.

It may not be amiss to point out at the very start the essential agreement between Froebel and Herbert Spencer in this fundamental principle of unification. Of course, it will be necessary in this comparison to keep in mind that Froebel applies the principle to education in its practical bearings as an interpretation of thought in life, whereas Spencer applies it to philosophy, as the interpretation of life in thought. To Spencer " knowledge of the lowest kind is *ununified* knowledge; science is *partially-unified* knowledge; philosophy is *completely-unified* knowledge." In the concluding paragraphs of " First Principles " he sets forth the " power of which no limit in time or space can be conceived " as the " inexpugnable consciousness in which religion and philosophy are at one with common sense," and as " likewise that on which all exact science is based." He designates " unification " as the " characteristic of developing thought," just as Froebel finds in it the characteristic of developing life; and Spencer's faith in the " eventual arrival at unity " in thought is as firm as Froebel's faith in the eventual arrival at unity in life.— *Translator.*]

§ 3. The knowledge of that eternal law, the insight into its origin, into its essence, into the totality, the connection, and intensity of its effects, the knowledge of life in its totality, constitute *science, the science of life;* and, referred by the self-conscious, thinking, intelligent being to representation and practice through and in himself, this becomes *science of education.*

The system of directions, derived from the know
edge and study of that law, to guide thinking, intelligent beings in the apprehension of their life-work and
in the accomplishment of their destiny, is *the theory of
education.*

The self-active application of this knowledge in the
direct development and cultivation of rational beings
toward the attainment of their destiny, is *the practice
of education.*

The object of education is the realization of a faithful, pure, inviolate, and hence holy life.

Knowledge and application, consciousness and realization in life, united in the service of a faithful, pure,
holy life, constitute the *wisdom of life*, pure wisdom.

§ 4. *To be wise is the highest aim of man*, is the
most exalted achievement of human self-determination.

To educate one's self and others, with consciousness,
freedom, and self-determination, is a twofold achievement of wisdom : it *began* with the first appearance of
man upon the earth ; it *was manifest* with the first appearance of full self-consciousness in man ; it *begins
now* to proclaim itself as a necessary, universal requirement of humanity, and to be heard and heeded as such.
With this achievement man enters upon the path which
alone leads to life ; which surely tends to the fulfillment
of the inner, and thereby also to the fulfillment of the
outer, requirement of humanity ; which, through a faithful, pure, holy life, attains beatitude.

§ 5. By education, then, the divine essence of man
should be unfolded, brought out, lifted into consciousness, and man himself raised into free, conscious obedi-

ence to the divine principle that lives in him, and to a free representation of this principle in his life.

Education, in instruction, should lead man to see and know the divine, spiritual, and eternal principle which animates surrounding nature, constitutes the essence of nature, and is permanently manifested in nature; and, in living reciprocity and united with training, it should express and demonstrate the fact that the same law rules both (the divine principle and nature), as it does nature and man.

Education as a whole, by means of instruction and training, should bring to man's consciousness, and render efficient in his life, the fact that man and nature proceed from God and are conditioned by him—that both have their being in God.

Education should lead and guide man to clearness concerning himself and in himself, to peace with nature, and to unity with God; hence, it should lift him to a knowledge of himself and of mankind, to a knowledge of God and of nature, and to the pure and holy life to which such knowledge leads.

§ 6. In all these requirements, however, education is based on considerations of the innermost.

The inner essence of things is recognized by the innermost spirit (of man) in the outer and through outward manifestations. The inner being, the spirit, the divine essence of things and of man, is known by its outward manifestations. In accordance with this, all education, all instruction and training, all life as a free growth, start from the outer manifestations of man and things, and, proceeding from the outer, act upon the inner, and form its judgments concerning the inner.

Nevertheless, education should not draw its inferences concerning the inner from the outer directly, for it lies in the nature of things that always in some relation inferences should be drawn inversely. Thus, the diversity and multiplicity in nature do not warrant the inference of multiplicity in the ultimate cause—a multiplicity of gods—nor does the unity of God warrant the inference of finality in nature; but, in both cases, the inference lies conversely from the diversity in nature to the oneness of its ultimate cause, and from the unity of God to an eternally progressing diversity in natural developments.

The failure to apply this truth, or rather the continual sinning against it, the drawing of direct inferences concerning the inner life of childhood and youth from certain external manifestations of life, is the chief cause of antagonism and contention, of the frequent mistakes in life and education. This furnishes constant occasion for innumerable false judgments concerning the motives of the young, for numberless failures in the education of children, for endless misunderstanding between parent and child, for so much needless complaint and unseemly arraignment of children, for so many unreasonable demands made upon them. Therefore, this truth, in its application to parents, educators, and teachers, is of such great importance that they should strive to render themselves familiar with its application in its smallest details. This would bring into the relations between parents and children, pupils and educators, teacher and taught, a clearness, a constancy, a serenity which are now sought in vain : for the child that seems good outwardly often is not good inwardly, i. e., does not desire the good spontaneously, or from love, respect, and appreciation;

similarly, the outwardly rough, stubborn, self-willed child that seems outwardly not good, frequently is filled with the liveliest, most eager, strongest desire for spontaneous goodness in his actions; and the apparently inattentive boy frequently follows a certain fixed line of thought that withholds his attention from all external things.

§ 7. Therefore, education in instruction and training, originally and in its first principles, should necessarily be *passive, following* (only guarding and protecting), *not prescriptive, categorical, interfering.*

[This should in no way be interpreted as a pretext for letting the child alone, giving him up wholly to his own so-called self-direction, allowing him possibly to drift into vicious lawlessness instead of training him upward into free obedience to law. Froebel, indeed, sees in the child a fresh, tender bud of progressing humanity, and it is with reference to the divinity that to him lies in the child thus viewed that he calls for passive following and vigilant protection. He would have the educator study the child as a struggling expression of an inner divine law; and it is this he would have us obey and follow, guard and protect, in our educational work. It is evident that this involves constant activity in judicious adjustment of surroundings, so that the child may be free from temptation and from the growth of unhealthy whims and pernicious tendencies; while, on the other hand, he may be supplied with ample incentives and opportunities to unfold aright.

Spencer says, with the same thought: "A higher knowledge tends continually to limit our interference with the processes of life. As in medicine, etc., . . . so in education, we are finding that success is to be achieved only by rendering our measures subservient to that spontaneous unfolding which all minds go through in their progress to maturity."—*Tr.*]

§ 8. Indeed, in its very essence, education should have these characteristics; for the undisturbed operation of the Divine Unity is necessarily good—can not be otherwise than good. This necessity implies that the young human being—as it were, still in process of creation—would seek, although still unconsciously, as a product of nature, yet decidedly and surely, that which is in itself best; and, moreover, in a form wholly adapted to his condition, as well as to his disposition, his powers, and means. Thus the duckling hastens to the pond and into the water, while the young chicken scratches the ground, and the young swallow catches its food upon the wing and scarcely ever touches the ground. Now, whatever may be said against the previously enounced law of converse inference, and against this other law of close sequence, as well as against their application to and in education, they will be fully vindicated in their simplicity and truth among the generations that trust in them fully and obey them.

We grant space and time to young plants and animals because we know that, in accordance with the laws that live in them, they will develop properly and grow well; young animals and plants are given rest, and arbitrary interference with their growth is avoided, because it is known that the opposite practice would disturb their pure unfolding and sound development; but the young human being is looked upon as a piece of wax, a lump of clay, which man can mold into what he pleases. O man, who roamest through garden and field, through meadow and grove, why dost thou close thy mind to the silent teaching of nature? Behold even the weed, which, grown up amid hindrances and constraint, scarcely yields an indication of inner law; behold it in nature, in field or garden, and see how perfectly it conforms to law—what a pure inner life it shows, harmonious in all parts and features : a beautiful sun, a radiant star, it has burst from the earth ! Thus, O parents, could your children, on whom you force in tender years forms and aims against their nature, and who, therefore, walk with you in morbid and un. natural deformity—thus could your children, too, unfold in beauty and develop in all-sided harmony !

In accordance with the laws of divine influence, and in view of the original soundness and wholeness of man, all arbitrary (active), prescriptive and categorical, interfering education in instruction and training must, of necessity, annihilate, hinder, and destroy. Thus— to take another lesson from nature—the grape-vine must, indeed, be trimmed ; but this trimming as such does not insure wine. On the other hand, the trimming, although done with the best intention, may wholly destroy the vine, or at least impair its fertility and productiveness, if the gardener fail in his work passively and attentively to follow the nature of the plant. In the treatment of the things of nature we very often take the right road, whereas in the treatment of man we go astray ; and yet the forces that act in both proceed from the same source and obey the same law. Hence, from this point of view, too, it is so important that man should consider and observe nature.

Nature, it is true, rarely shows us that unmarred original state, especially in man ; but it is for this reason only the more necessary to assume its existence in every human being, until the opposite has been clearly shown ; otherwise that unmarred original state, where it might exist contrary to our expectation, might be easily impaired. If, however, there is unmistakable proof from

his entire inner and outer bearing that the original
wholeness of the human being to be educated has been
marred, then directly categorical, mandatory education
in its full severity is demanded.

On the other hand, however, it is not always possible, and often difficult, to prove with certainty that the
inner being is marred; at least, this applies to the
point, the source in which the marring originates and
whence it derives its tendency. Again, the last essentially infallible criterion of this lies only in the human
being himself. Hence, from this point of view, too,
education in training and in all instruction should be
by far more passive and following than categorical and
prescriptive; for, by the full application of the latter
mode of education, we should wholly lose the pure, the
sure and steady progressive development of mankind—
i. e., the free and spontaneous representation of the
divine in man, and through the life of man, which, as
we have seen, is the ultimate aim and object of all education, as well as the ultimate destiny of man.

Therefore, the purely categorical, mandatory, and
prescriptive education of man is not in place before
the advent of intelligent self-consciousness, of unity in
life between God and man, of established harmony and
community of life between father and son, disciple and
master; for then only can truth be deduced and known
from insight into the essential being of the whole and
into the nature of the individual.

Before any disturbance and marring in the original
wholeness of the pupil has been shown and fully determined in its origin and tendency, nothing, therefore,
is left for us to do but to bring him into relations and

surroundings in all respects adapted to him, reflecting his conduct as in a mirror, easily and promptly revealing to him its effects and consequences, readily disclosing to him and others his true condition, and affording a minimum of opportunities for injury from the outbreaks and consequences of his inner failings.

§ 9. The prescriptive, interfering education, indeed, can be justified only on two grounds: either because it teaches the clear, living thought, self-evident truth, or because it holds up a life whose ideal value has been established in experience. But, where self-evident, living, absolute truth rules, the eternal principle itself reigns, as it were, and will on this account maintain a passive, following character. For the living thought, the eternal divine principle as such demands and requires free self-activity and self-determination on the part of man, the being created for freedom in the image of God.

[Self-activity, in Froebel's sense of the word, implies not merely that the learner shall do all himself, not merely that he will be benefitted only by what he himself does: it implies that at all times *his whole self shall be active*, that the activity should enlist his entire self in all the phases of being. The law of self-activity demands not activity alone, but all-sided activity of the whole being, the whole self.

There is much difference between the self-activity of Pestalozzi and that of Froebel. The former has reference more to acquisitive or learning processes that fill the memory with little that bears directly on mental expansion; it is much concerned with long lists of names, verbal facts and formulas, recitation, and with imitation even in reading, writing, singing, and drawing. Froebel's self-activity applies to the whole being; it would have all that is in the child self-actively growing, simultaneously and continuously. He looks upon the child as an individuality distinctly separated from all other individualities that make up the universe, but with an all-sided instinctive yearning for unification with these, with points eager for contact in all directions of being, and his self-activity applies to these outward tendencies, to *doing* in its widest sense, as much as it does to the inward tendencies, or to *seeing* in its widest sense.

Froebel, consequently, lays more stress than Pestalozzi on spontaneity of action, on the adaptation of all activities to the child's power, and on the full, whole-hearted, sympathetic, active co-operation of the teacher, whom he urges "to live (to learn and do) with the children."

Froebel's self-activity is necessarily coupled with joy on the part of the child. To him joy is the inward reaction of self-activity. Here, too, he is closely followed by Spencer, who asks that "throughout youth, as in early childhood and maturity, the process (of intellectual education) shall be one of self-instruction"; and "that the mental action induced by this process shall be throughout intrinsically grateful."

It is a matter of great regret that Spencer, who seems to be quite familiar with Pestalozzi, was unacquainted with Froebel's work. What a weapon of strength Froebel's thoughts and suggestions would have proved in Spencer's hands!—*Tr.*]

§ 10. Again, a life whose ideal value has been perfectly established in experience never aims to serve as model in its form, but only in its essence, in its spirit. It is the greatest mistake to suppose that spiritual, human perfection can serve as a model in its form. This accounts for the common experience that the taking of such external manifestations of perfection as examples, instead of elevating mankind, checks, nay, represses, its development.

§ 11. Jesus himself, therefore, in his life and in his teachings, constantly opposed the imitation of external perfection. Only spiritual, striving, living perfection is to be held fast as an ideal; its external manifestation —on the other hand—its form should not be limited. The highest and most perfect life which we, as Christians, behold in Jesus—the highest known to mankind—

is a life which found the primordial and ultimate reason of its existence clearly and distinctly in its own being; a life which, in accordance with the eternal law, came from the eternally creating All-Life, self-acting and self-poised. This highest eternally perfect life itself would have each human being again become a similar image of the eternal ideal, so that each again might become a similar ideal for himself and others; it would have each human being develop from within, self-active and free, in accordance with the eternal law. This is, indeed, the problem and the aim of all education in instruction and training; there can and should be no other. We see, then, that even the eternal ideal is following, passive, in its requirements concerning the form of being.

§ 12. Nevertheless, in its inner essence (and we see this in experience), the living thought, the eternal spiritual ideal, ought to be and is categorical and mandatory in its manifestations: and we see it, indeed, sternly mandatory, inexorable, and inflexible, but only when the requirement appears as a pronounced necessity in the essence of the whole, as well as in the nature of the individual, and can be recognized as such in him to whom it is addressed; only where the ideal speaks as the organ of necessity, and, therefore, always relatively. The ideal becomes mandatory only where it supposes that the person addressed enters into the reason of the requirement with serene, child-like faith, or with clear, manly insight. It is true, in word or example, the ideal is mandatory in all these cases, but always only with reference to the spirit and inner life, never with reference to outer form.

In good education, then, in genuine instruction, in

true training, necessity should call forth freedom; law, self-determination; external compulsion, inner free-will; external hate, inner love. Where hatred brings forth hatred; law, dishonesty and crime; compulsion, slavery; necessity, servitude; where oppression destroys and debases; where severity and harshness give rise to stubbornness and deceit—all education is abortive. In order to avoid the latter and to secure the former, all prescription should be adapted to the pupil's nature and needs, and secure his co-operation. This is the case when all education in instruction and training, in spite of its necessarily categorical character, bears in all details and ramifications the irrefutable and irresistible impress that the one who makes the demand is himself strictly and unavoidably subject to an eternally ruling law, to an unavoidable eternal necessity, and that, therefore, all despotism is banished.

§ 13. All true education in training and instruction should, therefore, at every moment, in every demand and regulation, be simultaneously double-sided—giving and taking, uniting and dividing, prescribing and following, active and passive, positive yet giving scope, firm and yielding; and the pupil should be similarly conditioned: but between the two, between educator and pupil, between request and obedience, there should invisibly rule a third something, to which educator and pupil are equally subject. This third something is the *right*, the *best*, necessarily conditioned and expressed without arbitrariness in the circumstances. The calm recognition, the clear knowledge, and the serene, cheerful obedience to the rule of this third something is the particular feature that should be constantly and clearly manifest in the bearing and conduct of the educator and teacher, and often firmly and sternly emphasized by him. The child, the pupil, has a very keen feeling, a very clear apprehension, and rarely fails to distinguish, whether what the educator, the teacher, or the father says or requests is personal or arbitrary, or whether it is expressed by him as a general law and necessity.

§ 14. This obedience, this trustful yielding to an unchangeable third principle to which pupil and teacher are equally subject, should appear even in the smallest details of every demand of the educator and teacher. Hence, the general formula of instruction is: *Do this and observe what follows in this particular case from thy action, and to what knowledge it leads thee.* Similarly, the precept for life in general and for every one is: *Exhibit only thy spiritual essence, thy life, in the external, and by means of the external in thy actions, and observe the requirements of thy inner being and its nature.*

Jesus himself charges man in and with this precept to acknowledge the divinity of his mission and of his inner life, as well as the truth of his teaching; and this is, therefore, the precept that opens the way to the knowledge of all life in its origin and nature, as well as of all truth (see § 23).

This explains and justifies, too, the next requirement, and indicates, at the same time, the manner of its fulfillment: *The educator, the teacher, should make the individual and particular general, the general particular and individual, and elucidate both in life; he should make the external internal, and the internal ex-*

ternal, and indicate the necessary unity of both; he should consider the finite in the light of the infinite, and the infinite in the light of the finite, and harmonize both in life; he should see and perceive the divine essence in whatever is human, trace the nature of man to God, and seek to exhibit both within one another in life (see § 25).

This appears from the nature of man the more clearly and definitely, the more distinctly and unmistakably, the more man studies himself in himself, in the growing human being, and in the history of human development.

§ 15. Now, the representation of the infinite in the finite, of the eternal in the temporal, of the celestial in the terrestrial, of the divine in and through man, in the life of man by the *nursing* of his originally divine nature, confronts us unmistakably on every side as the only object, the only aim of all education, in all instruction and training. Therefore man should be viewed from this only true standpoint immediately with his appearance on earth; nay, as in the case of Mary, immediately with his annunciation, and he should be thus heeded and nursed while yet invisible, unborn.

With reference to his eternal immortal soul, every human being should be viewed and treated as a manifestation of the Divine Spirit in human form, as a pledge of the love, the nearness, the grace of God, as a gift of God. Indeed, the early Christians viewed their children in this light, as is shown by the names they gave them.

Even as a child, every human being should be viewed and treated as a necessary essential member of humanity; and therefore, as guardians, parents are responsible to God, to the child, and to humanity.

Similarly, parents should view their child in his necessary connection, in his obvious and living relations to the present, past, and future development of humanity, in order to bring the education of the child into harmony with the past, present, and future requirements of the development of humanity and of the race (see § 24). For *man*, as such, gifted with divine, earthly, and human attributes, *should be viewed and treated as related to God, to nature, and to humanity; as comprehending within himself unity* (God), *diversity* (nature), *and individuality* (humanity), *as well as also the present, past, and future* (see §§ 18, 61).

§ 16. Man, humanity in man, as an external manifestation, should, therefore, be looked upon not as perfectly developed, not as fixed and stationary, but as steadily and progressively growing, in a state of ever-living development, ever ascending from one stage of culture to another toward its aim which partakes of the infinite and eternal.

It is unspeakably pernicious to look upon the development of humanity as stationary and completed, and to see in its present phases simply repetitions and greater generalizations of itself. For the child, as well as every successive generation, becomes thereby exclusively imitative, an external dead copy—as it were, a cast of the preceding one—and not a living ideal for its stage of development which it had attained in human development considered as a whole, to serve future generations in all time to come. Indeed, each successive generation and each successive individual human

being, inasmuch as he would understand the past and
present, must pass through all preceding phases of human development and culture, and this should not be
done in the way of dead imitation or mere copying, but
in the way of living, spontaneous self-activity (see § 24).
Every human being should represent these phases spontaneously and freely as a type for himself and others.
For in every human being, as a member of humanity
and as a child of God, there lies and lives humanity as a
whole; but in each one it is realized and expressed in a
wholly particular, peculiar, personal, unique manner;
and it should be exhibited in each individual human
being in this wholly peculiar, unique manner, so that
the spirit of humanity and of God may be recognized
ever more clearly and felt ever more vividly and distinctly in its infinity, eternity, and as comprehending
all existing diversity.

Only this exhaustive, adequate, and comprehensive
knowledge of man and of the nature of man, from
which diligent search derives spontaneously, as it were,
all other knowledge needful in the care and education
of man—only this view of man, from the moment of
his conception, can enable true, genuine education to
thrive, blossom, bear fruit, and ripen.

[Herbert Spencer, in his ' Education," states this less broadly
in these words: "The education of the child must accord both in
mode and arrangement with the education of mankind as considered
historically; or, in other words, the genesis of knowledge in the in
dividual must follow the same course as the genesis of knowledge in
the race." He attributes the enunciation of this doctrine to M.
Comte. Inasmuch as M. Comte published the first volume of his
"Positive Philosophy" in 1830, and Froebel issued his "Education
of Man" in 1826, the question of priority is easily settled. However, the thought was in the atmosphere of that period. It would

be easy to show traces of it in Pestalozzi, in Richter and Goethe, in Kant and Hegel, and certainly in Herbart; Froebel himself clearly foreshadows it in writings from the years 1821 and 1822. (See, also, note, § 24.)—*Tr.*]

§ 17. From this all that parents should do before and after the annunciation follows readily, clearly, and unmistakably—to be pure and true in word and deed, to be filled and penetrated with the worth and dignity of man, to look upon themselves as the keepers and guardians of a gift of God, to inform themselves concerning the mission and destiny of man as well as concerning the ways and means for their fulfillment. Now, the destiny of the *child as such* is to harmonize in his development and culture the nature of his parents, the fatherly and motherly character, their intellectual and emotional drift, which, indeed, may lie as yet dormant in both of them, as mere tendencies and energies. Thus, too, the destiny of *man as a child of God and of nature* is to represent in harmony and unison the spirit of God and of nature, the natural and the divine, the terrestrial and the celestial, the finite and the infinite. Again, the destiny of the child as *a member of the family* is to unfold and represent the nature of the family, its spiritual tendencies and forces, in their harmony, all-sidedness, and purity; and, similarly, it is the destiny and mission of man as a *member of humanity* to unfold and represent the nature, the tendencies and forces, of humanity as a whole.

§ 18. Now, although the nature of the parents and of the family as a whole may still lie concealed in them, unrecognized even in its dimmest foreshadowings, it will be developed and represented most purely and

perfectly by the children, if each unfolds and represents his own being, as perfectly, purely, and universally as possible; and, on the other hand, as much as
possible in accordance with his own individuality and
personality. Thus, too, the spirit of God and of humanity—although as yet concealed and unrecognized—
is revealed most purely and perfectly by man as a child
of God and of humanity as a whole, if he unfolds and
represents his own being as much as possible in accordance with his individuality and personality. This is
done if man develops and perfects himself in *that* manner and according to *that* law by which all things are
developed and perfected, have been developed and perfected, and which is supreme wherever Creator and
creature, God and nature, are found; if man in his life
reveals his being in inner and outer *unity;* in *individuality,* pure and perfect, in all individual outward reactions; in *diversity* so far as all he does and all that
proceeds from him has diverse relations. Only and
alone in this threefold, yet in itself *one* and *united,* representation, is the inner being perfectly shown, manifested, and revealed. Wherever one phase of this threefold representation is really lacking, or, indeed, only
imperfectly known or understood, we find imperfect,
incomplete representation—imperfect, hindering insight.
Only in this way each thing is manifested and revealed
in its unity, all-sidedly, and in accordance with its nature;
only by the recognition and application of this triune
representation of each thing whose nature is to be completely manifested and revealed, can a true knowledge
of each thing, a true understanding of its nature, be
reached (see §§ 15, 61).

§ 19. Therefore the child should, from the very time of his birth, be viewed in accordance with his nature, treated correctly, and given the free, all-sided use of his powers. By no means should the use of certain powers and members be enhanced at the expense of others, and these hindered in their development; the child should neither be partly chained, fettered, nor swathed; nor, later on, spoiled by too much assistance. The child should learn early how to find in himself the center and fulcrum of all his powers and members, to seek his support in this, and, resting therein, to move freely and be active, to grasp and hold with his own hands, to stand and walk on his own feet, to find and observe with his own eyes, to use his members symmetrically and equally. At an early period the child should learn, apply, and practice the most difficult of all arts— to hold fast the center and fulcrum of his life in spite of all digressions, disturbances, and hindrances.

§ 20. The *child's first utterance is that of force.* The operation of force, of the forceful, calls forth counter-force; hence the first crying of the child, his push ing with his feet against whatever resists them, the holding fast of whatever touches his little hands.

Soon after, and together with this, there is developed in the child sympathy. Hence his *smile*, his enjoyment, his delight, his vivacity in comfortable warmth, in clear light, in pure, fresh air. This is the beginning of self-consciousness in its very first germs.

Thus the first utterances of the child—of *human* life—are rest and unrest, joy and sorrow, smiles and tears.

Rest, joy, and smiles indicate whatever in the child's

feeling is adapted to the pure, undisturbed development of his nature, of his human nature, to the child's life, to human life in the child. To foster and guard these should be the first concern of all educating influences, of life-development, life-elevation, and life-representation.

Unrest, sorrow, tears, indicate in their first appearance whatever is opposed to the development of the child, of the human being. These, too, should be considered in education; it should strive and labor to find their cause or causes, and to remove them.

In the very first—but generally only in the very first—manifestations of fretting, restlessness, and crying, the child is unquestionably wholly free from stubbornness and willfulness; but, as soon as the little one feels—we know not how and in what degree—that he is left arbitrarily or from negligence or indolence to whatever may give him discomfort or pain, these faults begin to germinate.

Whenever this unfortunate feeling has been, as it were, inoculated, willfulness, the first and most hideous of all faults, has been begotten—nay, is born—a fault that threatens to destroy the child and his surroundings, and which can scarcely be banished without injury to some trait of his better nature; a fault that soon becomes the mother of deceit, of falsehood, defiance, obstinacy, and a host of subsequent sad and hideous faults.

However, in choosing the right way, too, we may err in the manner and form of proceeding.

In accordance with the spirit and destiny of humanity, man should be trained to learn, by the endurance of small, insignificant suffering, how to bear heavy suffering and burdens that threaten destruction. If, then, parents or attendants are firmly and surely convinced that all the fretting, restless child may need at the time has been supplied—that all that is or can be injurious has been removed—they should calmly and quietly leave the fretting, restless, or crying child to himself; calmly give him time *to find himself*. For, if the little one has once or repeatedly compelled sympathy and help from others in illusory suffering or slight discomfort, parents and attendants have lost much, almost all, and can scarcely retrieve their loss by force ; for the little ones have so keen a sense, so correct a feeling for the weaknesses of attendants, that they would rather put forth their native energy in the easier way of control of others—for which the weakness of attendants gives them the opportunity—than to exercise and cultivate it in themselves, in patience, endurance, and activity.

At this stage of development the young and growing human being is called *Säugling* (suckling), and this he is in the fullest sense of the word; for *sucking in* (absorbing) is as yet the almost exclusive activity of the child. Does he not, indeed, *suck in* (absorb) the condition of surrounding human beings? Therefore, the above-named manifestations—his smiles and frettings—remain as yet wholly within himself, are as yet the direct, undifferentiated concomitants of that activity.

At this stage the human being absorbs and takes in only diversity from without ; he *s—augt;* his whole being is, as it were, only an appropriating *Auge.** For

* This is a play upon the words *saugen* (to suck) and *Auge* (eye), by which Froebel desires to emphasize the statement that, at this stage, the

this reason even this first stage of development is of
the utmost importance for the present and later life of
the human being. It is highly important for man's
present and later life that at this stage he absorb nothing morbid, low, mean; nothing ambiguous, nothing
bad. The looks, the countenances of attendants should,
therefore, be pure; indeed, every phase of the surroundings should be firm and sure, arousing and stimulating
confidence, pure and clear: pure air, clear light, a clean
room, however needy it may be in other respects. For,
alas! often the whole life of man is not sufficient to
efface what he has absorbed in childhood, the impressions of early youth, simply because his whole being,
like a large eye, as it were, was opened to them and
wholly given up to them. Often the hardest struggles
of man *with himself*, and even the later most adverse
and oppressive events in his life, have their origin in
this stage of development; for this reason the care of
the infant is so important.

Positive testimony to this can be borne by mothers
who have nursed some of their children themselves,
have relegated the nursing of others to attendants, and
have observed both in later life. Similarly, mothers
also know that the first smile of the child marks a very
definite epoch in the child's life and development; that
it is the expression, at least, of the first physical finding-
of-self (*Sich-Selbst-findens*), and may be much more.
For that first smile originates not only in the physical
feeling of his individuality, but in a still higher physical
feeling of community between mother and child; then

---

almost exclusive activity of the child is to take in hosts of impressions
through the senses, of which the *eye* is the chief one.—*Tr.*

with father and brothers and sisters; and, later, between
these and humanity on the one hand and the child on
the other.

§ 21. This feeling of community, first uniting the
child with mother, father, brothers, and sisters, and resting on a higher spiritual unity, to which, later on, is
added the unmistakable discovery that father, mother,
brothers, sisters, human beings in general, feel and know
themselves to be in community and unity with a higher
principle—with humanity, with God—this feeling of
community is the very first germ, the very first beginning of all true religious spirit, of all genuine yearning
for unhindered unification with the Eternal, with God.
Genuine and true, living religion, reliable in danger and
struggles, in times of oppression and need, in joy and
pleasure, must come to man in his infancy; for the
Divine Spirit that lives and is manifest in the finite, in
man, has an early though dim feeling of its divine origin; and this vague sentiment, this exceedingly misty
feeling, should be fostered, strengthened, nurtured, and,
later on, raised into full consciousness, into clear apprehension.

It is, therefore, not only a touching sight for the
quiet and unseen observer, but productive of eternal
blessings for the child, when the mother lays the sleeping infant upon his couch with an intensely loving, soul-
ful look to their heavenly Father, praying him for
fatherly protection and loving care.

It is not only touching and greatly pleasing, but
highly important and full of blessings for the whole
present and later life of the child, when the mother,
with a look full of joy and gratitude toward the heav-

enly Father, and thanking him for rest and new vigor, lifts from his couch the awakened child, radiant with joyous smiles; nay, for the whole time of the related life between child and mother this exerts the happiest influence. Therefore, the true mother is loath to let another put the sleeping child to bed, or to take from it the awakened child.

The child thus cared for by his mother is well-conditioned in a human, earthly, and heavenly point of view. Prayer gives peace;* through God man rests in God, the beginning and end of all created things.

If father and mother would give to their children, as the choicest portion for life, this never-failing hold, this ever-steady point of support, parent and child must ever be in intimate inner and outer unity, when in prayer—in the silent chamber or in open nature—they feel and acknowledge themselves to be in union with their God and Father. Let no one say, "The children will not understand it," for thereby he deprives them of their greatest good. If only they are not already degenerate, if only they are not already too much estranged from themselves and their parents, they understand it, and will understand it: they understand it not through and in the thought, but through and in the heart. Religious spirit, a fervid life in God and with God, in all conditions and circumstances of life and of the human mind, will hardly, in later years, rise to full vigorous life, if it has not grown up with man from his infancy. On the other hand, a religious spirit thus fostered and nursed (from early infancy) will rise supreme

* *Gebet bettet*—literally, prayer gives a bed—another of Froebel's plays on words.— *Tr.*

in all storms and dangers of life. This is the fruit of earlier and earliest religious example on the part of the parents, even when the child does not seem to notice it or to understand it. Indeed, this is the case with all living parental example (see § 60).

§ 22. Not only in regard to the cultivation of the divine and religious elements in man, but in his entire cultivation, it is highly important that his development should proceed continuously from *one* point, and that this *continuous* progress be seen and ever guarded. Sharp limits and definite subdivisions within the continuous series of the years of development, withdrawing from attention the permanent continuity, the living connection, the inner living essence, are therefore highly pernicious, and even destructive in their influence. Thus, it is highly pernicious to consider the stages of human development—infant, child, boy or girl, youth or maiden, man or woman, old man or matron—as really distinct, and not, as life shows them, as continuous in themselves, in unbroken transitions; highly pernicious to consider the child or boy as something wholly different from the youth or man, and as something so distinct that the common foundation (*human being*) is seen but vaguely in the idea and word, and scarcely at all considered in life and for life. And yet this is the actual condition of affairs; for, if we consider common speech and life *as it actually is*, how wholly distinct do the child and the boy appear! Especially do the later stages speak of the earlier ones as something quite foreign, wholly different from them; the boy has ceased to see in himself the child, and fails to see in the child the boy; the youth no longer sees in himself the boy and

the child, nor does he see in these the youth—with
affected superiority he scorns them; and, most pernicious of all, the adult man no longer finds in himself
the infant, the child, the boy, the youth, the earlier
stages of development, nor in these the coming adult
man, but speaks of the child, the boy, and the youth as
of wholly different beings, with wholly different natures
and tendencies.

These definite subdivisions and sharp limitations
have their origin in the want of early and continuously
growing attention to the development and self-observation of his own life.   It is possible only to indicate, but
not to point out in their full extent, the unspeakable
mischief, disturbance, and hindrance in the development
and advancement of the human race, arising from these
subdivisions and limitations.   Suffice it to say that only
rare inner force can break through the limits set up
around the human being by those who influence him.
Even this can be accomplished only by a violent effort
that threatens to destroy, or, at least, to check and disturb, other phases of development.   Therefore, there is
throughout life somewhat of violence in the actions of
a man who has done this at any stage of his development.

How different could this be in every respect, if parents were to view and treat the child with reference
to all stages of development and age, without breaks
and omissions; if, particularly, they were to consider
the fact that the vigorous and complete development
and cultivation of each successive stage depends on the
vigorous, complete, and characteristic development of
each and all preceding stages of life!   Parents are espe-

cially prone to overlook and disregard this. When the human being has reached the age of boyhood, they look upon him as a boy; when he has reached the age of youth or manhood, they take him to be a youth or a man. Yet the boy has not become a boy, nor has the youth become a youth, by reaching a certain age, but only by having lived through childhood, and, further on, through boyhood, true to the requirements of his mind, his feelings, and his body; similarly, adult man has not become an adult man by reaching a certain age, but only by faithfully satisfying the requirements of his childhood, boyhood, and youth. Parents and fathers, in other respects quite sensible and efficient, expect not only that the child should begin to show himself a boy or a youth, but, more particularly, that the boy, at least, should show himself a man, that in all his conduct he should be a man, thus jumping the stages of boyhood and youth. To see and respect *in* the child and boy the germ and promise of the coming youth and man is very different from considering and treating him as if he were already a man; very different from asking the child or boy to show himself a youth or man; to feel, to think, and to conduct himself as a youth or a man. Parents who ask this overlook and forget that they themselves became mature and efficient only in so far as they lived through the various stages in natural succession and in certain relationships which they would have their child to forego (see § 28).

This disregard of the value of earlier, and particularly of the earliest, stages of development with reference to later ones, prepares for the future teacher and educator of the boy difficulties which it will be scarcely

possible to overcome. In the first place, the boy so conditioned has also a notion that it is possible for him to
do wholly without the instruction and training of the
preceding stage of development; in the second place,
he is much injured and weakened by having placed before himself, at an early period, an extraneous aim for
imitation and exertion, such as preparation for a certain
calling or sphere of activity. *The child, the boy, man,
indeed, should know no other endeavor but to be at every
stage of development wholly what this stage calls for.*
Then will each successive stage spring like a new shoot
from a healthy bud; and, at each successive stage, he
will with the same endeavor again accomplish the requirements of this stage: for only the adequate development of man at each preceding stage can effect and
bring about adequate development at each succeeding
later stage.

§ 23. It is especially needful to consider this in the
development and cultivation of human activity for the
pursuits of practical industry.

At present the popular notions of work and the pursuits of practical industry are wholly false, superficial,
untenable, oppressive, debasing, devoid of all elements
of life.

*God creates and works productively in uninter-
rupted continuity.* Each thought of God is a work, a
deed, a product; and each thought of God continues to
work with creative power in endless productive activity
to all eternity. Let him who has not seen this behold
Jesus in his life and works; let him behold genuine life
and work in man; let him, if he truly lives, behold his
own life and work.

The Spirit of God hovered over chaos, and moved it; and stones and plants, beasts and man took form and separate being and life. *God created man in his own image; therefore, man should create and bring forth like God.* His spirit, the spirit of man, should hover over the shapeless, and move it that it may take shape and form, a distinct being and life of its own. This is the high meaning, the deep significance, the great purpose of work and industry, of productive and creative activity. We become truly godlike in diligence and industry, in working and doing, which are accompanied by the clear perception or even by the vaguest feeling that thereby we represent the inner in the outer; that we give body to spirit, and form to thought; that we render visible the invisible; that we impart an outward, finite, transient being to life in the spirit. Through this godlikeness we rise more and more to a true knowledge of God, to insight into his Spirit; and thus, inwardly and outwardly, God comes ever nearer to us. Therefore, Jesus so truly says in this connection of the poor, "Theirs is the kingdom of heaven," if they could but see and know it and practice it in diligence and industry, in productive and creative work. Of children, too, is the kingdom of heaven; for, unchecked by the presumption and conceit of adults, they yield themselves in childlike trust and cheerfulness to their formative and creative instinct (see § 49).

[How deeply Froebel valued the creative activity, and how constantly he studied to keep it from degenerating into destructiveness, appears from the account of "a visit to Froebel," by Bormann. He writes, in speaking of the building-games: "Two things seemed to me particularly interesting and significant. Froebel never permitted the children to destroy an old form built by them for the

sake of building a new one with the same material, but insisted that
the new formations should be made (by suitable changes) from the
old ones. Thus he avoids haste, and awakens thoughtfulness and
patience, and, on the other hand, inspires respect for existing things,
and teaches at an early period not to build from the ruins of destroyed things, but to build up in an orderly manner from the
things that are."—*Tr.*]

The debasing illusion that man works, produces,
creates only in order to preserve his body, in order to
secure food, clothing, and shelter, may have to be en-
dured, but should not be diffused and propagated. Primarily and in truth man works only that his spiritual,
divine essence may assume outward form, and that
thus he may be enabled to recognize his own spiritual,
divine nature and the innermost being of God. Whatever food, clothing, and shelter he obtains thereby
comes to him as an insignificant surplus. Therefore
Jesus says, "Seek ye first the kingdom of heaven," i. e.,
the realization of the divine spirit in your life and
through your life, and whatever else your finite life
may require will be added unto you.

Again, Jesus says, "My meat is to do the will of
him who sent me," to work and accomplish whatever
God has enjoined me to do and as he has enjoined me
to do.

Thus the lilies of the field—which, in the ordinary
human sense, do not toil—are clothed by God more
splendidly than Solomon in all his glory. But does
not the lily put forth leaves and blossoms ; does it not
in its whole outward being reveal the inner being of
God ?

The fowls of the air, in a human sense, neither sow
nor toil, but do they not in their song, in the building

of their nests, in all their manifold and varied actions,
reveal the spirit and life which God has put into them?
And God feeds and keeps them.

Thus should man learn from the lilies of the field
and from the fowls of the air to reveal in his outward
work and deeds—however small and trifling, or great
and weighty they may be at the time—the spirit that
God has breathed into him, as place and time, position or calling in life may require. Then his sustenance will take care of itself. God will show him a
hundred ways; his intelligence will surely always indicate to him within himself or in his surroundings *one*
way or means—and what more does he need?—to satisfy his earthly necessities. And if all about him should
fail him, he has left within himself—not only undiminished, but, indeed, developed in a higher degree—the
divine power of allaying want by patient endurance.

Now, all spiritual effects as finite manifestations suppose a succession of time and events. If, therefore, at
any time in his life man has neglected to respect in the
use of his powers their divine nature and to exalt them
to work, or, at least, to develop them for work, he will
necessarily and unavoidably be overtaken by want in
proportion to his neglect. At least, he will not, at
some time, reap what he could have reaped, had he, in
the use of his powers, in his calling, always respected
their divine nature; for, in accordance with the earthly
and universal laws under which we live, the results of
that neglected activity would have appeared at some
time. Now, if the activity was neglected, how can its
results appear? If, then, at any time such want over-
take him, man has no other alternative than to let the

second side of his spiritual power, renunciation and endurance, come into play in order to allay the want, and to labor most diligently in order to avoid all similar want for the future.

The young, growing human being should, therefore, be trained early for outer work, for creative and productive activity. For this there exists a double reason, an inner and an outer requirement; and the former, inasmuch as it includes the latter, is of the greatest importance and eternal. The requirement is supported, too, by the nature of man as such (see § 87).

The activity of the senses and limbs of the infant is the first germ, the first bodily activity, the bud, the first formative impulse; play, building, modeling are the first tender blossoms of youth (see § 30); and this is the period when man is to be prepared for future industry, diligence, and productive activity. Every child, boy, and youth, whatever his condition or position in life, should devote daily at least one or two hours to some serious activity in the production of some definite external piece of work. Lessons through and by work, through and from life, are by far the most impressive and intelligible, and most continuously and intensely progressive both in themselves and in their effect on the learner. Notwithstanding this, children—mankind, indeed—are at present too much and too variously concerned with aimless and purposeless pursuits, and too little with work. Children and parents consider the activity of actual work so much to their disadvantage, and so unimportant for their future conditions in life, that educational institutions should make it one of their most constant endeavors to dispel this delusion. The domestic and scholastic education of our time leads children to indolence and laziness; a vast amount of human power thereby remains undeveloped and is lost. It would be a most wholesome arrangement in schools to establish actual working hours similar to the existing study hours; and it will surely come to this. By the current practice of using his powers so sparingly and in reference only to outer requirements, man has lost their inner and outer measure, and, therefore, fails adequately to know, appreciate, respect, and faithfully guard them.

As for religion, so, too, for *industry*, early cultivation is highly important. Early work, guided in accordance with its inner meaning, confirms and elevates religion. Religion without industry, without work, is liable to be lost in empty dreams, worthless visions, idle fancies. Similarly, work or industry without religion degrades man into a beast of burden, a machine. Work and religion must be simultaneous; for God, the Eternal, has been creating from all eternity. Were this fully recognized, were men thoroughly impressed with this truth, were they to act and work in conformity to it in life, what a height could mankind soon attain!

Yet human power should be developed, cultivated, and manifested, not only in inner repose, as religion and religious spirit; not only in outward efficiency, as work and industry; but also—withdrawing upon itself and its own resources—in abstinence, temperance, and frugality. Is it needful to do more than indicate this to a human being not wholly at variance with himself? Where *religion*, *industry*, and *temperance*, the truly undivided trinity, rule in harmony, in true pristine unity, there, indeed, is heaven upon earth—peace, joy, salvation, grace, blessedness.

Thus is seen in the child man as a whole; thus the unity of humanity and of man appears in childhood; thus the whole future activity of man has its germs in the child. And it can not be otherwise. If we would develop man and in him humanity as a whole, we must view him even in the child as a unit and in all his earthly relations. Now, since unity in the finite manifestations implies diversity, and since all all-sidedness in the finite manifestations implies a succession in time, the world and life are unfolded for the child and in the child in diversity and succession. Similarly, powers and tendencies, the activities of the senses and limbs, should be developed in the order in which they appear in the child.

[Froebel's demand for manual training in education has been adopted quite generally. However, the utterances of this need relate largely to industrial considerations. It is claimed that the chiefly literary character of school education does not meet the demands of the world's industrial interests; that there is a dearth of talent and skill in industrial pursuits, and a consequent excess of applicants for the learned professions and for commercial and clerical work; that labor is shunned as degrading, instead of being sought as ennobling; and that consequently pauperism and crime, as the results of enforced idleness, are on the increase.

There is much force in these claims, and, unquestionably, manual training will do much to meet the evils they disclose. Yet the need of manual training as an educational factor lies deeper—in the demand for full, all-sided development in all relations of life. In this sense manual training is as much a need of the professional and literary man, of the merchant and clerk, of the capitalist and land-owner, as it is of the artist and artisan, of the laborer and farmer; as much a need of woman as it is of man: its need rests on the immanent being of man more than on a transient industrial need.

It has long been conceded that experience, and, primarily, direct personal experience, furnishes the material for human insight and conduct. Until quite lately, however, the school has recognized this fact only in the in-leading processes of intellectual growth, which are now largely based on direct personal contact with things and life. In the out-leading processes of intellectual growth, in the expression of ideas, the school is still satisfied with words and ignores the value of things; it recognizes, indeed, the debt of gratitude the intellect owes to the reflex influence which comes from efforts to formulate knowledge in words, but neglects the plastic expression of ideas by the hands which hold to their formulation in words the same relation that things hold to symbols in impression.

Thus, in the study of the cube, the child will probably first see the cube, handle it, use it in his plays, and thus gain many notions concerning its shape. These may be expressed in words, and plastically in clay. Both modes of expression will react favorably upon the child's idea of the shape; but the efforts at plastic representation will be found much more effectual in clearing the idea of inaccuracies and imperfections. At every step the child has opportunities to compare the representation of his idea with the idea and with the original, to correct faults and to supply omissions.

While, therefore, this manual training gives skill for industrial pursuits, and lifts work to a high place in the respect and gratitude of the child, it supplies imperative needs of permanent self-expansion as no other educational agency can do. Of course, this manual training should adapt the material of work to the capacities and needs of the little workers, so that it may yield readily to their limited skill, adapt itself without worry to their aims, and thus secure for manual expression an automatism similar to that of speech. Again, the external products of this manual training are more symbolical than practical—the real product lies *in* the child. In this it passes beyond mere industrial training, whose products are chiefly practical and external. Similarly, this manual training would lead beyond the mere artisanship of industrial training to true creative art.

With proper guidance this systematic manual training becomes the most powerful agency in securing for the pupil the habit of success, a calm sense of power, a firm conviction of mastership, which are so essential to fullness of life, and almost indispensable to the success of the school.

That Froebel, in his recommendations of the school workshop, was guided by these larger views, appears from his announcement of the *Volkserziehungsanstalt* at Helba, a project which he, unfortunately, never realized. This announcement was made in 1829, in the full flush of the hopes kindled in Froebel's breast by the recently won favor of the Duke of Meiningen. In the announcement he writes: " The institution will be fundamental, inasmuch as in training and instruction it will rest on the foundation from which proceed all genuine knowledge and all genuine practical attainments; it will rest on life itself and on creative effort, on the union and interdependence of *doing* and *thinking, representation* and *knowledge, art* and *science.* The institution will base its work on the pupil's personal efforts in work and expression, making these, again, the foundation of all genuine knowledge and culture. Joined with thoughtfulness, these efforts become a direct medium of culture; joined with reasoning, they become a direct means of instruction, and thus make of work a true subject of instruction."

Froebel proposed to devote the forenoon to instruction in the current subjects of school study, and the afternoon to work in the field, the garden, the forest, in and around the house. His list of occupations comprised the preparation of wood for the kitchen and the furnace; the making of simple wooden kitchen utensils; the weaving and binding of mats for the table and for the floor; the binding of books and the ruling of slates and practice-paper; the making of a variety of collections of objects of nature and art, and of suitable boxes for these objects; the care of the garden, the orchard, the field; the plaiting of straw mats for the hot-beds, and basket-making; the care of pigeons, chickens, ducks, etc. ; the preparation of artistic and geometrical forms with paper in folding, cutting, and mounting, pricking, weaving, interlacing, etc. ; the use of pasteboard in the making of stars, wheels, boxes, napkin-rings, cardbaskets, lamp-shades, etc. ; play with splints, tablets, sticks and peas; the whittling of boats, windmills, water-wheels, etc. ; the making of chains and baskets from flexible wire; modeling with clay; drawing and painting; and many other things.

Froebel's project failed ; yet much of the seed he had scattered broadcast had fallen on good soil. A stray grain had taken root in distant Finland, where, in 1866, Cygnaeus, an ardent admirer of Froebel, introduced *slöjd* (wood-work) as an obligatory branch of instruction in the schools of his country. The success of Finland aroused Sweden, and brought support to Clauson-Kaas in Denmark.

In 1875 this man was invited by admirers of Froebel to visit Dresden to bring to them a gospel which Germany is gradually recognizing as the neglected gift of one of her own sons. In the mean while the thought had found an earnest advocate in Dr. Schwab, at Vienna, through whose vigorous agitation Austria-Hungary is dotted all over with school gardens and school workshops; and in 1882 France decreed that in her common schools "boys and girls shall devote two or three hours per week to instruction in manual work (*travaux manuels*)."

In the further special directions for carrying out this law in the schools of France, the following points are of interest : Boys from seven to nine years old are to be instructed in manual exercises to develop manual dexterity, in cutting geometrical figures from pasteboard, in basket-making, in modeling geometrical figures and simple objects; boys from nine to eleven years old are to be taught the manufacture of pasteboard articles to be covered with glazed paper, in bending and plaiting iron wire, in the manufacture of objects from wire and wood (e. g., bird-cages), in the modeling of architectural ornaments, in the use of the commonest tools; boys from eleven to thirteen years old have practice in drawing and modeling, in the use of tools for working in wood (planes, saws, simple joints, turning-lathes), and in the use of the file and other tools for smoothing metal casts and working in iron.

In all these cases the educational influence of work as a creative and expressional activity constitutes the chief consideration. They look to the establishment of true *school* workshops, i. e., workshops that serve the purposes of the school, which center in the adequate development of the physical and psychical powers of a complete human being, destined to the mastership of inner and outer life. They differ in this respect from manual training-schools, technical schools, industrial schools of all names, whose specific aim is preparation for efficiency in engineering or industrial pursuits. Of course, in the latter, too, the work will not be without educational influence, but this is a secondary consideration of little moment compared with the specific objects of the schools in question. Schools of this character existed in all the countries named above long before the introduction of the school workshop as an adjunct of the common school.—*Tr.*]

MAN IN THE PERIOD OF EARLIEST CHILD-HOOD.

§ 24. ALTHOUGH in itself at all times made up of the same objects and of the same organization, the external world comes to the child at first out of its void—as it were, in misty, formless indistinctness, in chaotic confusion—even the child and the outer world merge into each other. At an early period there come, too, on the part of the parents, corresponding words which at first separate the child from the outer world, but afterward reunite them. With the help of these words, these objects present themselves, at first singly and rarely, but later in various combinations and more frequently, in their self-contained fixed individuality. At last man—the child—beholds himself as a definite individual ob-ject, wholly distinct from all others.

Thus, in the mind of man, in the history of his mental development, in the growth of his consciousness, in the experience of every child from the time of his appearance on earth to the time when he consciously beholds himself in the garden of Eden, in beautiful nature spread out before him, there is repeated the history of the creation and development of all things, as the holy books relate it. Similarly, in each child there is repeated at a later period the deed which marks the beginning of moral and human emancipation, of the dawn of reason—essentially the same deed that marked, and, inasmuch as the race was destined for freedom, must mark, the moral and human emancipation, the dawn of reason in the race as a whole.

Every human being who is attentive to his own development may thus recognize and study in himself the history of the development of the race to the point it may have reached, or to any fixed point. For this purpose he should view his own life and that of others at all its stages as a continuous whole, developing in accordance with divine laws. Only in this way can man reach an understanding of history, of the history of human development as well as of himself, the history and phenomena, the events of his own development, the history of his own heart, of his own feelings and thoughts; only in this way can he learn to understand others ; only in this way can parents hope to understand their child (see § 16).

[Of course, this is to be taken in a general sense. Froebel's idea is not that each human being must imitate the various phases of human development from savagery to present civilization, and laboriously wade through the grossness, ignorance, and wickedness of past generations to the refinement, culture, and good-will of our day. Froebel's thought is, rather, that the various instincts and tendencies of life are developed in each human being in the same general order in which we find them developed in humanity as a whole. This is amply illustrated in the pages of this work, and needs no additional elucidation. (See also note, § 16.)—*Tr.*]

§ 25. To make the internal external, and the external internal, to find the unity for both, this is the gen-

eral external form in which man's destiny is expressed
(see § 14). Therefore, every external object comes to
man with the invitation to determine its nature and re
lationships. For this he has his senses, the organs that
enable him to meet that invitation. This is exhaustively
indicated in the word *S-inn* (sense), or *s*elf-active *inter*-
nalization.*

Every thing and every being, however, comes to be
known only as it is connected with the opposite of its
kind, and as its unity, its agreement with this opposite,
its equation with reference to this is discovered; and
the completeness of this knowledge depends upon the
completeness of this connection with the respective
opposite, and upon the complete discovery of the connecting thought or link.

[The law of the connection of contrasts Froebel designates variously as the law of development and as the law of unification. To
Fichte and Hegel this is a law of mere thought; to Froebel it is
more a law of life. In a letter to Krause, written in 1828, he states
this quite clearly in these words: "I see the simple course of development progressing from analysis to synthesis, which appears in
pure thought, also in the development of every living thing." When,
in 1850, Poesche and Benfey in his presence compared this law
with Fichte's law of the idealistic constitution of things, and with
Hegel's dialectic method, he said: "It is both of these, and yet has
nothing in common with either of them; it is the law which the
contemplation of nature has taught me, and which I offer to children to guide them in their development." The high place it occupied in his life he revealed to Diesterweg in 1849: "The pantheistic
view of life belongs to the past: we see no longer an inseparable
One, but a Three. *Trinity* has become a corner-stone which people
had rejected because they did not understand its meaning. To
eyes that can see, the trinity of God is manifest in all his works. Do

---

* A play on the word *Sinn* and S*elbsthätige* Inn-*erlichmachung* (sense
and self-active internalization).—*Tr.*

we not everywhere see the Three in *contrasts and their connection?*
And where do we find *absolute* contrasts, contrasts (opposites) that
have not somewhere or somehow a connection? In action and re,
action the contrasts that we see everywhere give rise to the motions
in the universe as they do in the smallest organism. This implies
for all development a *struggle*, which, however, sooner or later will
find its adjustment; and this adjustment is the connection of contrasts resulting in harmony among all the parts of the whole." A
comparatively concise statement of the principal applications of this
law in education will be found in the italicized words near the close
of § 14.

A favorite external illustration of this law Froebel finds in his
Second Gift, consisting of the ball, cube, and cylinder. The ball
and cube are clear contrasts; they represent the one and the many
(in the faces), rest and motion, straight and curved. They find their
connection in the cylinder, which has *one curved* face on which it
moves, and *many* (two) *straight* faces on which it *rests*. In his Ham-
burg lectures of 1849 he furnishes the following systematic presentation of all development, in which (—) designates fixed or constant,
and (+) fluid or variable elements, and (±) the connection of the
two:

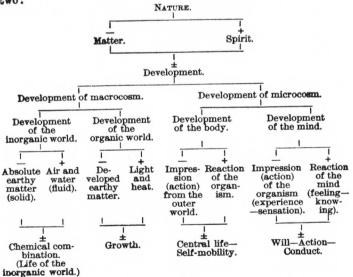

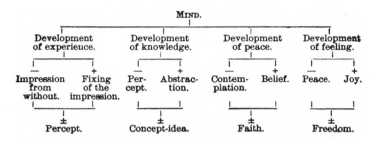

In a highly instructive paper on this subject, Dr. Hohlfeld gives the following account of contrasts and their mediation or connection:

In their *quality*, the terms of a contrast are either both affirmative (*contrary*), such as man and woman, science and art, God and world, or only one of the terms is affirmative, the other negative (*contradictory*), such as yes and no, ego and non-ego, good and notgood. The latter exist only in abstraction; the contradictory contrast simply comprehends in a convenient fashion the sum of all the contrary contrasts of a given idea. Thus the non-ego comprehends all existence with the exception of the ego.

In their *direction*, the terms of a contrast are either *right* or *oblique*. Of these the former are either *co-ordinate* or *sub-ordinate*. Nature and mind, man and woman, art and science are co-ordinate contrasts. In the contrast of God and world, whole and part, body and member, the second term is subordinate to the first. Man and animal, animal and plant, science and a particular art, are oblique contrasts.

In their modality, contrasts are temporal, eternal, or combine the two.

The " mediation," or connection, of contrasts is either *direct* or *indirect* (true " mediation "), and the former is either more *external* or more *internal*. Examples of more external direct contrasts we have in the combination of a horizontal and vertical line into a right angle or a right cross, and in the juxtaposition of blue and red. Examples of more internal contrasts we have in the slanting line which partakes of both the horizontal and vertical direction, in the mixture of blue and red into violet, in the combination of sulphur and mercury into cinnabar. These inner direct connections are excellent " mediating " links between the simple terms of the con-

trasts. Thus, slanting mediates between horizontal and vertical
violet between blue and red, etc.—*Tr.*]

§ 26. The objects of the external world present
themselves to man in a more or less solid, liquid, or
gaseous condition. Accordingly, man finds himself endowed with senses that apprehend more or less fully
the solid, liquid, or gaseous conditions.

Again, every object comes to man in a state of predominating rest or motion; and, accordingly, each of
these senses is again distributed between two distinct
organs, of which one is fitted more to give a knowledge
of objects at rest, and the other to give a knowledge
of objects in motion. Thus the sense for the gaseous
(aëriform) is distributed between the eye and the ear,
the sense for the liquid between the organs of taste and
smell, the sense for the solid between the organs of
feeling and touch.*

In accordance with the law of contrasts in the development of knowledge, the sense of hearing is the
first to be developed in the child; later on, there follows, guided and incited by hearing, the sense of sight.
The development of these two senses in the child, then,
enables parents and attendants to establish a most intimate union between objects and their opposites, *words*
and *symbols*, connecting them into one, as it were,
thus leading the child to see and, later on, to know
them.

[Concerning the order of development of the senses, Froebel's
position may require modification. Darwin's child "had his eyes
fixed on a candle as early as the ninth day, and up to the forty-fifth

---

* The sense of feeling determines the temperature and mere contac
prisence, that of touch the hardness and smoothness of a body.—*Tr.*

day nothing else seemed thus to fix them"; "on the forty-ninth day his attention was attracted by a bright-colored tassel, as was shown by his eyes becoming fixed and the movements of his arms ceasing." It is true that "during the first fortnight he often started on hearing any sudden sound," and once, when he was sixty-six days old, he was frightened into nervous crying by his father's sneezing; but these were probably reflex movements, and had little to do with true hearing, for, even when one hundred and twenty-four days old, he found it difficult "to recognize whence a sound proceeded." All this would indicate that, in time of development, sight had the precedence. Mr. Champneys reports that his child had his eyes fixed on a candle when a week old; not until the fourteenth day did he turn to his mother when she spoke to him, and "even then did not start at sudden noises, however loud, unless accompanied by jerks or vibrations." M. Taine finds the first positive evidence of true hearing at two and a half months, when the child, "hearing her grandmother's voice, turns her head to the side from which it comes." It will be noticed that all these observers find the test for accomplished hearing in the turning of the head (or eyes) toward the point whence the sound proceeded. This seems to imply that the sense of sight is used as the criterion, and must, therefore, have been previously developed.

Preyer found his child decidedly sensitive to light "long before the lapse of the first day"; on the second day the eyes were rapidly closed on the approach of a candle; on the ninth, the head is at the same time energetically averted; on the tenth day the candle, held at the distance of one metre, is viewed without flinching; on the eleventh, it is viewed with evidences of pleasure. Color seems to make an impression on the twenty-third day; and after the first month brilliant objects are the signal for exclamations of joy. Con cerning the sense of hearing, Preyer mentions the difficulty of separating the convulsive movements of the eyelids, due to reflex action from other causes, from similar movements due to sound-impressions. Not until the first half of the fourth day can he convince himself that his boy has ceased to be deaf: at this time the clapping of hands close to the child causes him suddenly to open his half-closed eyes; on the same day whistling near his ears stops his crying; on the eleventh and twelfth day the father's voice has a soothing effect; on the twenty-fifth day still less doubtful symptoms of sensitiveness to sound are noticed; in the sixth week he shows for the first time appreciation of musical sound, being soothed by the mother's singing, which he receives with *eyes wide open.*

Thus, along the entire line, sight seems to be in advance: the child is decidedly sensitive to light on the first day, but, to sound, not before the fourth day; color impresses the child on the twenty-third day, and musical sound not before the thirty-sixth. Additional proof might be furnished, but this must suffice here. It seems to indicate clearly enough that Froebel's position concerning these two senses is untenable.

Later on, however, Preyer shows that to neither of these two senses belongs the first place in the order of development, but that this belongs to the sense of taste, which, even at birth, distinguishes sweet things from bitter, sour, and salt things. Similarly, certain parts of the body, such as the tongue and the lips, are sensitive to contact with external things at birth; and many observations point to a similar, though less definite, sensitiveness to certain odors. This seems to be in full accord with the biological history of the senses, which shows that they are all differentiations from a general contact sense that pervades the entire mass of the lowest forms of individualized protoplasm.

When the senses, however, are once established, it seems natural that in their further development sight, hearing, and specialized touch should take the lead. More than the other senses—taste, smell, and the general contact sense—they enable the human being in his efforts to separate self from not-self for the sake of securing control of the latter. And in this further development, too, sight and touch, leading man further from self in insight, will excel hearing in relative importance and development.—*Tr.*]

§ 27. With the advancing development of the senses, there is developed in the child, simultaneously and symmetrically, the use of the body, of the limbs; and this, too, in a succession determined by their nature and the properties of corporeal objects.

External objects are themselves near, at rest, and invite rest; or they are in motion, moving away, and invite seizure, grasping, holding fast; or they are fixed in distant places or spaces, and thus invite him who would bring them nearer to move toward them.

Thus is developed the use of the limbs in sitting and lying, in grasping and holding, in walking and running.

Standing represents the use of the body and limbs in their most complete totality; it is the finding of the center of gravity of the body.

This bodily standing is as significant for this stage as the first smile, the physical finding of self, was for the preceding stage, and as moral and religious equipoise is for the highest stage of human development.

At this stage of development the young, growing human being cares for the use of his body, his senses, his limbs, merely for the sake of their use and practice, but not for the sake of the results of this use. He is wholly indifferent to this; or, rather, he has as yet no idea whatever of this. For this reason the child at this stage begins to *play* with his limbs—his hands, his fingers, his lips, his tongue, his feet, as well as with the expression of his eyes and face (see § 30).

Now, as has been just indicated, these movements of the face and body are, at first, in no way representations of the internal in the external; indeed, this is reserved for the next stage of development. Yet these plays, as the first utterances of the child, should be carefully observed and watched, lest the child contract habitual bodily and, particularly, *facial* movements that have no inner meaning (e. g., distortions of the eyes and face), thus inducing at an early period a separation between gestures and feelings, between body and mind, between the inner and the outer. This separation, in its turn, might lead either to hypocrisy or to the formation of habitual movements and manners which refuse obedience to the will and accompany man like a mask through all his life.

From a very early period, therefore, children should never be left too long to themselves on beds or in cradles without some external object to occupy them. This precaution is needful, too, in order to avoid bodily enervation, which necessarily gives rise to mental enervation and weakness.

In order to avoid this enervation, the bed of children should from the beginning, from the very first moment, not be too soft. It should consist of pillows of hay, sea-grass, fine straw, chaff, or, possibly, horse-hair, but never of feathers. So, too, the child should be but lightly covered while asleep, securing for it the influence of fresh air.

In order to avoid leaving the child on its bed mentally unoccupied while going to sleep, and, still more, just after waking, it is advisable to suspend in a line with the child's natural vision, a swinging cage with a lively bird.* This secures occupation for the senses and the mind, profitable in many directions.

§ 28. As soon as the activity of the senses, of the body and the limbs is developed to such a degree that the child begins self-actively to represent the internal outwardly, the stage of infancy in human development ceases, and the stage of *childhood* begins.

---

* The women of Appenzell, naturally great lovers of liberty, substituted for this an artificial bird cut from bright-colored paper. Froebel himself, at a later period, proposed the substitution of the balls of the first gift. — *Tr.*

Up to this stage the inner being of man is still un-
organized, undifferentiated.

With language, the expression and representation of
the internal begin ; with language, organization, or a
differentiation with reference to ends and means, sets in.
The inner being is organized, differentiated, and strives
to make itself known (*Kund* thun), to announce itself
(ver*künd*igen) externally. The human being strives by
his own self-active power to represent his inner being
outwardly, in permanent form and with solid material;
and this tendency is expressed fully in the word *Kind*
(child), *K-in-d*,* which designates this stage of development.

At this stage of childhood — when there become
manifest the tendency and endeavor to represent the
inner in and through the outer, and to unite the two, to
find the unity that connects them—the actual education
of man begins, and attention and watchful care are directed less to the body and more to the mind.

But man and his education are, at this stage, wholly
intrusted to the mother, the father, the family, who, together with the child, constitute a complete, unbroken
unity.   For language—the medium of representation—
audible speaking is at this stage in no way differentiated
from the human being.   He does not, as yet, know or
view it as having a being of its own.   Like his arm, his
eye, his tongue, it is one with him, and he is uncon-
scious of its existence.

§ 29. However, it is impossible to establish among
the various stages of human development and cultiva-

---

* A play on the word *Kind*, probably referring back to the words
Kund *thun* and *ver*künd*igen* in the same paragraph. — *Tr.*

tion any definite order with reference to their relative
degrees of importance, except the necessary order of
succession in their appearance in which the earlier is
always the more important.   In its place and time each
stage is equally important.   Nevertheless, inasmuch as
it contains the development of the first points of connection and union with surrounding persons and things,
the first approaches toward their interpretation and understanding, toward the comprehension of their inner
being, this stage (of childhood) is of paramount importance (see § 22).

This stage is, indeed, important, for it matters much
to the developing human being whether the outer world
seem to him noble or ignoble; low, dead, as a thing
made only for the enjoyment of others—to be used,
consumed, destroyed, or as having a destiny of its own—
high, living, spiritual, animated, and divine; whether
it seem to him pure or impure, ennobling and uplifting,
or debasing and oppressive; whether he see and know
things in their true or in false distorted relations.

Therefore, the child at this stage should see all
things rightly and accurately, and should designate them
rightly and accurately, definitely and clearly; and this
applies to things and objects themselves, as well as to
their nature and properties.

He should properly designate the relations of objects in space and time, as well as with one another;
give each its proper name or word, and utter each word
in itself clearly and distinctly according to its constituent vocal elements.

[Mothers and other attendants of children not unfrequently re-
tard this unification of language and thought by excessive indul-

gence in so-called "baby-talk." The child struggles against many difficulties of speech—calls cows, *tows;* calves, *talves;* bread, *bed;* brown, *bown.* Fond mothers and attendants find these imperfections of speech so very sweet that they imitate them, and are loath to have the children lose these charming defects. In the pernicious indulgence of their selfish delight they even intensify the faults and invent new ones, which they force upon the child. Such inventions are *hannies,* for hands; *hootsy-tootsies,* for feet; *pets, mammas, dinks,* and other unmeaning plural for corresponding singular forms. In all such cases it is the mother's clear duty to speak plainly and correctly, in order to aid her child in overcoming the troublesome difficulties of speech involved. She need not on this account address her child any less tenderly, fondly, and soothingly.

There are, indeed, phases of "baby-talk" that are not open to these objections. These we find in thoughtful efforts to aid the child through judicious adaptation of our efforts to his difficulties. Thus, as soon as the child begins his meaningless monologues, practicing certain sounds, such as *tattattatta . . ., appappappapp . . ., dadadada . . ., rrrrrr . . .,* the attendants may sometimes carefully join in these exercises. This will probably teach the child to listen to others as well as to himself more attentively, and will hasten the time when he will find himself able to imitate sounds uttered by others. More or less onomatopoetic words may, for a time at least, be received into the legitimate vocabulary of the child. Such words are *moo,* for cow; *tin-tin,* for bell; *tchoo-tchoo,* for locomotive, etc. Yet even in these cases the ordinary name should soon be connected regularly with the onomatopoetic name, and at last the latter dropped entirely by the attendants.

On the other hand, when the child, in his efforts to imitate the language of his surroundings, fails, saying *wah-wah,* for water; *shoo-mum,* for sugar; *kean,* for clean—the only way to help the child is always to speak the correct words clearly and distinctly. Here there should be no yielding, inasmuch as the peculiarities of the child's speech are due wholly to imperfections of hearing or speaking; and, so far as the child's attendants are concerned, only persistent purity in their *model* speech can remove these imperfections. Of course, this does not imply that the attendants should use "big words" or complex forms of expression. On the contrary, the forms should be simple and closely adapted to the child's understanding. Thus the words, "Baby—drink?" "See—dog," "Milk—sweet," accom-

panied by some deliberate, suitable gesture and a sympathetic countenance, will be solidly helpful to the child without loss of endear-
ment and mutual joy. On the other hand, "Does mamma's little
darling pet want a drink? Well, it shall have some. Mamma will
give it just all it wants, and more, too," are largely unmeaning chat-
ter to the child; only now and then he recognizes a word that
arouses in him corresponding thought, as the sea-faring man now
and then espies an island in an ocean of water.

The observations of E. S. Holden and M. W. Humphreys, which
are corroborated by the experience of all thoughtful mothers with
whom I have conversed on the subject, indicate that children will
learn most readily nouns, and then in their order verbs, adjectives,
adverbs, pronouns, conjunctions, and prepositions. Professor Holden found that at the close of the second year two children had
acquired the following vocabulary:

	Nouns.	Verbs.	Adjectives.	Adverbs.	Miscellaneous.	Total.
FIRST CHILD :	285	107	34	29	28	483
SECOND CHILD :	230	90	37	17	25	399

He excluded from his lists some 500 words which the children could
use only in connection with nursery-rhymes they had learned, and
many names of pictures concerning which the children's understanding was doubtful. Humphreys found that a two-year-old girl
possessed a vocabulary of 592 nouns, 283 verbs, 114 adjectives, 56
adverbs, 35 pronouns, 28 prepositions, 5 conjunctions, and 8 inter-
jections. He, too, excluded the words which the child knew only
in nursery-rhymes, numerals, the names of the week-days, and many
proper names.

The observations of these men, as well as those of many others,
seem to indicate that a normal child, after the lapse of his second
year, need no longer be in the trammels of the imperfections of pronunciation, of needless suffixes, and of affected reduplications that
characterize ordinary so-called "baby-talk."—*Tr.*]

Now, since this stage of human development requires that the child should learn to designate all things
rightly, clearly, and distinctly, it is essentially needful
that all things should be brought before him rightly,
clearly, and distinctly, so that he may see and know

them rightly, clearly, and distinctly. These things are inseparable and reciprocally dependent (see § 33).

However, inasmuch as at this stage language is still undifferentiated or one with the speaking human being, names are for the speaking child still one (united) with the things—i. e., he can not as yet separate the name and the thing, as he can not separate matter and spirit, soul and body. To him they are still one and the same. This is seen particularly in the play of children at this time; how eagerly and (if he can do so) how much the child speaks during his play.

Play and speech constitute the element in which the child lives. Therefore, the child at this stage imparts to each thing the faculties of life, feeling, and speech. Of everything he imagines that it can hear. Because the child himself begins to represent his inner being outwardly, he imputes the same activity to all about him, to the pebble and chip of wood, to the plant, the flower, and the animal.

And thus there is developed in the child at this stage his own life, his life with parents and family, his life with a higher invisible spirit, common to both, and particularly his life in and with nature, as if this held life like that which he feels within himself. Indeed, life in and with nature and with the fair, silent things of nature should be fostered at this time by parents and other members of the family as a chief fulcrum of child-life; and this is accomplished chiefly in play, in the cultivation of the child's play, which at first is simply natural life.

§ 30. *Play.*—*Play* is the highest phase of child-development—of human development at this period:

for *it is self-active representation of the inner—representation of the inner from inner necessity and impulse* (see § 27).

Play is the purest, most spiritual activity of man at
this stage, and, at the same time, typical of human life
as a whole—of the inner hidden natural life in man and
all things. It gives, therefore, joy, freedom, contentment, inner and outer rest, peace with the world. It
holds the sources of all that is good. A child that
plays thoroughly, with self-active determination, perse-
veringly until physical fatigue forbids, will surely be a
thorough, determined man, capable of self-sacrifice for
the promotion of the welfare of himself and others. Is
not the most beautiful expression of child-life at this
time a playing child ?—a child wholly absorbed in his
play ?—a child that has fallen asleep while so absorbed ?

As already indicated, play at this time is not trivial,
it is highly serious and of deep significance. Cultivate
and foster it, O mother ; protect and guard it, O father!
To the calm, keen vision of one who truly knows human
nature, the spontaneous play of the child discloses the
future inner life of the man.

The plays of childhood are the germinal leaves of
all later life ; for the whole man is developed and shown
in these, in his tenderest dispositions, in his innermost
tendencies. The whole later life of man, even to the
moment when he shall leave it again, has its source in
the period of childhood—be this later life pure or impure, gentle or violent, quiet or impulsive, industrious
or indolent, rich or poor in deeds, passed in dull stupor
or in keen creativeness, in stupid wonder or intelligent
insight, producing or destroying, the bringer of har-

mony or discord, of war or peace. His future relations
to father and mother, to the members of the family, to
society and mankind, to nature and God—in accordance
with the natural and individual disposition and tendencies of the child—depend chiefly upon his mode of life
at this period; for the child's life in and with himself,
his family, nature, and God, is as yet a unit. Thus, at
this age, the child can scarcely tell which is to him
dearer—the flowers, or his joy about them, or the joy
he gives to the mother when he brings or shows them
to her, or the vague presentiment of the dear Giver of
them.

Who can analyze these joys in which this period is
so rich?

If the child is injured at this period, if the germinal
leaves of the future tree of his life are marred at this
time, he will only with the greatest difficulty and the
utmost effort grow into strong manhood; he will only
with the greatest difficulty escape in his further development the stunting effects of the injury or the one-
sidedness it entails.

[Much has been said concerning the value and importance of
play by educators at all times. Plato thinks that "the plays of
children have the mightiest influence on the maintenance or non-
maintenance of laws"; that during the first three years the "soul of
the nursling" should be made "cheerful and kind" by keeping
away from him "sorrow and fears and pain," and by soothing him
with song, the sound of the pipe, and rhythmic movement; that at
the next period of life, when the children "almost invent" their
games, they ought to come together at the temples and play under
the supervision of nurses, who are to "take cognizance of their behavior." He foreshadows Froebel even in the demand for the regulation of play by music. "From the first years," he says, "the plays
of children ought to be subject to laws; for, if these plays and those

who take part in them are arbitrary and lawless, how can children ever become virtuous men, abiding by and obedient to law? If, on the contrary, children are trained to submit to laws in their plays, the love for law enters their souls with the music accompanying the games, never leaves them, and helps in their development." Aristotle, too, believes that children (until they are five years old) "should be taught nothing, not even necessary labor, lest it hinder growth; but should be accustomed to use so much motion as to avoid an indolent habit of body; and this can be acquired by various means, among others by play, which ought to be neither illiberal nor too laborious nor lazy." Elsewhere he insists on the need of "entertaining employment" for children, and praises the "rattle of Archytas" as a useful contrivance, "keeping children from breaking things about the house." Even Quintilian, while he covets instruction at an early period, and, inasmuch as "they must do something," would have them learn to read "after they are able to speak," yet would labor to render the instruction "an amusement to the child," and does not object to the use of "ivory figures of letters to play with." He looks upon playing as "in itself a mark of activity of mind," and thinks that "children who play in a slow and spiritless manner will not show any remarkable aptitude for any branch of science."

Luther severely censures those who "despise the plays of children," and informs us that "Solomon, who was a judicious schoolmaster, did not prohibit scholars from play at the proper time, as the monks do their pupils, who thus become mere logs and sticks." . . . "A young man shut up in this way, and kept apart from men," he says, "is like a young tree which ought to bear fruit, but is planted in a pot." Rabelais has his Pantagruel redeemed from the stultifying effects of over-training by placing him in the hands of a wise tutor, who knew how to make his studies amusing, interesting, and profitable, by making them "*active*" and connecting them with life. Fénelon believes in the efficacy of play. Locke thinks that "all their innocent folly, playing, and child-like actions are to be left perfectly free and unrestrained"; that "to restrain the natural gayety of that age serves only to spoil the temper both of body and mind"; that "this gamesome humor which is wisely adapted by Nature to their age and temper should be encouraged to keep up their spirits and improve their health and strength"; and that "the chief art is to make all that they have to do sport and play." Further on he finds that "free liberty permitted them in their recreation will discover their natural tempers, show their inclinations and aptitudes."

In his "Letters on Æsthetic Education," Schiller says: "The plays of children often have very deep meaning, for, to speak plainly and concisely, man plays only where he is a human being in the fullest sense of the word, and he has reached full humanity only where he plays. This proposition, which at present may appear paradoxical, will acquire great and deep significance when we shall learn to refer it to the doubly serious ideas of duty and destiny; it will then, I am sure, sustain the entire superstructure of æsthetic art and of the yet more difficult *art of life*." With still keener insight into child-nature, Richter says in his incomparable "Levana": "Activity alone can bring and hold serenity and happiness. Unlike our games, the plays of children are the expressions of serious activity, although in light, airy dress. . . . Play is the first poetical (creative) utterance of man."

To Froebel, however, belongs the credit of having found the true nature and function of play, and of regulating it in such a way as to lead it gradually and naturally into work, securing for work the same spontaneity and joy, the same freedom and serenity, that characterize the plays of childhood, realizing in all directions of human activity what Prof. Pillans (quoted by Herbert Spencer) asserts concerning school-work, that "where young people are taught as they ought to be, they are quite as happy in school as at play, seldom less delighted, nay, often more, with the well-directed exercise of their mental energies than with that of their muscular powers." In his gifts and occupations he found for the two contrasts of play and work the living connection, making them both utterances of the same *one* creative activity. In play, it is the exercise of this activity that forms the purpose of the exertion and rewards it with joy unspeakable; in work, the external product, the outcome of the activity, becomes the purpose and additional reward of the exertion. Froebel has shown how both may be combined, how the human being— the child, the boy or girl, the youth or maiden, man or woman—may learn to secure both enjoyments through the same effort, delighting in the activity which leads to a coveted result, however distant and difficult of attainment.

Preyer, in his work on "The Soul of the Child," after speaking of the pleasurable sensations aroused in his boy on being carried out into the open air, etc., says: "A new kind of pleasurable sensations, with some admixture of intellectual elements, is noticed when the child begins to effect some change of form by his own activity, gradually gaining some knowledge of his own power. Not only the effects of the voice, especially crying and the first consciously made sounds, are concerned in this, but a number of 'plays.' At first it was, in the fifth month, the crumpling of a sheet of paper, which the boy repeated with evident pleasure. From this time on to his third year he found great pleasure in the tearing and rolling up of newspapers. With similar pleasure he engaged in pulling a glove from side to side (until his fourth year), in pulling the hairs of my beard, in ringing a small bell for an insufferably long time. Later he found enjoyment in the movement of his own body, in marching and in purely intellectual plays, packing and unpacking of things, cutting with scissors, turning the leaves of a book, looking at pictures. At last there came imagination, which animates clumsy pieces of wood, changes the leaves of trees into delicious articles of food, etc.

"On the whole, however, during the first period of their life, children owe many more pleasurable feelings to the removal of conditions of discomfort than to the creation of conditions of positive pleasure. The removal of hunger, thirst, wet, cold, tight clothing, gives rise to pleasurable sensations that are stronger than those generated by soft light, moving tassels, tepid baths, singing, and the kindliness of parents, or as strong as these. Not before the fourth month new pleasurable sensations are added by the first successful attempts to take hold."

He is inclined to look upon the cries, the laughter, and the various movements attending these pleasurable sensations as instinctive or reflex in their character for quite a long time. Even the stamping with the foot in the eleventh month, the stiffening of the body as a measure of resistance in the tenth month, he does not consider intentional. About this time, however, a number of plays and experiments seem to indicate the awakening of will. "Thus, in the eleventh month," he writes, "my child would frequently beat with a spoon against a paper or some other object held in the other hand, then suddenly exchange the two objects, and move the spoon with the other hand, as if he desired to determine whence the noise proceeded."

At a still later period, between the fifteenth and twentieth months, the pleasure of the child's plays seems to be due to the "reproduction of familiar thought-images attended with pleasurable feelings which have been crystallized out, as it were, into relative clearness from the great mass of vague perceptions. Most of the plays which the children invent themselves may be reduced to this, even the game of hide-and-seek (in the seventeenth and eighteenth months), and, related to this, the game of 'hunting for' scraps of paper, pieces of biscuits, buttons, and other favorite things (in the fifteenth month)."

Much that goes by the name of play, Preyer considers as true experimenting, more particularly with reference to the study of changes produced by the child's own activity. In this connection he mentions the tearing of paper into small bits, continued with remarkable patience even between the forty-fifth and fifty-fifth weeks. For this he finds the explanation in the "gratification on the part of the child to find himself the cause of so remarkable a change." The same he holds to be true with reference to "the shaking of a bunch of keys; the opening and closing of a box or purse (thirteenth month); the pulling out, emptying, refilling, and replacing of a table-drawer; the piling up and scattering of gravel; turning the leaves of a book (thirteenth to nineteenth month); burrowing and working in sand; the arranging of shells, pebbles, buttons (twenty-first month); the filling and emptying of bottles, cups, watering-pots (thirty-first to thirty-third month); the throwing of stones into the water. The zeal with which these seemingly aimless movements are executed is remarkable. The sense of gratification must be very great, and is probably due to the feeling of his own power, and of being the cause of the various changes."—*Tr.*]

§ 31. In these years of childhood the child's food is a matter of very great importance, not only at the time —for the child may by its food be made indolent or active, sluggish or mobile, dull or bright, inert or vigorous—but, indeed, for his entire future life. For impressions, inclinations, appetites which the child may have derived from his food, the turn it may have given to his senses, and even to his life, as a whole, can only with difficulty be set aside even when the age of self-dependence has been reached. They are one with his whole physical life, and therefore intimately connected with his spiritual life; at any rate, with his sensations and feelings.

Therefore, after the mother's milk, the first food of the child should be plain and simple, not more artificial and refined than is absolutely needful, in no way stimulating and exciting through an excess of spices, nor rich, lest it hinder the inner organs in their activity.

Parents and nurses should ever remember, as underlying every precept in this direction, the following general principle: that simplicity and frugality in food and in other physical needs during the years of childhood enhance man's power of attaining happiness and vigor—true creativeness in every respect.

Who has not noticed in children, over-stimulated by spices and excess in food, appetites of a very low order, from which they can never again be freed—appetites which, even when they seem to have been suppressed, only slumber, and in times of opportunity return with greater power, threatening to rob man of all his dignity, and to force him away from his duty?

If parents would consider that not only much individual and personal happiness, but even much domestic happiness and general prosperity, depend on this, how very differently they would act!

But here the foolish mother, there the childish father, is to blame. We see them give their children all kinds of poison, and in every form, coarse and fine. Here it comes in the oppressing quantity which does not allow the body to digest it, which is often given only to drive away the *ennui* that torments the unoccupied child; again, it comes in over-refinement in

the preparation of food, by which the physical side
of the child's life is stimulated without true spiritual
cause, consuming and weakening the body.   Here indolence and sluggishness are considered as needful rest;
there the child's physical mobility, a symptom of over-
stimulation, and independent of true spiritual causes, is
greeted as true increase and development of life.

It is by far easier than we think to promote and
establish the happiness and welfare of mankind.   All
the means are simple and at hand ; yet we see them not.
We see them, perhaps, but do not notice them.   In
their simplicity, naturalness, availability, and nearness,
they seem too insignificant, and we despise them.   We
seek help from afar, although help is only in and through
ourselves.   Hence, at a later period, half or all our ac-
cumulated wealth can not procure for our children what
greater insight and a clearer vision discern as their
greatest good.   This they now must miss, or can enjoy
but partially and scantily.   It might have been theirs
without effort, as it were, had we in their childhood
attended to it but a little more ; indeed, it would have
been theirs in full measure had we expended very much
less for their physical comfort.

Would that to each young, newly married couple
there could be shown, in all its vividness, only one of
the sad experiences and observations in its small and
seemingly insignificant beginnings, and in its incalcu-
lable consequences, that tend utterly to destroy all the
good of later education !—only one of these sad experiences, of which the educator is compelled to make hun-
dreds, and whose knowledge can help him but little to
counteract the injurious consequences of the respective

faults in the later life of those in whom he observes them; for who does not know the mighty influence of early impressions?

And here it is easy to avoid the wrong and to find the right. Always let the food be simply for nourishment—never more, never less. Never should food be taken for its own sake, but only for the sake of promoting bodily and mental activity. Still less should the peculiarities of the food, its taste or delicacy, ever become an object in themselves, but only a means to make it good, pure, wholesome nourishment; else, in both cases, the food destroys health.

Let the food of the child, then, be as simple as the circumstances in which the child lives can afford; and let it be given in quantities proportioned to his bodily and mental activity.

§ 32. In order to enable the child at this period to move and play, to develop and grow freely, and without hindrance, his clothing should be free from lacing and pressure of all kinds; for such clothing would oppress and fetter also the spirit of the child. The clothing of the child, in this as well as in the next period, should not bind the body;* for it will have on the mind, on the soul, of the child, the same effect it has on the body. Clothes, in form and color and cut, should never become an object in themselves, else they will soon direct the child's attention to his appearance instead of his real being, make him vain and frivolous—dollish—a puppet instead of a human being. Clothing, therefore, is by no means an unimportant concern, either for the child or

---

* By tight lacing, close-fitting seams, and multiplicity of articles of clothing.— *Tr.*

the adult man, as it is desirable for him, even as a Christian, to be able to say, " Without piece and without seam, only a continuous whole, like the garment of Jesus, was also his life and work, and his doctrine."

§ 33. The aim and object of the parental care of the child, in the domestic and family circle, then, is to awaken and develop, to quicken all the powers and natural gifts of the child, to enable all the members and organs of man to fulfill the requirements of the child's powers and gifts.

[Herbert Spencer, who, although ignorant of Froebel's work, has so many points of contact with him, finds the proper function of education in "preparation for complete living," which is the free exercise of all our faculties. There seems to be little fundamental difference, too, between the physiological, psychological, sociological, and ethical limitations of complete living on the part of Spencer, and the life-unity with self, mankind, nature, the universe, and God demanded by Froebel. (Compare § 19.)— Tr.]

The natural mother does all this instinctively, without instruction and direction ; but this is not enough : it is needful that she should do it consciously, as a conscious being acting upon another being which is growing into consciousness (see § 56), and consciously tending toward the continuous development of the human being, in a certain inner living connection (see § 2).

[That instinct alone is not sufficient to enable the mother to guide the child aright is amply shown by the many cruel practices to which children are subjected among barbarous tribes, and by the survival of many senseless and even pernicious customs in the nurseries of even the most cultured communities of our day. Conscientious mothers everywhere point with expressions of deepest regret to the many oversights and neglects of which they were unwittingly guilty, the many misunderstandings and misapplications that blurred their efficiency, the many blunders whose pernicious effects years of

subsequent toil could not efface. Insight will add a conscious purpose to the instinct; it will arouse the sense of duty in the soul, it
will enable the head to help the heart, add wisdom to love, avoid
waste, and insure success.—*Tr.*]

By sketching her work, therefore, I hope to show it
to her in its nature, significance, and connection. It is
true, the plainest thoughtful mother could do this more
fully, more perfectly, and more deeply; but through
imperfection man rises to perfection. I trust, therefore,
that this sketch may awaken faithful and calm, thoughtful and rational parental love, and show us the course
of development in childhood in unbroken succession.

"Give me your arm." "Where is your hand?"
In such words the mother strives to teach the child to
feel the complexity of his body and the difference between his limbs.

"Bite your finger." This is an especially well-con-
ceived action, which a deep natural feeling has suggested
to the thoughtful mother playing with her child. It
induces reflection in its earliest phases, by tending to
bring to the child's knowledge an object which, although
it has an individuality of its own, is yet united with the
child.

Not less important is the mother's pleasantly playful
manner of leading the child to a knowledge of the members which he can not *see*, the nose, the ears, the tongue,
and teeth. The mother gently pulls the nose or ear, as
if she meant to separate them from head or face, and,
showing to the child the half-concealed end of her finger
or thumb, says, "Here I have the ear, the nose," and
the child quickly puts his hand to his ear or nose, and
smiles with intense joy to find them in their right places.

In this action the mother first arouses and directs in the child a desire to know even what he can not see externally.

All this tends to lead the child to self-consciousness, to reflection about himself in the approaching period of boyhood. Thus, a boy ten years old, similarly guided by instinct, believing himself unobserved, soliloquized: "I am not my arm, nor my ear; all my limbs and organs I can separate from myself, and I still remain myself; I wonder what I am ; who and what this is which I call myself ? "

In the same spirit, maternal love continues with the child, in order to lead him to use these things. " Show me your tongue." " Show me your tooth." " Bite it with your tooth." " Slip the foot into the stocking— into the shoe." " There is the foot in the stocking—in the shoe."

Thus maternal instinct and love gradually introduce the child to his little outside world, proceeding from the whole to the part, from the near to the remote.

Similarly, as she at first sought to bring to the child's notice objects as such, and in their relative positions, she soon directs attention to their attributes and qualities. In this, of course, she first shows them in their actions, and only later in their passive conditions.

She says, " The candle burns," as she cautiously holds the child's finger toward the flame, enabling him to feel the heat without being really burned, and guarding him against an unknown danger. Or, she says, " The knife pricks," as she carefully and gently presses the point of the knife against the child's finger. Or, " The soup burns your mouth."

At a later period, as if she would direct the child to the permanence of the active quality, or to its cause, the mother says, " The soup *is hot*, it *burns* you." " The knife is sharp, it pricks, it cuts; let it alone." From a knowledge of the effect, the mother leads to the immanent lasting cause, *sharp ;* and, later, from a knowledge of the immanent quality to a knowledge of the effect, pricking, cutting, as such, *without* the direct personal experience of these effects.

Further on, the mother leads the child first to feel his own action, and then to contemplate the action itself. Thus, the mother delightfully teaching him in all she does and says, requests the child who is to take food, " Open your mouth "; or, when he is to be washed, " Close your eyes "; or she teaches the child to find the object of his action. Thus, when she lays the child in his little bed, she says, " Go to sleep "; or, as she lifts a spoonful of food to his lips, " Eat, my pet." And, in order to direct his attention to the effect of the food upon the nerves of taste and upon the relation between the food and the body, she says, " How good that tastes ! " In order to direct his attention to the smell of flowers, the mother imitates the noise of snuffing, and says, " How good that smells ! Would you like to smell it ? " Or, on the other hand, she turns with the expression of displeasure her face away from the flower, which she removes from the child.

Thus, the plainest mother, who with her beloved child withdraws almost bashfully into privacy—lest unconsecrated eyes profane the sanctuary — seeks in the most natural manner to arouse to full activity all his limbs and senses.

Unfortunately, our conceit induces us to lose sight of this natural and divine starting-point of all human development; we stand perplexed, having lost beginning and end, and therefore the right direction. Having denied God and nature, we seek counsel from human knowledge and wit. We build houses of cards; but there is no room in them for the ways of the natural mother, for divine influence; and the slightest utterance of the child, impelled by the joy and instinct of life, throws them down. If they should stand, the child must be, if not bodily, yet intellectually fettered.

Where has this discussion taken us? Into the nursery of the worldly-wise, of the so-called refined people, who scarcely believe that there are in the child germs which, if they are to thrive, must be developed early; who know still less that all the child is ever to be and become, lies—however slightly indicated—in the child, and can be attained only through development from within outward.

How dead, therefore, does everything seem here; how cold, or, at best, how loud and noisy! But, is not the mother here? Alas! it is not the mother's room, it is only the nursery.

Away! and let us again go where not only the room of child and mother is one, but where even mother and child are still one; where the mother is loath to give the care of her child to strangers. Let us see and hear how the mother, there, shows to the child objects in their motions: "Hark! the bird sings! The dog says, 'bow-wow!'" And then, directly from the word to the name, from hearing to sight, "Where is Peep-peep? Where is Bow-wow?" The mother even ventures to lead from the contemplation of the thing and its quality in their connection to the contemplation of the quality as distinct from the thing. "The bird flies," she says at first about the actual bird that flies. "See the little bird," she says later, on beholding the flitting, unsteady light-reflection that comes from the moving surface of water or of a mirror. Then, in order to teach the child that this is an incorporeal phenomenon which shares with the bird only its mobility, she says, "Catch the little bird," and asks the child to cover the reflection with his hands.

Again, in order to lead the child to the contemplation of the motion alone, the mother says, when she beholds the pendulum oscillations of some object, "swing-swong," or "To-fro."

Similarly, she seeks to attract the child's attention to the mutability of things—e. g., showing the lighted candle, "Here is the light"; taking it away, "All gone, light"; or, "Papa comes," and, "By-by, papa." Again, showing the self-mobility of things, "Come, kitty, to my pet," and, "Run, kitty, run." She incites the child to bodily activity—"Hold the flower," "Catch the kitty," or, slowly rolling the ball, "Catch the ball."

All-embracing mother-love seeks to awaken and to interpret the feeling of community between the child and the father, brother, and sister, which is so important, when she says, "Love dear papa"; or as she caressingly passes the child's hand over the father's cheek, "Dear, dear papa"; or, "Love little sister," etc.

In addition to the sense of community as such, the germ of so much glorious development, the mother's love seeks also through movements to lead the child to feel his own inner life. By regular, rhythmic movements—and this is of special importance—she brings this life within the child's conscious control when she dandles him up and down on her hand or arm in rhythmic movements and to rhythmic sounds.

Thus the genuine, natural mother cautiously follows in all directions the slowly developing, all-sided life in the child. She strengthens it, and thus arouses to ever-greater activity the still more all-sided life within, and develops this.

Others suppose the child to be empty, wish to inoculate him with life, make him as empty as they think him to be, and deprive him of life, as it were. Thus, too, there are lost again in word and tone those means of cultivation that lead so simply and naturally to the development of rhythm and obedience to law in all human life-utterances, for their significance is recognized by few persons, and by still fewer persons considered and further unfolded in connection with the further development of life in the human being.

Nevertheless, an early, pure development of rhythmic movement would prove most wholesome in the succeeding life-periods of the human being. We rob ourselves as educators, and we still more rob the child as pupil by discontinuing so soon the development of rhythmic movements in early education. It would be easier for him to compass the legitimate, proper measure of his life. Much willfulness, impropriety, and coarseness would be taken out of his life, his movements, and actions. He would secure more firmness and moderation, more harmony; and, later on, there would be de·

veloped in him a higher appreciation of nature and art, of music and poetry (see § 80).

Even very small children, in moments of quiet, and particularly when going to sleep, will hum little strains of songs they have heard ; this, too, has not escaped the attention of the observant, thoughtful mother, and should be heeded and developed even more in the education of little children as the first germ of future growth in melody and song. Undoubtedly this would soon lead in children to a self-activity similar to that attained in speech, and children whose faculty of speech has been thus developed and trained, find, seemingly without effort, the words for new ideas, peculiar associations and relations among newly discovered qualities.

Thus, a very little girl, brought up in child-like purity by maternal thoughtfulness, after long and thoughtful examination of the soft and downy leaves of a plant, exclaimed joyfully, "Oh, how woolly !" The mother could not recollect that she had ever directed the child's attention to such a quality.

Similarly, the same child, on beholding the two most brilliant planets quite near each other in the clear, starry sky, exclaimed joyfully, "Father and mother stars !" Yet the mother had not the least idea how this association with the stars had been called up in the child's mind.

§ 34. In teaching the child to stand and walk, we should use neither perambulators nor leading-strings. He should stand when he is strong enough to keep his balance freely and independently ; and he should walk when, freely moving forward, he can independently keep his balance. He should not stand before he can sit erect, draw himself up by some tall object near by, and thus keep his balance without support. He should not walk before he can creep, rise freely, maintain his balance, and proceed by his own effort. At first, when at some distance from his mother, he has raised himself by his own effort, the return to the mother's lap will invite him to go forward. Soon, however, the child feels strength in his own feet, rejoices intensely over it, and, for his own pleasure, repeats the new art for its own sake, as formerly he repeated the art of standing. In a short time he begins the practice of the art without strain or effort; he is attracted by the bright, round, smooth pebble, by the gayly-colored, fluttering bit of paper, by the smooth, symmetrical, three- or four-cornered piece of board, by the rectangular blocks of wood for building, by the brilliant, quaint leaf, and he tries to get hold of these with the help of the newly acquired use of his limbs, to bring like things together, and to separate things that are unlike. Look at the child that can scarcely keep himself erect, and that can walk only with greatest care—he sees a twig, a bit of straw; painfully he secures it, and, like the young bird in spring, carries it to his nest, as it were.

Behold, again, the child laboriously stooping and slowly going forward on the ground, under the eaves of the roof. The force of the rain has washed out of the sand small, smooth, bright pebbles, and the ever-observing child gathers them as building-stones, as it were, as material for future building. And is he wrong? Does not the child, in truth, collect material for his future life-building? Like things must here be ranged to·ᵒether, things unlike must be separated. Not crude

things, but things wrought out of their crudeness, are
to be joined together.

§ 35. If the building is to be sound, all the material
must be known not only by its name, but also by its
qualities and uses; and, that the child desires this, is
shown in his child-like, quiet, busy activity. We call
it childish because we do not understand it, because we
have not eyes to see, nor ears to hear, and, still less,
feeling to feel with the child; we are dull, therefore
the child's life seems dull to us. We do not know its
meaning; how, then, can we interpret it for the child?
And yet it is the longing for this interpretation that
urges the child to appeal to us. How can we impart
a language to the things of child-life when they are
dumb in us? And yet it is the intense desire for this
that urges the child to bring his treasures to us and to
lay them in our laps. The child loves all things that
enter his small horizon and extend his little world. To
him the least thing is a new discovery; but it must not
come dead into the little world, nor lie dead therein,
lest it obscure the small horizon and crush the little
world.

Therefore, the child would know himself why he
loves this thing; he would know all its properties, its
innermost nature, that he may learn to understand himself in his attachment. For this reason the child examines the object on all sides; for this reason he tears
and breaks it; for this reason he puts it in his mouth
and bites it. We reprove the child for his naughtiness
and foolishness; and yet he is wiser than we who reprove him.

The child would know the inner nature of the thing.

An innate instinct which, properly appreciated and guided, would seek to find God in all his works, urges him to this. God gave him understanding, reason, language. Those who lead his life do not, can not gratify this instinct. Where, then, shall the child seek gratification for this instinct of research, if not from the object itself ?

It is true the broken object, too, is dumb; yet it reveals in its fragments at least either like or unlike parts, as is instanced in the broken stone, the torn flower, and this means an extension of knowledge. Do adults extend their knowledge in a different way ? Is not the inside of the plant pithy, hollow, or woody ? Is not its cross-section circular, triangular, square, polygonal ? Is not the fracture even or uneven, smooth or rough, impervious or porous, splintery or conchoidal, or hackly or fibrous ? Are not the fragments sharp or blunt-edged ? Is it not brittle, or does it not rather yield to the blows without breaking ?

All this the child does in order that from the diversity of outer manifestations of the object its inner nature and its relation to him may become revealed to him, that he may know the cause of his liking, his fondness of the object ? And do we adults who seek knowledge proceed differently ?

We overlook this in the child's activity, and we do not recognize its value and significance until the teacher does it, and requests our sons to do it.

Therefore, even the lucid word of the most lucid teacher frequently has no influence upon our sons; for they are asked to learn now with the teacher what they should have learned in childhood with the help of our quickening explanations; what, indeed, childhood meant they should learn almost without effort.

And yet how little is needed from attendants to aid childhood in this tendency! It is only needful to designate, to name, to put into words what the child does, sees, and finds.

Rich, indeed, is the life of the child ripening into boyhood; but we see it not. Real is his life, but we feel it not. His life accords with the destiny and mission of humanity, but we know it not. We not only fail to guard, nurse, and develop the inner germ of his life, but we allow it to be stifled and crushed by the weight of his own instincts, or to find vent on some weaker side in unnaturalness. We then see the same phenomenon which, in the plant, we call wild-shoot, or water-shoot, a misdirection of the energies, of the desires and instincts in the child (the human plant).

Now, at last, we would fain give another direction to the energies, desires, and instincts of the child growing into boyhood; but it is too late. For the deep meaning of child-life passing into boyhood we not only failed to appreciate, but we misjudged it; we not only failed to nurse it, but we misdirected and crushed it.

§ 36. A child has found a pebble. In order to determine by experiment its properties, he has rubbed it on a board near by, and has discovered its property of imparting color. It is a fragment of lime, clay, redstone, or chalk.

See how he delights in the newly discovered property, and how busily he makes use of it! Soon the whole surface of the board is changed.

At first the boy took delight in the new property.

then in the changed surface—now red, now white, now
black, now brown—but soon he began to find pleasure
in the winding, straight, curved, and other forms that
appear.   These linear phenomena direct his attention
to the linear properties of surrounding objects.   Now
the head becomes a circle, and now the circular line
represents the head, the elliptical curve connected with
it represents the body ; arms and legs appear as straight
or broken lines, and these again represent arms and legs ;
the fingers he sees as straight lines meeting in a common
point, and lines so connected are, for the busy child,
again hands and fingers; the eyes he sees as dots, and
these again represent eyes ; and thus a new world opens
within and without.   For what man tries to represent
or do he begins to understand.

The perception and representation of linear relations
open to the child on the threshold of boyhood a new
world in various directions.   Not only can he represent
the outer world in reduced measure, and thus comprehend it more easily with his eyes ; not only can he reproduce outwardly what lives in his mind as a remi-
niscence or new association, but the knowledge of a
wholly new invisible world, the world of forces, has its
tenderest rootlets right here.

The ball that is rolling or has been rolled, the stone
that has been thrown and falls, the water that was
dammed and conducted into many branching ditches—
all these have taught the child that the effect of a force,
in its individual manifestations, is always in the direction of a line.

Thus the representation of objects by lines soon
leads the child to the perception and representation of

the direction in which a force acts. "Here flows a brook," and, saying this, the child makes a mark indicating the course of a brook. The child has drawn lines signifying to him a tree. "Here grows another branch, and here still another," and as he speaks he draws forth from the tree, as it were, the lines indicating the branches.

Very significantly the child says, "Here comes a bird flying," and draws in the direction of the supposed flight a winding line.

Give the child a bit of chalk or the like, and soon a new creation will stand before him and you. Let the father, too, in a few lines, sketch a man, a horse. This man of lines, this horse of lines, will give the child more joy than an actual man, an actual horse would do.

§ 37. Mothers and attendants, would you know how to lead the child in this matter? See and observe the child ; he will teach you what to do.

Here a child traces a table by passing its fingers along its edges and outlines, as far as he can reach them. Thus the child sketches the object on the object itself, as it were. This is the first, and, for the child, the safest step by which he first becomes aware of the outlines and forms of objects. In like manner he sketches and studies the chair, the bench, the window.

Soon, however, the child advances. He draws lines across four-sided boards — the table, the seat of the chair or bench — vaguely anticipating that this is the method for retaining the forms and relations of surfaces. A little later he draws the form in reduced measure.

Behold! here he has sketched the table, the chair, the bench, and many other things, on the table-top.* Do you not see how he developed and grew spontaneously to this attainment?

Objects which he could move, which he could take in at one glance, he laid on a board or bench or table, and sketched their outline by passing his hand around them. Later on, scissors and boxes, and still later, leaves and twigs, nay, the child's own hand and the shadows of objects, are sketched in this way.

Many things are gained by these proceedings of the child—more than I can enumerate—a clear conception of forms, the power to represent the forms independently, the fixing of the forms as such, strengthening and practice of the arm and hand in free representation of these.

The attentive mother, the thoughtful father, the sympathetic family (without any of them having ever drawn, without an artist among them), may lead the child growing into boyhood to draw with tolerable accuracy a straight line, a diagonal or diameter, even rectangular objects in vertical position (e. g., mirrors, windows, and many other things), with some degree of resemblance.

---

* It was formerly not uncommon to find table-tops made of large slabs of slate-stone. There was such a table in my father's house when I was a boy. I still connect with it many a fruitful memory of earnest studies of form and outline, of delightful trains of fancy, and of vigorous struggles of invention that made the ugliest weather a boon. A small portable blackboard is an excellent substitute for such a table. It will accomplish more for the child's understanding of things, and for the vigorous development of a healthy imagination, than the most earnest talks, and the most ideal story-books could do.—*Tr.*

It is not only conducive but necessary to the devel
opment and strengthening of the child's power and skill
that parents should, without being pedantic or too exact-
ing, connect the child's actions with suitable language,
e. g., "Now I draw a table, a mirror; now I draw the
diagonal of the slate, of the board."

This enhances the inner and the outer power, increases knowledge, awakens the judgment and reflection,
which avoids so many blunders, and which, *in a natural
way*, can not be aroused too soon. For the word and
the drawing * are always mutually explanatory and com-
plementary; for neither one is, by itself, exhaustive and
sufficient with reference to the object represented. The
drawing properly stands between the word and the
thing, shares certain qualities with each of them, and is,
therefore, so valuable in the development of the child.
The true drawing has this in common with the thing,
that it seeks to represent it in form and outline; like
the word, however, it never is the thing itself, but only
an image of the thing. The word and the drawing are
again clearly opposed in their nature: for the drawing
is dead, while the word lives; the drawing is visible, as
the word is audible. The word and the drawing, therefore, belong together inseparably, as light and shadow,
night and day, soul and body do. The faculty of drawing is, therefore, as much innate in the child, in man, as
is the faculty of speech, and demands its development
and cultivation as imperatively as the latter; experience
shows this clearly in the child's love for drawing, in the
child's instinctive desire for drawing.

---

* I translate *Zeichen* here by *drawing*, not symbol, inasmuch as Froebel has reference to the drawings just described.—*Tr.*

[Drawing offers the child the full connection between the innei and the outer, so far as the eye is concerned. Here outer objects are freed of all the attributes of corporeality; and yet their images have a visible reality, and vividly recall the absent attributes. Here the child gives visible expression to his ideas. Here he feels the full delight of creating, as it were, whatever his fancy dictates. This accounts for the evident eagerness with which he returns, again and again, to slate and pencil, and for the satisfaction with which he lingers with them.— *Tr.*]

§ 38. The representation of objects by and in drawing induces and implies clear perception, and this soon leads the child to the ready recognition of the constantly repeated association of certain numbers of similar objects—e. g., two eyes and two arms, five fingers and five toes, the six legs of the beetle and of the fly. Thus the drawing of the object leads to the discovery of number (see §§ 75, 99). The repeated return of one and the same object leads to counting. The fixed distinctive sum of objects similar in certain respects constitutes the number of these objects. Thus, by a new discovery, by the development and cultivation of the number-faculty in the child, his sphere of knowledge, his world, is again extended; and an essential need of his inner being, a certain yearning of his spirit, is satisfied by this development. For the child has heretofore viewed his greater or smaller quantities of similar and dissimilar objects with a certain longing, a vague feeling that he still lacks a certain means of knowledge. He was still unable to recognize and to determine the relative quantities of these different heaps of things; but now he knows he has two large and three small pebbles, four white and five yellow flowers, etc. The knowledge of number relations adds very much to the child's life.

The mind of the child requires, however, that the mother and other attendants should, from the very beginning and early, develop in the child the number-faculty in accordance with the nature of number, and with the specific laws of human thought.

If the child is quietly observed, it will be easy to see how he follows spontaneously the road implied by the laws of human thought, proceeding from the visible to the invisible and more abstract. He does this unconsciously, it is true, but surely. At first the child places together similar objects, and obtains thus, e. g., apples, pears, nuts, beans.

Let, now, the mother or some other attendant add the explanatory word; in other words, let them join the visible with the audible, thus bringing it nearer the child's insight and knowledge, nearer his inner perception, by naming these objects.

Who has not observed and had frequent opportunities to see how the child arranges the objects of each kind singly in a row? Let the mother here again add the explanatory, quickening word, saying, e. g.:

Apple, apple, apple, apple, etc.; all apples.

Pear, pear, pear, pear, etc.; all pears;

or whatever else the child may have placed in the rows—nuts, beans, pebbles, or leaves—of each kind of objects there are always several. Now, in order to enable the child particularly to see this, let the mother speak the words in common with the child, as just indicated.

Later, when the mother has the child to arrange the objects one after the other, let her describe this proceeding with the child definitely and clearly, thus:

One apple, another apple, still another apple ; many apples.

One pear, another pear, still another pear; many pears.

And so on with other objects. The quantity of each kind of objects is continually increased by the regular addition of a new object of the same kind.

Instead of the indefinite words "another," "still another," the mother subsequently uses the numerals definitely indicating the increase, counting together with the child, thus :

One apple, two apples, three apples, etc.

One pear, two pears, three pears, four pears, etc.

Again, let the mother place several objects of each kind in naturally increasing quantities, in successive sets, and indicate in words what she does, thus :

<table>
<tr><td>* apple,</td><td>* pear,</td></tr>
<tr><td>* * apples,</td><td>* * pears,</td></tr>
<tr><td>* * * apples, etc.</td><td>* * * pears, etc.</td></tr>
</table>

Subsequently, again, let mother and child pronounce together. At last let the child do the arranging as well as the speaking, counting alone.

While here with each number the kind of object was still named, let, subsequently, the numbers only be named and reserve the name of the kind of object for the last number, thus :

* (one), * * (two), * * * (three), * * * * (four apples) ;
* (one), * * (two), * * * (three), * * * * (four pears), etc.

Here the successive groups of objects are considered chiefly with reference to their numbers, the consideration of the kind of object lying in the background.

Lastly, the mother names only the numbers in the

series, leaving the kind of objects wholly out of consideration, thus:

* (one), * * (two), * * *(three), * * * * (four), * * * * *(five), etc.
This is the abstract consideration and perception of groups in their natural succession, the perception of numbers as such.

In this way a clear and sure knowledge of numbers (at least up to ten) should be developed in the period of childhood. But at no time should the numerals be given to the child as empty, unmeaning sounds and be thus repeated by him; by such a method the child might be led to count two, four, seven, eight, one, five, two, if it were not rescued at last by the native power of the human mind, throwing off all things unnatural.

For a long time the child should never say the numerals, which, in themselves, are empty and meaningless to him, without the aid of objects which he actually counts.

In this presentation of the development of number ideas there has been given, at the same time, an illustration in what manner and according to what laws the child ascends from the perception of individual things to the more general and the most general conceptions. It is true, in experience, this transition is often quite sudden.

§ 39. What wealth, what abundance and vigor of inner and outer life, do we now find in the rightly guided and guarded child toward the close of childhood and entrance into the period of boyhood! Where will the coming man find an object of thought and feeling, of knowledge and skill, that does not have its tenderest rootlets in the years of childhood? What subject of future instruction and discipline does not germinate in childhood?

Language and nature lie open before the child. He begins to apprehend the properties of number, form, magnitude, the knowledge of space, the nature of forces, the effects of substances. Color, rhythm, melodious sound, and shapeliness have impressed him in their ultimate germs and in their peculiar significance. He has begun to distinguish, with some degree of definiteness, nature and the world of art, and has commenced, with some degree of certainty, to contrast himself with the outer world; already there has been aroused in him the consciousness of an inner world of his own. Nevertheless, we have as yet not touched nor even considered an important side of child-life, the side of association with father and mother, brother and sister, in their domestic cares, in their professional duties.

§ 40. I look about me: I see the scarcely two-year-old child of a day-laborer leading his horse; the father has placed the halter in the child's hands. Calmly and deliberately the little fellow walks before the horse, and looks back with steady eye to see if the horse is following. It is true, the father holds the check-reins in his hand, still the child firmly believes that he leads the horse, that the horse must obey him. For, see, the father stops to speak to an acquaintance, and, of course, the horse stops too; but the child, thinking the horse willful, pulls the halter with all his might to make it go on.

My neighbor's son, scarcely three years old, tends his mother's goslings near my garden-hedge. The space to which he is to confine the lively little creatures in their search for food is small. They escape from the little swain, who may have been busy in other ways, seeking food for his mind. The goslings get into the road, where they are exposed to injury. The mother sees this, and calls out to the child to be careful. The little boy who, by the ever-renewed efforts for freedom on the part of the goslings, probably had been often disturbed in his own pursuits, retorts in his vexation, " Mother, you seem to think it is not hard to tend the goslings."

Who can indicate the present and future developments which the child reaps from this part of the parent's work, and which he might reap even more abundantly, if parents and attendants heeded the matter and made use of it later on in the instruction and training of their children ?

Behold here the little child of the gardener. He is weeding; the child wishes to help, and he teaches the little fellow to distinguish hemlock from parsley, to observe the differences in the brilliancy and odor of the leaves.

There the forester's son accompanies his father to the clearing that, at some previous time, they together had sown. Everything looks green. The child sees only young pine-plants; but the father teaches him to recognize the cypress-spurge and to distinguish it from the pine-plant by its different properties.

Again, the father takes aim and fires; he hits the mark, and teaches the attentive child that three points that lie in the same direction always lie in one and the same straight line; that in order to direct a line—the barrel of the rifle—toward a certain point, three points must be laid in this direction, and that, when this has been done, all other points of the gun-barrel lie in the same line and direction.

In another place the child sees his father striking the hot iron, and is taught by the father that the heat makes the iron softer; and, again, as the father tries in vain to push the heated iron rod through an opening through which before it passed so easily, that heat expands the iron.

[Froebel here continues through three pages to furnish similar illustrations from a variety of professions and trades, showing the exhaustless wealth of information and discipline that may come to the child from this loving intercourse with a kind and thoughtful father in his daily work.—*Tr.*]

The child—your child, ye fathers—feels this so intensely, so vividly, that he follows you wherever you are, wherever you go, in whatever you do. Do not harshly repel him; show no impatience about his ever-recurring questions. Every harshly repelling word crushes a bud or shoot of his tree of life. Do not, however, tell him in words much more than he could find himself without your words. For it is, of course, easier to hear the answer from another, perhaps to only half hear and understand it, than it is to seek and discover it himself. To have found one fourth of the answer by his own effort is of more value and importance to the child than it is to half hear and half understand it in the words of another; for this causes mental indolence. Do not, therefore, always answer your children's questions at once and directly; but, *as soon as they have gathered sufficient strength and experience,* furnish them with the means to find the answers in the sphere of their own knowledge.

Let parents—more particularly fathers (for to their special care and guidance the child ripening into boyhood is confided)—let fathers contemplate what the fulfillment of their paternal duties in child-guidance yields to them; let them feel the joys it brings. It is not possible to gain from anything higher joy, higher enjoyment, than we do from the guidance of our children, from living with and for our children. It is inconceivable how we can seek and expect to find anywhere higher joy, higher enjoyment, fuller gratification of our best desires than we can find in intercourse with our children; more recreation than we can find in the family circle, where we can create joy for ourselves in so many respects.

We should be deeply impressed with the truth of these statements could we but see in his plain home-surroundings, in his happy, joyous family, the father who, from his own resources, has created what here has been but partially described. In a few words he sums up his rule of conduct: "To lead children early to think, this I consider the first and foremost object of child-training."

To give them early habits of work and industry seemed to him so natural and obvious a course as to need no statement in words. Besides, the child that has been led to think will thereby, at the same time. be led to industry, diligence — to all domestic and civic virtues.

Those words are a seed from which springs a shady

evergreen tree of life, full of fragrant blossoms and sound, ripe fruit. May those of us who allow our children to grow up thoughtless and idle, and therefore dull and dead, hear and heed this!

§ 41. But—it is hard to say it, yet its truth will appear if, in our intercourse and life with our children, we cast a searching glance upon the condition of our minds and hearts—we are dull, our surroundings are dull to us. With all our knowledge, we are empty for our children. Almost all we say is hollow and empty, without meaning and without life. Only in the few rare cases, when our discourse rests on intercourse with life and nature, we enjoy its life.

Let us hasten, then! Let us impart life to ourselves, to our children; let us through them give meaning to our speech and life to the things about us! Let us live with them, and let them live with us; thus shall we obtain through them what we all need.

Our words, our discourses in social life, are dull, are empty husks, lifeless puppets, worthless chips; they are devoid of inner life and meaning; they are evil spirits, for they have neither body nor substance.

Our surroundings are dead and dull. Objects are matter. They crush, instead of lifting us, for they lack the quickening word that gives them significance and meaning.

We do not feel the meaning of what we say, for our speech is made up of memorized ideas, based neither on perception nor on productive effort. Therefore, it does not lead to perception, production, life; it has not proceeded, it does not proceed, from life.

Our speech is like the book out of which we have

tearned it, at third or fourth hand. We do not ourselves see what we say, we can not give outer form to
what we say. Therefore, our speech is so empty and
meaningless. For this reason, and only for this, our
inward and outward life, as well as the life of our children, is so poor, because our speech is not born from a
life, rich inwardly and outwardly, in seeing and doing;
because our speech, our word, is not based on the perception of the thing it designates. Therefore, we hear
the sound, it is true, but we fail to get the image; we
hear the noise, but see no movement.

§ 42. Fathers, parents, let us see that our children
may not suffer from similar deficiencies. What we no
longer possess—the all-quickening, creative power of
child-life—let it again be translated from their life into
ours.

Let us learn from our children, let us give heed to
the gentle admonitions of their life, to the silent demands of their minds.

Let us live with our children: then will the life of
our children bring us peace and joy, then shall we begin
to grow wise, to be wise.

[This celebrated saying, "*Kommt, lasst uns unsern Kindern le-
ben!*" is frequently translated, "Come, let us live *for* our children!"
Unsern Kindern is the dative case. and implies here devotion *to*, ab-
sorption *in*, harmony *with*, the life of our children. It seems to me
that this is more fully expressed by the preposition *with*. *With* implies that both, we and the children, are equally active; *for* seems
to place the burden on *us*, and renders the children passive recipients
of our bounty.

Living with our children means entering fully into their simple
ways of seeing and saying, of feeling and thinking, of willing and
doing; it means placing at their service our wider knowledge, our
greater strength, patiently helping them, guarding and guiding

them in their life, in their spontaneous search for light and love; it means joining them in their simple truthfulness, their childish faith in man, and leading them on the basis of this to a higher and mightier faith in the immutable laws of nature and of God; it means being true with them so that they may reach higher truth; it means loving with them what they love, so that with our help they may learn to love the highest good.

Living with our children implies on our part sympathy with childhood, adaptability to children, and knowledge and appreciation of child-nature; it implies genuine interest in all that interests them, to rejoice and grieve with them in the measure of *their* joy and grief, not merely in the measure of our appreciation of loss or gain, of substance or shadow; it implies seeing ourselves with the eyes of a child, hearing ourselves with the ears of a child, judging ourselves with the keen intuition of a child.

Froebel even sees in it the expression of a universal law in its application to the lite of humanity; it means to him the realization in consciousness of the organic connection of human life in successive generations. "The loving heart," he says elsewhere, "feels it in all things, the eager mind sees it in all things as a cosmic thought; the heart and the mind find it in the universe of which man himself is only an organic part. Does not the sun proclaim it to the earth and all her creatures, all her children? Do not the elements—earth, water, air, light, and heat—proclaim it to each other with reference to all earthly things? Do not, again, in each plant all the various parts proclaim this to each other with reference to the seed growing in quiet seclusion? In all nature, wherever there are life and activity, we find this thought: 'Come, let us live with our children'—revealed as a law comprehending all life."—*Tr.*]

§ 43. During the period of human development heretofore considered, the objects of the external world were intimately connected with the word, and through the word with the human being.

This period, therefore, is pre-eminently the period of development of the faculty of speech. Therefore, in all the child did, it was so indispensable that whatever he did should be clearly and definitely designated by the word, connected with the word. Every object every thing became such, as it were, only through the word; before it had been named, although the child might have seemed to see it with the outer eyes, it had no existence for the child. The name, as it were, created the thing for the child; hence the name and the thing seemed to be one, like the stem and the marrow, the branch and the twig. Yet, in spite of this intimate connection of the object with its name, and, through this, with man—and this can not be too clearly noticed and too carefully followed by the educator—every object at this stage of human development is again so entirely distinct from all others, each object and each whole, too, shows in its parts no organic connection. The destiny of man and of things, however, tends in a very different direction. Not only should man consider each thing as an undivided whole, but he should also look upon it as organized in its parts for a common purpose. He is to view it not only as an independent whole, an individual unit, but he should also view it as a member of a relatively greater and higher whole, fulfilling a higher common purpose. Of each thing he is to know not only its external conditions and associations, but its inner relationships, its inner unity with what seems to be outwardly distinct from it.

§ 44. Yet the totality of what surrounds man as his outer world can not be known by him in its oneness; he can find it only in the knowledge of the peculiar nature of each thing, the individuality and personality of each object.

Now, man finds it difficult to recognize a thing—

the inner nature of a thing—if it is brought too close
to him inwardly and outwardly; and the difficulty is
increased in the measure in which it approaches him
too closely, inwardly and outwardly. The misunderstandings between parent and child in the family circle
furnish frequent and speaking proofs for this. For
this reason man finds it so difficult to know himself.
On the other hand, external separation often brings
about inner unity, inner recognition and appreciation.
Thus, alas! man knows many foreign things—foreign
objects, other times, other men—better than his home
surroundings, his own time, better than himself. If
man would know himself truly, he must represent himself externally, must place himself over against himself, as it were. Now, if man in obedience to his destiny is truly and thoroughly to know each thing of the
surrounding world; if, with the aid of each thing, he
is truly and thoroughly to know himself, the period of
childhood which unites man and object must be fol
lowed by a new period opposed to its predecessor in
its nature; a period which separates man and object,
which outwardly opposes them to one another, but
unites them inwardly; a period which brings the objects inwardly nearer to man by separating the object
from its name, considers the object and the word as
separate, distinct, yet uniting things. This period
when language assumes an independent existence, is the
one that now follows.

When he learns to separate the name from the
thing, and the thing from its name, the speech from
the speaker, and *vice versa ;* when, later on, language
itself is externalized and materialized in signs and

writing, and begins to be considered as something actually corporeal, man leaves the period of childhood and enters the *period of boyhood.*

[In an additional paragraph, Froebel indulges in a play on the word *Knabe, boy,* seeking to fix the idea that this is the period when man, by his own strength, consciously appropriates the external.—*Tr.*]

III.

THE BOYHOOD OF MAN.

§ 45. As the preceding period of human development, the *period of childhood*, was predominantly that
of *life* for the sake merely of living, for making the internal external, so the *period of boyhood* is predominantly the period for *learning*, for making the external
internal.

On the part of parents and educators the period of
infancy demanded chiefly *fostering care*. During the
succeeding period of childhood, which looks upon man
predominantly as a unit, and would lead him to unity,
training prevails. The period of boyhood leads man
chiefly to the consideration of particular relationships
and individual things, in order to enable him later on
to discover their inner unity. The inner tendencies
and relationships of individual things and conditions are
sought and established (see § 56).

Now, the consideration and treatment of individual
and particular things, as such, and in their inner bearings and relationships, constitute the essential character
and work of instruction; therefore, *boyhood is the period in which instruction predominates.*

This instruction is conducted not so much in accordance with the nature of man as in accordance with the

fixed, definite, clear *laws* that lie in the nature of things, and more particularly the laws to which man and things are equally subject. It is conducted not so much in the method in which the universal, eternal law finds peculiar expression in man as rather in the method in which this law finds peculiar expression in each external thing, or simultaneous expression in both man and thing. It is conducted, then, in accordance with fixed and definite conditions lying *outside* the human being; and this implies knowledge, insight, a conscious and comprehensive survey of the field.

Such a process constitutes the *school* in the widest sense of the word. The school, then, leads man to a knowledge of external things, and of their nature in accordance with the particular and general laws that lie in them; by the presentation of the external, the individual, the particular, it leads man to a knowledge of the internal, of unity, of the universal. Therefore, on entering the period of boyhood, man becomes at the same time a *school-boy*. With this period school begins for him, be it in the home or out of it, and taught by the father, the members of the family, or a teacher. School, then, means here by no means the school-room, nor school-keeping, but *the conscious communication of knowledge, for a definite purpose and in definite inner connection* (see § 56).

§ 46. On the other hand, as it has appeared and continues to appear in every aspect, the development and cultivation of man, for the attainment of his destiny and fulfillment of his mission, constitute an unbroken whole, steadily and continuously progressing, gradually ascending. The feeling of community, awakened in the infant, becomes in the child impulse, inclination; these lead to the formation of the disposition and of the heart, and arouse in the boy his intellect and will.

To give firmness to the will, to quicken it, and to make it pure, strong, and enduring, in a life of pure humanity, is the chief concern, the main object in the guidance of the boy, in instruction and the school.

§ 47. Will is the mental activity, ever consciously proceeding from a definite point in a definite direction toward a definite object, in harmony with the man's nature as a whole.

This statement contains everything, and indicates all that parent and educator, teacher and school, should be or should give to the boy in example and precept during these years.

The starting-point of all mental activity in the boy should be energetic and sound; the source whence it flows, pure, clear, and ever flowing; the direction, simple, definite; the object, fixed, clear, living and life-giving, elevating, worthy of the effort, worthy of the destiny and mission of man, worthy of his essential nature, and tending to develop it and to give it full expression.

In order, therefore, to impart true, genuine firmness to the natural will-activity of the boy, all the activities of the boy, his entire will, should proceed from and have reference to the development, cultivation, and representation of the internal. Instruction in example and in words, which later on become precept and example, furnishes the means for this. Neither example alone nor words alone will do: not example alone, for it is particular and special, and the word is needed to give to particular individual examples universal applicability ; not words alone, for example is needed to interpret and explain the word which is general, spiritual, and of many meanings.

But instruction and example alone and in themselves are not sufficient : they must meet a good, pure heart, and this is an outcome of proper educational influences in childhood.

Therefore, the cultivation of boyhood rests wholly on that of childhood ; therefore, activity and firmness of the will rest upon activity and firmness of the feelings and of the heart. Where the latter are lacking, the former will scarcely be attainable.

§ 48. The pure and good heart and the thoughtful and gentle sympathies of the child constitute in themselves a unity. Hence their utterance is an intense longing to find for the many externally separate things that surround the child an inner necessary unity, such as he feels in himself, a quickening spiritual bond and law —a bond and law by which these things may gain at least the significance of life and significance for life.

Now, it is true, for the period of childhood this longing is gratified in the complete enjoyment of living play. By this, in the period of childhood, man is placed in the center of all things, and all things are seen only in relation to himself, to his life. Yet above all it is family-life that gratifies this longing fully. Family-life alone secures the development and cultivation of a good heart and of a thoughtful, gentle disposition in their full intensity and vigor, so incomparably important for every period of growth, nay, for the whole life of man (see § 86).

Now, inasmuch as that desire for unity is the basis of all genuinely human development and cultivation, and inasmuch as every separating tendency hinders pure human development, man, even in child-hood, refers everything to family-life, beholds everything through family-life, as is shown so clearly in childhood.

For the child, therefore, the life of his own family becomes itself an external thing and a type of life. Parents should consider this fact : that the child in his own life would fain represent this type in the purity, harmony, and efficiency in which he sees it.

[On the great value of family-life, see also § 86. The family is to Froebel the type of unified human life. In it the triune essence of humanity—light, love, and life—is individualized in father, mother, and child ; light predominating in the father, love in the mother, life in the child. Of these, love is the center and fulcrum, as the mother, too, is at the center and fulcrum of the family. Light may secure individual existence and furnish insight, but love alone can make life worth living, love alone can lead to *the subordination of the whole being to a heart turned upward, taught lovingly and patiently*—as mothers teach—*to yearn for the Infinite*. This is in full agreement with his primary principle of life-unity ; for the emotional element of our being, the heart, is nearest the divinity within us. Head and hand are but the instruments of the heart from which they receive their direction.—*Tr.*]

§ 49. Now, in the family, the child sees the parents and other members of the family at work, producing, doing something ; the same he notices with adults generally in life and in those active interests with which his family is concerned. Consequently the child, at this stage, would like himself to represent what he sees. He would like to represent—and tries to do so—all he sees his parents and other adults do and represent in work, all which he thus sees represented by human power and human skill.

What formerly the child did only *for the sake of the activity*, the boy now does *for the sake of the result* or product of his activity; the child's instinct of activity has in the boy become a *formative instinct*, and this occupies the whole outward life, the outward manifes tation of boy-life at this period (see § 23).

How cheerfully and eagerly the boy and the girl at this age begin to share the work of father and mother— not the easy work, indeed, but the difficult work, calling for strength and labor !

Be cautious, be careful and thoughtful, at this point, O parents ! You can here at one blow destroy, at least for a long time, the instinct of formative activity in your children, if you repel their help as childish, use less, of little avail, or even as a hindrance.

Do not let the urgency of your business tempt you to say, " Go away, you only hinder me," or, " I am in a hurry, leave me alone."

Boys and girls are thus disturbed in their inner activity; they see themselves shut out from the whole with which they felt themselves so intimately united ; their inner power is aroused, but they see themselves alone, and do not know what to do with the aroused power ; nay, it becomes a burden to them, and they become fretful and indolent.

After a third rebuff of this character, scarcely any child will again propose to help and share the work. He becomes fretful and dull, even when he sees his parents engaged in work which he might share. Who has not later on heard the parents of such children complain : " When this boy (or girl) was small and could not help, he busied himself about everything; now that he knows something and is strong enough, he does not want to do anything " ?

Just so! In accordance with the nature of the spiritual principle working in man, as yet unconsciously and unrecognized, the first utterances of the instinct of activity, of the formative instinct, come without any effort on his part, and even against his will, as indeed happens to him even in later life. Now, if this inner impulse to formative activity in man, particularly in early youth, is met by an external obstacle, especially by one like the will of parents, which can not be set aside, the inner power itself is weakened, and a frequent repetition of this forces it back into complete inactivity.

When the child has been thus disturbed, he does not consider why his help was permissible at one time and not at another time ; he chooses that which is more agreeable to his physical nature. He abstains from the activity the more readily and willingly, because the will of his parents seems to make it his duty to do so.

The child becomes indolent—i. e., spirit and life cease to animate his physical being; the latter becomes a mere body to him, which now he must carry as a burden ; whereas, formerly, the sense of power led him to feel his body, not as such, but as the mighty source of the power that filled him.

Therefore, O parents, if you wish your children eventually to help you, foster in them at an early period the instinct of activity, and especially the formative instinct of boyhood, even though it should involve

some effort, some sacrifice on your part. It will re-
pay a hundred-fold, as does good wheat planted in
good soil.

[Here, as elsewhere, Froebel places himself broadly on the
thought that in the order of development, the lower is the necessary condition of the higher, and owes its value to the higher.
Later on, this will be shown in his presentation of the development
of conscious spontaneity from the mere energy as seen in the crystal. For the same reason he asks us here to foster this, as yet comparatively simple instinct, of more or less purposeless activity, which
appears almost like a reflex effect of the impressions that crowd in
upon the child. He sees in this activity the germ and promise of
higher developments, of the highest differentiations of conscious
purpose. Similarly, he would lead the child from apparently purposeless and frivolous play to the teeming fields of earnest labor;
not by contemning play but by fostering it, and by directing it in
its legitimate channels.— *Tr.*]

Strengthen and develop this instinct; give to your
child the highest he now needs; permit him to add his
power to your work—specially dear to him because it
is yours—so that he may not only gain the consciousness
of his power, but learn to appreciate its limitations.

If in his former activity (in childhood) he imitated
phases of domestic life, in his present activity (in boyhood) he shares the work of the house—lifting, pulling,
carrying, digging, splitting. The boy wants to try his
strength in everything, so that his body may grow
strong, that his strength may increase, and that he may
know its measure. The son accompanies his father
everywhere—to the field and to the garden, to the shop
and to the counting-house, to the forest and to the
meadow; in the care of domestic animals and in the
making of small articles of household furniture; in the
splitting, sawing, and the piling up of wood , in all the

work his father's trade or calling involves. Question upon question comes from the lips of the boy thirsting for knowledge—How? Why? When? What for? Of what?—and every somewhat satisfactory answer opens a new world to the boy. Language comes to him everywhere, in its independence, as a mediator.*

At this age the healthy boy, brought up simply and naturally, never evades an obstacle, a difficulty; nay, he seeks it, and overcomes it.

"Let it lie," the vigorous youngster exclaims to his father, who is about to roll a piece of wood out of the boy's way—"let it lie, I can get over it." With difficulty, indeed, the boy gets over it the first time; but he has accomplished the feat by his own strength. Strength and courage have grown in him. He returns, gets over the obstacle a second time, and soon he learns to clear it easily. If activity brought joy to the child, work now gives delight to the boy. Hence, the daring and venturesome feats of boyhood; the explorations of caves and ravines; the climbing of trees and mountains; the searching of the heights and depths; the roaming through fields and forests.

The most difficult thing seems easy, the most daring thing seems without danger to him, for his promptings come from his innermost heart and will.

However, it is not alone the desire to try and use his power that prompts the boy at this age to seek adventure high and low, far and wide; it is particularly the peculiarity and need of his unfolding innermost life, the desire to control the diversity of things, to see

---

* As a mediator between him and the outer world, bringing him the knowledge for which he thirsts.—*Tr.*

individual things in their connection with a whole, especially to bring near that which is remote, to comprehend (the outer world) in its extent, its diversity, its integrity; it is the desire to extend his scope step by step.

To climb a new tree means to the boy the discovery of a new world. The outlook from above shows everything so different from the ordinary cramped and distorted side-view. How clear and distinct everything lies beneath him! Could we but recall the feelings that filled our hearts and souls in boyhood, when the narrow limits of our surroundings sank before our extended view, we should not cry out to him : " Come down ; you might fall ! "

Not by walking and standing alone, do we learn to walk and stand. Not by walking and standing, sitting and crawling, do we learn to keep from falling ; the survey of our surroundings, too, is needed. And how different does the commonest thing look when viewed from above !

[More clearly than in any other passage, Froebel here indicates his position with reference to the much-abused maxim, " Learn to do by doing," which has sometimes been attributed to him by well-meaning but ill-informed persons. Froebel, it is true, would have skill in action imparted by practice; but he never makes skill as such an object of educational activity, deeming it of value only when it serves insight, which can come only from *seeing*. He would, indeed, have *doing*, but always as the expression of thought and feeling, which, again, are based on previous *seeing*. In this respect Froebel is a more faithful follower of Comenius than those over-zealous persons who seem to have caught nothing from the great Moravian teacher than this maxim, " Learn to do by doing." Comenius himself applies the saying only to the arts of the school—such as writing, speaking (or reading), singing, and ciphering—and treats of it

in a chapter subordinate to the "Method of the Sciences" which, as
he says, need "the eye, the object, and light.'

This is not vitiated by the fact that "every science is evolved out
of its corresponding art." An art is a complex empirical organism,
involving the co-operation of more or less extended systems of variously inter-related seeing and doing. The corresponding science
grows in the measure in which we learn to see it as a living, rationally constituted whole.—*Tr.*]

Should it not be our duty and our work to secure
for our boy at an early period this elevation of mind
and heart? Shall he not from a lofty standpoint clear
his understanding, and expand heart and mind by extending his view into the distance?

"But," you object, "the boy will become reckless;
I am never free from anxiety about him." The boy,
who from early youth has been led quietly and with
reference to the steady development of his power, will
never task his strength much more than his previous
trials justify. Thus he passes through all these dangers
like one led by a good genius; while another boy, who
knows neither his strength nor the difficulty of his task,
attempts to do what his little skill and strength do
not warrant him to undertake, and thus incurs danger
where even the most timid would deem himself safe.

Indeed, the most really venturesome boys are always
those who, without steadily practiced strength, are
taken with a sudden fit of power, and, at the same
time, are offered an opportunity for its use. They will
then, particularly if others observe them, easily get into
danger.

Not less significant and developing is the boy's inclination to descend into caves and ravines, to ramble in
the shady grove and in the dark forest. It is the de-

sire to seek and find the new, to see and discover the
hidden; the desire to bring to light and to appropriate
that which lies concealed in darkness and shadow.

From these rambles the boy returns with rich treasures of unknown stones and plants, of animals—worms,
beetles, spiders, and lizards—that dwell in darkness
and concealment. "What is this? what is its name?"
etc., are the questions to be answered; and every new
word enriches his world, and throws light upon his surroundings. Beware of greeting the boy with the excla-
mation, "Fie, throw that down; that is horrid!" or
"Drop that, it will bite you!" If the child obeys, he
drops and throws away also a considerable portion of
his power; and, when later on you say to him, or when
common sense and reason tell him, "See, this is a harm-
less creature," he will avert his eyes, and a great amount
of knowledge will be lost at the same time. On the
other hand, the little boy, scarcely six years old, may
tell you about the structure of the beetle and about the
peculiar uses it makes of its limbs; things that heretofore had remained unnoticed by you. It may be well
to caution him about taking hold of unknown creatures,
but not in such a way as to make him timid.

However, the genuine, vigorous boy at this age is by
no means always on the heights or in the depths. The
same desire that urges him to seek knowledge and insight on the mountains and in the valleys, attracts and
holds him also to the plain. Here he makes a little
garden under the hedge near the fence of his father's
garden; there he represents the course of the river in
his furrow and in his ditch; there he studies the effects
of the fall or pressure of water upon his little water-

wheel; here he observes a small piece of wood or a bit
ot light bark floating on a little pond he has dammed
up. He is particularly fond of occupying himself with
the clear, living, mobile water in which the boy who
seeks self-knowledge beholds the image of his soul as in
a mirror. For the same reason he is fond of busying
himself with plastic substances (sand, clay), which to
him are, as it were, a life-element. For he seeks now,
impelled by the previously acquired sense of his power,
to master the material, to control it. Everything must
submit to his formative instinct; there in the heap of
earth he builds a cellar, a cavern, and on it a garden, a
bench.

Boards, branches of trees, laths, and poles are made
into a hut, a house; the deep, fresh snow is fashioned
into the walls and ramparts of a fortress; and the rough
stones on the hill are heaped together to make a castle:
all this is done in the spirit and tendency of boyhood,
in the spirit and tendency of unification and assimila-
tion (see § 94).

There two boys, scarcely seven years old, with
their arms around each other, walk across the yard in
friendly, intimate consultation; they are on the way to
get tools in order to build in a dark grove, on the hill
behind the house, a hut with a table and bench, an outlook from which their eyes can take in the whole valley
at one glance, as a beautifully organized whole.

This unifying and, at the same time, self-reliant
spirit unites all things that come near and seem adapted to its nature, its wants, and inner status—unites
stones and human beings in a common purpose, a common endeavor. And thus each one soon forms for him-

self his own world; for the feeling of his *own power* implies and soon demands also the possession of his *own space* and his *own material* belonging exclusively to him.

Be his realm, his province, his land, as it were, a corner of the court-yard, of the house, or of the room; be it the space of a box, of a chest, or of a closet; be it a grotto, a hut, or a garden—the human being, the boy at this age, needs an external point, if possible, chosen and prepared by himself, to which he refers all his activity.

When the room to be filled is extensive, when the realm to be controlled is large, when the whole to be represented or produced is complex, then brotherly union of similar-minded persons is in place. And when similar-minded persons meet in similar endeavor, and their hearts find each other, then either the work already begun is extended, or the work begun by one becomes a common work.

[In this and the following passages Froebel foreshadows the kindergarten, which he meant to be *par excellence* the social nursery of the child—a place where the children's faculties might be directed without violence into social channels. In the educational practice of home and school this phase of child-nature is almost wholly ignored, and not unfrequently suppressed as detrimental to the child's individual welfare. To the mother the child is *her* child, to the school it is *a* child.

Perhaps this is well, so far as the mother is concerned, inasmuch as it is her special province to nurse the earliest germ of individual development which underlies the future social worth of the child, and inasmuch as the home rarely offers suitable conditions to train the child for life in a society of equals. With the school, however, this is different; here all the elements of a society of equals are given, opportunities for common enterprise are so abundant that isolation becomes a matter of great difficulty. Here, then, it would be easy to establish an atmosphere of universal good-will; to develop and foster habits of sympathy, gratitude, and helpfulness; to have the pupil grow surely and steadily into ever fuller appreciation of the value of social effort to himself, and of his own value to society; to fill the soul of each one brimful of a generous self-assertion and a rational self-sacrifice that shrink from no duty and yield no right.

In the kindergarten Froebel has provided an ideal society of equals which the child may enter at the very moment when his social instincts enter consciousness. The school would gain in every phase of its work, could it connect itself organically with the kindergarten and become an institution where the future men and women might learn the arts of co-ordination and subordination, of creative and directive leadership, of intelligent and cheerful helpfulness in the attainment of common purposes. Thus the school would strengthen the pupil's individuality, invigorate it through exercise, lead it to ever greater self-consciousness in practice, elevate his drift and character by giving him a tendency to seek worthy objects for a generous activity, enable him to become a leader in matters in which he has the stuff for leadership, and a contented follower in all affairs in which his powers assign him a humbler station.— *Tr.*]

Would you, O parents and educators, see in miniature, in a picture, as it were, what I have here indicated, look into this education-room * of eight boys, seven to eight years old.

On the large table of the much-used room there stands a chest of building-blocks, in the form of bricks, each side about one sixth of the size of actual bricks, the finest and most variable material that can be offered a boy for purposes of representation. Sand or sawdust, too, have found their way into the room, and fine, green moss has been brought in abundantly from the last walk in the beautiful pine-forest.

---

* A word formed in imitation of the word school-room, to indicate the wider scope of the place. — *Tr.*

[This is the first foreshadowing of what has since in the kindergarten been developed into *group-work*. In group-work several children, or the whole little society, unite their skill and energy in the use of the gifts and occupations for a common purpose. This purpose may lie within the limits of a single gift or occupation, or it may require a variety of these. A few instances will illustrate this: The group-work remains within the limits of a single gift or occupation when the children use the folding papers as paving-stones in building a sidewalk, when they use their third gifts in representing a farm-yard with its buildings and implements, when they combine to build a street railroad with the help of the fourth gift, when two children fold a dwelling-house from a large sheet of cardboard, while the others are busy folding from smaller sheets of paper all kinds of furniture—tables, chairs, sofas, beds, writing-desk, picture-frames, looking-glasses, etc.

Here the individuality of each child has full play, and yet is exercised in the service of a common purpose, subordinating itself to the claims and needs of the little society with no loss and much gain. This becomes still more evident when a variety of gifts and occupations are brought into play. Here is an instance: In one corner of a suitably prepared " sand-table " a few handfuls of sand are spread to receive yellow folding-papers, cut and rolled so as to represent a wheat-field; behind this a few children build a small village, from the fifth and sixth gifts; others erect near the center of the table a large mill, with the necessary out-houses; still others build a road, a brook, a bridge, with suitable material; a few boys are busy making bags of flour out of clay; two girls are constructing a wagon out of sticks, peas, and interlacing material. Thus all unite to express what they know about the history of wheat.

In the primary school it becomes desirable to develop these social tendencies methodically and in harmony with individual development. This is accomplished with the help of my group-table, first systematically used at La Porte (Indiana). The table is similar to the ordinary kindergarten-table, but in the shape of a square or hexagon, and of a size to accommodate four or six children, one at each side of the table. When the children work at this table with any given material, at respectively equal distances from the center or margin, the work will be strictly symmetrical and definitely related to the sides and angles, diagonals and diameters of the table-top. This symmetrical arrangement serves as a powerful connecting link among the individual workers. They soon learn to contribute their material and energy to the execution of social purposes with little or no thought of individual gain, and still less of individual supremacy.—*Tr.*]

It is intermission, and each one has begun his own work. There in a corner stands a chapel quite concealed, a cross and an altar indicate the meaning of the structure: it is the creation of a small, quiet boy. There on a chair two boys have united to undertake a considerably greater piece of work : it is a building of several stories, and probably represents a castle, which looks down from the chair as from a mountain into a valley. But what has quietly grown under the hands of that boy at the table? It is a green hill crowned by an old, ruined castle. The others, in the mean while, have erected a village in the plain below.

Now, each one has finished his work ; each one examines it and that of the others. In each one rises the thought and the wish to unite all in a connected whole ; and scarcely has this wish been recognized as a common one, when they establish common roads from the village to the ruin, from this to the castle, and from the castle to the chapel, and between them lie brooks and meadows.

At another time some had fashioned a landscape from clay, another had constructed from pasteboard a house with doors and windows, and a third had made miniature ships from nut-shells. Each one examines his work : it is good, but it stands alone. He sees his neighbor's work : it would gain so much by being united. And immediately the house, as a castle, crowns the hill, and the tiny ship floats on the small artificial lake, and, to the delight of all, the youngest brings his shepherd and sheep to graze between the mountain and the lake. Now, they all stand and behold with pleasure and satisfaction the work of their own hands.

Again, what busy tumult among those older boys at the brook down yonder! They have built canals and sluices, bridges and sea-ports, dams and mills, each one intent only on his own work. Now the water is to be used to carry vessels from the higher to the lower level; but at each step of progress one trespasses on the limits of another realm, and each one equally claims his right as lord and maker, while he recognizes the claims of the others. What can serve here to mediate? Only *treaties*, and, like states, they bind themselves by strict treaties. Who can point out the varied significance, the varied results of these plays of boys? Two things, indeed, are clearly established. They proceed from one and the same spirit of boyhood; and the playing boys made good pupils, intelligent, and quick to learn, quick to see and to do, diligent and full of zeal, reliable in thought and feeling, efficient and vigorous. Those who played thus are efficient men, or will become so.

Particularly helpful at this period of life is the cultivation of gardens owned by the boys, and their cultivation for the sake of the produce. For here man for the first time sees his work bearing fruit in an organic way, determined by logical necessity and law—fruit which, although subject to the inner laws of natural development, depends in many ways upon his work and upon the character of his work!

This work fully completes, in many ways, the boy's life with nature, and satisfies his curiosity concerning her workings, his desire to know her—a desire that urges him again and again to give thoughtful and continuous attention and observation to plants and flowers. Nature, too, seems to favor these promptings and occupations, and to reward them with abundant success ; for a glance upon these gardens of children reveals at once the fact that, if a boy has given his plants only moderate care and attention, they thrive remarkably well; and that the plants and flowers of the boys who attend to them with special care live in sympathy with these boys, as it were, and are particularly healthy and luxuriant.

If the boy can not have the care of a little garden of his own, he should have at least a few plants in boxes or pots, filled not with rare and delicate or double plants, but with common plants that have an abundance of leaves and blossoms, and thrive easily.

The child, or boy, who has guarded and cared for another living thing, although it be of a lower order, will be led more easily to guard and foster his own life. At the same time the care of plants will gratify his desire to observe other living things, such as beetles, butterflies, and birds, for these seek the vicinity of plants.

By no means, however, do all the plays and occupations of boys at this age aim at the representation of things ; on the contrary, many are predominantly mere practice and trials of strength, and many aim simply at display of strength. Nevertheless, the play of this period always bears a peculiar character, corresponding with its inner life. For, while during the previous period of childhood the aim of play consisted simply in *activity* as such, its aim lies now in a *definite, conscious purpose;* it seeks *representation* as such, or the thing to be represented in the activity. This character is developed more and more in the free boyish games as the boys advance in age. This is observable even with all games of physical movement, with games of running, boxing, wrestling, with ball-games, racing, games of hunting, of war, etc. (see § 30).

It is the sense of sure and reliable power, the sense of its increase, both as an individual and as a member of the group, that fills the boy with all-pervading, jubilant joy during these games. It is by no means, however, only the physical power that is fed and strengthened in these games; intellectual and moral power, too, is definitely and steadily gained and brought under control. Indeed, a comparison of the relative gains of the mental and of the physical phases would scarcely yield the palm to the body. Justice, moderation, self-control, truthfulness, loyalty, brotherly love, and, again, strict impartiality—who, when he approaches a group of boys engaged in such games, could fail to catch the fragrance of these delicious blossomings of the heart and mind, and of a firm will; not to mention the beautiful, though perhaps less fragrant, blossoms of courage, perseverance, resolution, prudence, together with the severe elimination of indolent indulgence? Whoever would inhale a fresh, quickening breath of life should visit the play-grounds of such boys. Flowers of still more delicate fragrance bloom, and the spirited, free boy spares them as the spirited horse spares the child that lies in the path of his dashing career. These delicate blossoms, resembling the violet and anemone, are forbearance, consideration, sympathy, and encouragement for the weaker, younger, and more delicate; fair ness to those who are as yet unfamiliar with the game.

Would that all who, in the education of boys, bare- ly tolerate play-grounds, might consider these things! There are, indeed, many harsh words and many rude deeds, but the sense of power must needs precede its cultivation. Keen, clear, and penetrating are the boy's eye and sense in the recognition of inner meaning; keen and decided, therefore, even harsh and severe, is his judgment of those who are his equals, or who claim equality with him in judgment and power.

Every town should have its own common play- ground for the boys. Glorious results would come from this for the entire community. For at this period games, whenever it is feasible, are common, and thus develop the feeling and desire for community, and the laws and requirements of community.

The boy tries to see himself in his companions, to feel himself in them, to weigh and measure himself by them, to know and find himself with their help. Thus, the games directly influence and educate the boy for life, awaken and cultivate many civil and moral virtues.

Yet the seasons and surroundings do not always permit the boy, free from the duties of home and school, to exercise and develop his powers in the open air, and at no time should boys be unoccupied. There- fore other kinds of external occupations and representa- tions of in-door life constitute at this age an essential part of the activity and guidance of boys, and are very important to him. This is particularly the case with so-called mechanical pursuits, such as paper and paste- board work, modeling, etc. (see § 22).

However, there is in man still another wish—a longing, a desire of the soul that can not be gratified by external occupations, by external activity. All that external occupation and activity can give man at this period does not by any means suffice him, does not meet the demands and needs of an education adequate to his nature : the present, however full and rich, can not suffice him.

The existence of the present teaches him the existence of the past. This, too, which was before he was, he would know. He would know the reason, the past cause of what now is. Indeed, he would that what has remained over from past time should reveal to him the reason of its existence, should tell him of that old time.

Who fails to remember the keen desire that filled his heart, more particularly in the period of his later years of boyhood, when he beheld old walls and towers, ruins, old buildings, monuments, and columns on the hills and on the road-side—to hear others give accounts of these things, of their time and their causes? Nay, who has not at such times noticed in himself a vague, undefinable feeling that at some time these things themselves could and would give an account of themselves and their time?

And who, judging by his experience and knowledge, can furnish him these accounts, if not those who lived before he did—his elders? That these might tell him, is his earnest wish; and thus there is developed in the boy at this age the desire and craving for tales, for legends, for all kinds of stories, and later on for historical accounts. This craving, especially in its first appearance, is very intense; so much so, that, when others fail to gratify it, the boys seek to gratify it themselves. particularly on days of leisure, and in times when the regular employments of the day are ended.

Who has not been filled with respect when noticing a group of boys of this age gathered around one whom a good memory and a lively imagination have designated as their story-teller? How attentively they all listen when his story gratifies their favorite wish and confirms their judgment by its plot and incidents—in short, when it brings before them words and deeds in harmony with their own inner thoughts and feelings!

However, even the present in which the boy lives still contains much that at this period of development he can not interpret, and yet would like to interpret; much that seems to him dumb, and which he would fain have speak; much that appears to him dead, and which he longs to see alive and active.

He wishes that others might furnish him this interpretation, and impart a language to the silent objects; that they might put into clear words the inner living connection of all things which his mind vaguely apprehends.

Yet these others frequently are quite unable to gratify the boy's wish, and thus there is developed in him the intense desire for fables and fairy-tales which impart language and reason to speechless things—the one within, and the other beyond the limits of human relations and human, earthly phenomena of life.

Surely all must have noticed this, if they have given more than superficial attention to the life of boys at this age. Similarly, they must have noticed that—if here, too, the boy's desire is not or can not be gratified by his attendants—he will spontaneously hit upon the invention and presentation of fairy-tales and fables, and either work them out in his own mind alone or enter-tain his companions with them.

[One of the most difficult arts of the kindergartner is the telling of stories; and it is, perhaps, equally difficult to give detailed directions concerning the practice of this art. Yet there are a few plain requirements which it may be well to mention here. In the first place, the story should be simple in plot and form; the events and words should be few and marked, and within the child's comprehension. Involved constructions, long words, unmeaning sentimentalities, and confusing moralizings should be omitted.

Again, the plot should be true—i. e., the events should be possible, and should have some logical connection. All that is hideous or vicious should be kept out. Cruel or wanton punishments or accidents and ludicrous situations should be avoided: they blunt or pervert the moral sense of the child. The story should take the child into an ideal world of truth and beauty and goodness, where he may always rest from the unpleasant experiences and gather strength from the struggle with their opposites in life. Here he should learn to love truth and beauty and goodness, so that when their opposites do come these may find no points of attraction in the child's soul. The stories, too, should be such that the child may easily imitate them by drawing on his slender stock of experiences, and by enlivening these with his ideals of whatever is lovely and good.—*Tr.*]

These fairy-tales and stories will then very clearly reveal to the observer what is going on in the innermost mind of the boy, though doubtless the latter may not be himself conscious of it (see § 97). Whatever he feels in his heart, whatever lives in his soul, whatever he can not express in his own words, he would fain have others express. Whatever his mind vaguely apprehends, whatever fills his heart with joy and pleasure, as the sense of power and the feeling of spring, he would fain express in words; but he feels himself unable to do so. He seeks for words, and, as he can not yet find them in himself, he rejoices intensely to hear them from others, especially in song.

How the serene, happy boy of this age rejoices in song! He feels, as it were, a new, true life in song. It is the sense of growing power that in his wanderings from the valley to the hill, and from hill to hill, pours forth the joyous song from his throat.

The intense desire to understand himself holds the boy; therefore he seeks the clear, pure, living water in lake or brook. In his play he ever returns to this, because in it he sees himself, the image of his soul, and because in and through it he hopes to get a knowledge of his spiritual nature.

What the water in brook and lake, what the pure air and wide expanse on the mountain-top are to the boy's soul, that, too, play is to him—a mirror of the life-struggles that await him; therefore, in order to gain strength for these, boys and youth seek obstacles, difficulties, and strife in their play.

The desire to gain a knowledge of the past and of nature attracts the boy again and again to flowers and to old walls and ruined vaults. The desire to express what fills his innermost heart and mind urges him to sing. Thus it is certain that very many of the external phenomena, very many things in the boy's conduct and actions, have an inner, spiritual significance; that they indicate his inner, spiritual life and tendency, and are, therefore, symbolic.

How salutary would it be for parents and child, for their present and future, if parents believed in this symbolism of childhood and boyhood, if they heeded the child's life in reference to this! It would unite parents and children by a new living tie; it would establish a new living connection between their present and their future life.

§ 50. Such is pure boy-life at this period. From this description of inner and outer pure boy-life and child-life, which fortunately for man we still meet occasionally—where natural views of education prevail in actual life possibly in greater beauty, richness, and intensity than has been represented—from this description let us cast a glance upon boy-life and child-life as we generally meet it more or less pronounced in actual life. Let us look particularly upon the life of the child and boy in his filial, brotherly, domestic relations, in his activity and work as a pupil and companion. We shall be compelled to confess frankly that many things are very different: that we meet stubbornness, obstinacy, supineness, mental and physical indolence, sensuality, vanity and self-conceit, dogmatism and despotism, an unbrotherly and unfilial spirit, emptiness and superficiality, aversion to work and even to play, disobedience and ungodliness, etc.

When we look for the sources of these and many other undeniable shortcomings in the life of children and boys, we are confronted ultimately by a double reason: in the first place, the complete neglect of the development of certain sides of full human life; secondly, the early faulty tendency—the early faulty and unnatural steps of development and distortion of the originally good human powers and tendencies by arbitrary and willful interference with the original orderly and logical course of human development.

§ 51. For, surely, the nature of man is in itself good, and surely there are in man qualities and tendencies in themselves good. Man is by no means naturally bad, nor has he originally bad or evil qualities and tendencies; unless, indeed, we consider as naturally evil, bad, and faulty the *finite*, the *material*, the *transitory*, the *physical* as such, and the logical consequences of the existence of these phenomena, namely, that man must have the possibility of failure in order to be good and virtuous, that he must be able to make himself a slave in order to be truly free. Yet these things are the necessary concomitants of the manifestation of the eternal in the temporal, of unity in diversity, and follow necessarily from man's destiny to become a conscious, reasonable, and free being.

Whoever is to do with self-determination and freedom that which is divine and eternal, must be at liberty to do that which is earthly and finite.

Since God wished to reveal himself in the finite, this could be done only with finite and transitory material.

Whoever, then, considers that which is finite, material, physical, as in itself bad, thereby expresses contempt for creation, nature, as such—nay, he actually blasphemes God.

Similarly, it is treason to human nature and to man to consider him in his essence as neither good nor bad or evil; how much more, then, is it treason to consider him in his nature as essentially bad or evil!

Man thereby denies God in humanity, for he denies His work, and hence the ways and means of truly knowing God, and thus puts into the world falsehood, the only source of all evil.

§ 52. If there is anything absolutely evil, it is this, for it is the origin of all evil. But falsehood has no real existence; it is already annihilated; and, as in its very nature it is annihilated, it must also be annihilated in its outward manifestations. For man has been created neither with nor for falsehood, but with and for truth. Again, man does not create falsehood out of himself, out of his own nature; he can and does create it only because God has created him for truth. Man creates falsehood by failing to recognize this fact for himself, or to lead others to recognize it. Man creates falsehood by hindering the recognition of this fact as proceeding from the pure fount of his being in and through himself.

Man, as an earthly phenomenon, is destined to have body and soul developed consciously and rationally, with a certain degree of symmetry and harmony. If man could only reach a clear and distinct knowledge of his nature—if, after having attained such knowledge wholly or in part, he were not so paralyzed in strength and will by evil habit and infirmity—he would immediately throw off all shortcomings, and even the manifestation of all evil that is in him and done by him—that clings to him, as it were, and hides him like a disguise. All these shortcomings and wrong-doings have their origin merely in the disturbed relations of these two sides of man: his *nature*, that which he has grown to be; and his *essence*, his innermost being. Therefore, a suppressed or perverted good quality—a good tendency, only repressed, misunderstood, or misguided—lies originally at the bottom of every shortcoming in man. Hence the only and infallible remedy for counteracting any shortcoming and even wickedness is to find the originally good source, the originally good side of the human being that has been repressed, disturbed, or misled into the shortcoming, and then to foster, build up, and properly guide this good side. Thus the shortcoming will at last disappear, although it may involve a hard struggle *against habit, but not against original depravity* in man; and this is accomplished so much the more rapidly and surely because man himself tends to abandon his shortcomings, for man prefers right to wrong.

§ 53. Thus, selecting one point for illustration, we can not deny that there is at present among children and boys little simplicity, little true gentleness, little mutual forbearance, brotherly patience, little true religious feeling; but, on the other hand, much egotism, unfriendliness, particularly rudeness, etc. This is clearly due not merely to the failure of arousing at an early period, and of subsequently cultivating in the child and boy a feeling of common sympathy, but also to the early annihilation of this feeling between parents and children.

If, then, true brotherly love, true simplicity, trustful and truly loving gentleness, friendliness, forbearance, and respect for the companion and fellow-man is to prevail again, this can be accomplished only by addressing ourselves to the feeling of common sympathy lingering—however much or little of it there may stil' be left—in the heart of every human being, and cultivating it with the greatest care. This would surely soon give back to us what we now miss so painfully in domestic, social, and religious life.

Another source of many boyish faults lies in precipitation, carelessness, frivolity, and thoughtlessness. The boy is apt to act in obedience to a possibly praiseworthy impulse that holds captive his mind and body ; but he has not as yet experienced in his life the consequences of gratifying this particular impulse, and it has, indeed, not even occurred to him to consider the consequences of the action (see § 6).

Thus a boy of by no means evil disposition took real delight in powdering his dear uncle's wig with plaster-of-Paris without any thought of wrong, and still more without considering that the hard grains of stone would necessarily injure the hair of the wig.

Another boy found in a large tub of water some deep, round bowls of porcelain. He observed accidentally that these bowls, when dropped upside down on the smooth surface of water, sprang back with an explosive noise. This gave him pleasure ; he frequently tried the experiment, perfectly sure, without doubt, that the bowl could not be broken in the deep, yielding water. He was frequently successful, and, in order to improve the result of the experiment, the bowl was dropped from greater and greater heights. At one time the bowl fell so horizontally upon the level water-surface, and from so great a height, that the imprisoned air could not escape in any direction, but was compressed so forcibly that it broke the bowl into two almost equal parts. Perplexed and distressed, the little self-teaching physicist stood before the unexpected result of his play that had delighted him so much.

Yet boys show a still greater—indeed, almost an incredible—degree of short-sightedness in obeying their impulses.

A boy throws stones for a long time at the small window of a house near by, trying very hard to hit it.   He
has no idea, nor does he realize that, if a stone strikes
the window, the latter must necessarily break.   At last
a stone hits the window, the window breaks, and the
amazed boy stands rooted to the spot.

Again, another boy—by no means malicious, but,
on the contrary, very good-natured and fond of pigeons
—aimed at his neighbor's beautiful pigeon on the roof,
with perfect delight and an intense desire to hit his
mark.   He did not consider that, if the bullet should
hit the mark, the pigeon would be killed, and still less
that this pigeon might be the mother of young ones
needing her care.   He fired, the bullet struck, the pigeon
fell, a beautiful pair of pigeons were separated, and a
number of unfledged young ones lost the mother who
had fed and warmed them.

It is certainly a very great truth—and failure to
appreciate it does daily great harm—that it generally
is some other human being, not unfrequently the educator himself, that first makes the child or the boy bad.
This is accomplished by attributing evil—or, at least,
wrong—motives to all that the child or boy does from
ignorance, precipitation, or even from a keen and praiseworthy sense of right or wrong.

Unfortunately, there still are such men of mischief
among educators.   To them children and boys are
always little malicious, spiteful, lurking sprites, where
others see at most a jest carried too far, or the effect of
too free an exercise of spirit.

Such birds of ill omen, especially when they are
educators, are the first to bring guilt upon such a child,

who, though not wholly innocent, is yet without *guilt;*
for they give him motives and incentives which were
as yet unknown to him; they make his actions bad,
though not, at first, his will; they kill him spiritually,
take away his (spiritual) life, and lead him to think
that this life does not come to him out of himself
and through himself, and that he can not secure it
by his own effort. When true (spiritual) life has thus
left him, and he can not secure it by his efforts, what
does mere knowledge avail him? what does a powerless
wish, devoid of energy, avail him? What they have
thus made evil and bad in the belief that not even the
child can attain heaven, can carry a heaven in his heart,
without first going, to speak mildly, through guilt—
this they would have made good again by God, and this
they call converting the child.

They act like the good-natured little boy who says
of his fly or beetle that is weak from maltreatment, or
has even lost its feet, "See, how tame!"

There still are children and boys who, in spite of
great external shortcomings from neglect or ignorance
of external relations of life, and in spite of total abandonment to momentary impulses, nevertheless have an
intense inner desire to become good and virtuous. It is
true, such boys ultimately also may become intrinsically
bad, but only because in their innermost desires they
have frequently been not only not understood, but misunderstood. Could they yet be appreciated in good
time, they would certainly still become good men.

Children and boys, indeed, are often punished by
parents and adults for faults and misdemeanors which
they had perhaps previously learned from these very

persons. Punishment, especially punishment by words, very often teaches children, or at least brings to their notice, faults of which they were wholly free.

§ 54. Man, therefore, sins much more against man, against the children, than he does against God. For what can the unworthy action of the naughty child effect against the dignity of the father whose virtue has been proved and is acknowledged? On the other hand, how much injury in body and soul may come to a younger child through the words and deeds of a naughty boy! This, too, indicates the relation of man to man, and of man to God.

§ 55. As already indicated, a deep and significant feeling of anticipation and longing aspiration occupies the boy's mind in all he does during this period. All he does bears a common character, for he seeks the unity that unites all things and beings, he seeks to find himself in and among all things.

An indefinable longing urges him to seek the things of nature, the hidden objects, plants and flowers, etc., in nature; for a constant presentiment assures him that the things which satisfy the longing of the heart can not be found on the surface; out of the depth and darkness they must be brought forth.

Educators not only neglect at an early period to nurture this longing, but, unfortunately, they disturb at too early a period even the boy's effort to nourish it from his own resources. For the boy of this age, who has been led naturally, however feebly and unconsciously, seeks, in fact, only the unity that unites all things, the absolute living Unity, the source of all things—God; not a god made and fashioned by human wit, but Him who is ever near the heart and mind, near the living spirit, and who, therefore, may be known in spirit and in truth, and who alone can be thus approached.

In his maturity, the boy is satisfied only when he has found Him to whom he has been drawn by indefinable yearning, because only then will he have found himself. We have thus reviewed the inner and outer life of the boy in free activity at school age. What, now, makes the school?

IV.

MAN AS A SCHOLAR OR PUPIL.

§ 56. THE *school* endeavors to render the scholar fully conscious of the nature and inner life of things and of himself, to teach him to know the inner relations of things to one another, to the human being, to the scholar, and to the living source and conscious unity of all things—to God (see § 45).

The aim of instruction is to bring the scholar to insight into the unity of all things, into the fact that all things have their being and life in God, so that in due time he may be able to act and live in accordance with this insight. Instruction itself offers the ways and means for attaining this aim (see § 45).

Therefore, the school and instruction place the external world and his own self, inasmuch as this forms a part of the external world, before the scholar as something separate, something different from him, something foreign to him.

Furthermore, the school points out the inner tendencies and relations among individual things and objects, and thus rises to ever higher generality and spirituality. Therefore, the boy, when he enters school, leaves the external view of things and enters upon a higher spiritual view of them.

It is this leaving of the outer and superficial view of things on the part of the child, and his entrance upon an inner view leading to knowledge, insight, and consciousness, it is this transition of the child from domestic order to the higher cosmic order of things that makes the boy a scholar and constitutes the essence of the school.

It is by no means the acquisition of a certain number of miscellaneous external facts that constitutes the essential characteristic of the school, but only the living spirit that animates all things and in which all things move.

Would that all whose business it is to direct and manage schools might carefully consider this!

Therefore, the school, as such, implies the presence of an intelligent consciousness which, as it were, hovers over and between the outer world and the scholar, which unites in itself the essence of both, holds the inner being of both, mediating between the two, imparting to them language and mutual understanding. This consciousness is the *master* in this art, who is called *master* also because for *most* things he is to point out the unity of things.* He is *school*master because it is his business to point out and render clear to himself and others the inner, spiritual nature of things.

Every school-child anticipates, expects, and requires this of the schoolmaster; and this anticipation and hope, this faith, is the invisible and efficacious tie between the two.

---

* Another of Froebel's strange plays on words that have no connection with each other—this time the words *Meister* and *meist* (*master* and *most*).— *Tr.*

It is probable, too, that this anticipation and hope, this childlike faith of children, enabled former school-masters to be much more efficient in the production of genuine inner life in their children than many school-teachers of our day, who acquaint the children with many things without showing them their necessary inner spiritual unity and connection.

Do not reply that, even if this higher view of the school is the true one, and if there exists an inner spiritual ideal of it, it could scarcely be shown to have an actual existence—at least, not where a tailor, as schoolmaster, sits enthroned on his working-table, and the children below him recite their a-b, ab, and their "sum total of all instruction," nor where an old wood-cutter in winter, in a dark, sooty room, drives into the heads of children the explanation of the small Lutheran catechism as he would his wedges for wood-splitting—that here certainly spirit, spiritual nature, and life have no place.

[Froebel's early life fell in the period when country schools were still, in many cases, intrusted to persons who earned their live-lihood chiefly in some other occupation, such as tailoring, shoemak-ing, weaving, etc. Not unfrequently in poorer communities the same man "kept school" in winter, and during the summer worked on farms, or acted as a communal shepherd. One and the same scanty school-book contained "the sum total of all instruction"—the bulk of which was made up of the Lutheran catechism.—*Tr.*]

But just here they have a place; how else could the blind show the way to the lame, and the cripple support the weak on his feet? It is only the child's anticipa-tion, his faith, his child-like simplicity, which hopes and trusts that the schoolmaster—simply because he is and is called schoolmaster—can give an inner spiritual unity to that which is externally separated, giving life to that which is dead, and meaning to that which lives.

This expectation alone, be it ever so misty and obscure, renders the schoolmaster's work efficient. This anticipation and faith are like the all-quickening air by which the stones, which he may offer his children to eat, are turned into food for them—if not for their head, yet for the heart. It is this anticipation, hope, and yearning, this all-quickening spirit and breath, that even in the dark, sooty room, make the school so dear to the school-boy.

The spirit, the genuine spirit of the school, like the spirit of Jesus and of God, does not come by external doings. Thus, too, spacious school-rooms, *as such*, are not sufficient if the good ventilation has taken the place of higher spiritual life. Airy, bright school-rooms are a great, precious boon, worthy the daily gratitude of teacher and pupil; but alone they are not sufficient.

Luther's words, " To fast and to deck out the body furnish, indeed, fine external discipline; but only he is truly worthy and well prepared who has faith and trust," find their application here, too.

The faith and trust, the hope and anticipation with which the child enters school, accomplish everything; they bring about stupendous results in such schools. For the child enters school with the child-like faith, the silent hope : " Here you will be taught something that you can not learn elsewhere; here you gain food for mind and spirit, elsewhere you can obtain food only for the body; here (this is literally the child's living hope and anticipation) you receive food and drink that still the hunger and thirst, elsewhere you are offered food and drink that only give occasion for new hunger and thirst."

With this faith he listens, too, to the ordinary words, the ordinary speech from the lips of the man who is the schoolmaster.

Even if there is no high spiritual meaning in his words, the child's faith discovers it there ; and the child's high power of spiritual digestion gets food from chips and straw.

Now, if even the tailor, wood-cutter, or weaver, when he teaches, ceases to be to the child tailor, wood-cutter, or weaver, and becomes schoolmaster, how much more will this be the case where the school-teacher in village or city—be he called organist, chorister, or rector —is truly a schoolmaster !

Ask every true school-child, let every one who in village or city has been a true school-child ask himself, with what feeling he approached the school-house, and still more with what feeling he entered it ; how he felt more or less keenly each day as if he had entered into a higher spiritual world.

How else could it be possible for children to repeat daily, not only for more than a quarter of an hour during a whole week, without tiring but with a feeling of heightened life, some text from Sunday's sermon—e. g., " Seek ye first the kingdom of God " ? How else could the children sing and memorize hymns abounding in strange figures, such as " How much it costs to follow Christ," or, " Let heart and spirit soar on high," daily, in sections, during a whole week, with true inner edification and a living influence on the life of every scholar ? How else could this be done at an early period of boy-life in such a way that in the storms of life the youth and the man rest on these things as on a rock?

The occasional excessive vivacity of the boys in school does not contradict this. The boy feels less restraint and moves more freely just because of the influence of the school, because of the heightened inner spiritual power which has been fed by the school. The genuine school-boy should never be dispirited and indolent, but full of life and spirit, strong in body and mind. Therefore the truly high-spirited boy who follows his natural vivacity full of joy surely never thinks of any injurious effect on outer life.

It is a great mistake to think that the energetic, animating, uniting (intensive) power of man increases with years and cultivation. The energetic, animating, uniting power decreases; and the expansive, productive, creative, modifying (extensive) power increases.

The feeling and consciousness of this extending, creative power in man unfortunately have a tendency to destroy the recognition and appreciation of the former energetic, animating, uniting power. This, with the confounding of the two in their nature and manifestation, leads us in life, in the management of schools and of the education of children, to great and frequent errors, and robs the life of each one of its true basis.

We now trust too little to the energetic and uniting power in the child and boy—we respect it too little as a spiritually quickening power. Therefore, too, it has too little influence in the later years of boyhood. For the neglect of this inner power causes the inner power itself to vanish.

Or we play with this power when it manifests itself in children. Hence we fare with them as with a magnet which we leave hanging or even lying inactive and without a burden, or with whose magnetic power we play irregularly and regardless of magnetic laws. In both cases the power is diminished or lost; when, later on, the magnet is to show its power, it is found weak and inefficient. So it is with those children; when, later on, they are expected to bear some physical or moral burden, they are found wanting.

Would that, in judging and estimating the inner power of children and boys, we might never forget the words of one of our greatest German writers: that there is a greater advance from the infant to the speaking child than there is from the school-boy to a Newton!

Now, if the advance is greater, the power, too, must be greater; this we should consider. The later extent, diversity, directness, and concentration of man's knowledge and insight (their extensiveness) dim and weaken our apprehension of the former unity and mobility (intensiveness) of human power.

It is the spirit alone, then, that makes the school and the school-room; not the increasing analysis and isolation of what is already isolated—a process that has no limits, and supplies ever-new data for further analysis and reduction—but the unification of that which is isolated and separate by attention to the uniting spirit that lives in all isolation and diversity. This it is that makes the school.

Never forget that *the essential business of the school is not so much to teach and to communicate a variety*

*and multiplicity of things as it is to give prominence
to the ever-living unity that is in all things.*

[This is not to be construed as meaning that schooling should be
chiefly for "power" or "mental discipline," as is claimed by the ad-
vocates of chiefly formal studies. No one could be more opposed
than Froebel to the various school practices of "threshing empty
straw" for the sake of gaining "threshing power." What he demands in the above sentence is the teaching of principles as opposed
to the teaching of isolated facts and rules. He is filled with the
same thought which Herbert Spencer subsequently expressed as follows: "Between a mind of rules and a mind of principles, there exists a difference, such as that between a confused heap of materials,
and the same materials organized into a complete whole, with all its
parts bound together." In both cases, it will be seen, material contents are implied, and mere formalism is excluded.—*Tr.*]

Because this is so frequently forgotten and placed
in the background disregarded, there are at present so
many school-*teachers* and so few school-*masters*, so many
institutions of learning and so few *schools*.

Possibly they do not know, or, at least, they may
not have recognized with sufficient clearness and distinctness, what spirit it is that pervaded and even now
sometimes pervades genuine schools, what spirit it is
that ought to animate schools. Even the genuine, faithful schoolmaster, in the simplicity of his vocation, may
not have recognized it nor formulated it; in the faithful performance of his work, thoroughly absorbed in
his calling, he may not recognize it nor be able to formulate it. For this reason, no doubt, it has glided away
so rapidly, and continues to vanish.

Unfortunately, we see here again confirmed what to
our sorrow confronts us so often in life: that even the
highest and most precious blessing is lost by man, if he
does not know what he possesses, if he does not hold it

fast and represent it in his life consciously, freely, and from his own choice (see § 33). The anticipation and hope, the trust and disposition of childhood indeed show the way, but man is to follow it with conscious insight and self-determination, persisting in what he knows to be right. For man is destined for consciousness, for freedom, and for self-determination.

§ 57. Furthermore, a vivid presentation of the requirements of the school shows that the subject *in* which the boy is to be instructed is also the one *about* which he should be instructed—else instruction and learning are thoughtless play and without effect upon head and heart, the intellect, and the feelings.

What has been said will also answer, or, at least, make it easy to answer, the questions : Do we need schools ? Why do we need schools and instruction ? What shall they be, and how shall they be constituted ?

As spiritual and material beings, we are to become thinking, conscious, intelligent (self-consciously feeling and perceiving), efficient human beings. We should first seek to cultivate our powers, our spirit, as received from God ; to represent the divine in our lives, knowing that thereby all that is earthly will, too, have its claims satisfied. We are to grow in wisdom and understanding with God and men, in human and divine things. We should know that we are and ought to be and to live in that which is our Father's. We should know that we in our earthly being and all earthly things are a temple of the living God. We should know that we are to be perfect as our Father in heaven is perfect ; and in accordance with this knowledge we should act and live. To this knowledge the school is to lead us ; for this the school and instruction are needed; in accordance with this aim they should be constituted.

§ 58. What, now, shall the school teach? In what shall the human being, the boy as scholar, be instructed?

Only the consideration of the nature and requirements of human development at the stage of boyhood will enable us to answer this question. But the knowledge of this nature and these requirements can be derived only from the observation of the character of man in his boyhood.

Now, in accordance with this character, this manner of being, in what things is the boy to be instructed?

The life and outward being of man in the beginning of boyhood show him, in the first place, to be animated by a spiritual self of his own; they show, too, the existence of a vague feeling that this spiritual self has its being and origin in a higher and Supreme Being, and depends on this Being in which, indeed, all things have their being and origin, and on which all things depend. The life and outward being of man in boyhood show the presence of an intense feeling and anticipation of the existence of a living, quickening Spirit, in which and by which all things live, by which all things are invisibly surrounded, as a fish is surrounded by water and man and all creatures by the clear, pure atmosphere.

In his boyhood, in the beginning of his school-life, man seems to feel the power of his spiritual nature, to anticipate vaguely God and the spiritual nature of all things. He shows, at the same time, a desire to attain ever more clearness in that feeling, and to confirm his anticipation.

Man, in boyhood, approaches the outer world, placed over against him, with the feeling and hope and belief that it, too, is animated and ruled by a spirit, like that which animates and rules him; and he is filled by an intense, irresistible longing—which returns with every new spring and every new fall, with every new, fresh morning and calm evening, with every peaceful festive day—a longing to know this all-ruling spirit, to make it his own, as it were.

The outer world confronts man in boyhood in a two-fold character—first, as the product of human requirements and human power, and, secondly, as the outcome of the requirements of the power that works in nature.

Between this outer world (the world of form and matter) and the inner world (the world of mind and spirit), language appears—originally united with both, but gradually freeing itself from both, and thereby uniting the two.

§ 59. Thus the *mind* and the *outer world* (first as *nature*), and *language* which unites the two, are the poles of boy-life, as they also were the poles of mankind as a whole in the first stage of approaching maturity (as the sacred books show). Through them the school and instruction are to lead the boy to the threefold, yet in itself one, knowledge—to the knowledge of himself in all his relations, and thus to the knowledge of man as such; to the knowledge of God, the eternal condition, cause, and source of his being and of the being of all things; and to the knowledge of nature and the outer world as proceeding from the Eternal Spirit, and depending thereon.

Instruction and the school are to lead man to a life in full harmony with that threefold, yet in itself one, knowledge. By this knowledge they are to lead man from desire to will, from will to firmness of will, and thus in continuous progression to the attainment of his destiny, to the attainment of his earthly perfection.

V.

THE CHIEF GROUPS OF SUBJECTS OF INSTRUCTION.

A. Religion and Religious Instruction.

§ 60. *Religion* is the endeavor to raise into clear knowledge the feeling that originally the spiritual self of man is one with God, to realize the unity with God which is founded on this clear knowledge, and to continue to live in this unity with God, serene and strong, in every condition and relation of life.

Religion is not something fixed, but an ever-progressing and, for this very reason, ever-present tendency.

Religious instruction quickens, confirms, explains the feeling that man's own spiritual self, his soul, his mind and spirit, have their being and origin in God and proceed from God; it shows that the qualities and the nature of the soul, of the mind and spirit, have their being in and through God; it gives an insight into the being and working of God; it gives an insight into the relation of God to man, as it is clearly manifested in the mind and life of every one, in life as such, and particularly in the life and development of mankind, as they are preserved and revealed in the sacred books; it applies this knowledge to life as such, and particularly to and in the life of each one, and to the progressive development of mankind, so that the divine may be represented in the human, and that man may know and do his duty; it presents and points out the ways and means by which the desire to live in true unity with God may be gratified, and by which this unity, if impaired, may be restored.

For this reason *religious instruction always assumes some degree of religion, however weak.* Religious instruction can bear fruit, can affect and influence life only in so far as it finds in the mind of man true religion, however indefinite and vague. If it were possible that a human being could be without religion, it would also be impossible to give him religion.

This should be considered by thoughtless parents who allow their children to grow to school age without giving the slightest care to the religious tendency of the young minds (see § 21).

Intelligent insight into the nature of religion—simple as it is, founded in the very nature of man, and so in harmony with the nature of man—is nevertheless so rarely pure, because man, who is also material and occupies space, finds it difficult to understand original unity without assuming and premising previous separation, and because in the mind of man the conception of unification is always associated with the conception of union in space or time. But God, the spiritual, eternally self-developing, must ever remain an undivided one, simply because he is spiritual; and, as *true original unity* by no means implies, but absolutely *excludes, previous separation,* so *unification* neither supposes nor requires, but absolutely *excludes, union in space and time.*

Human experience and observation offer by far more proofs than are needed to demonstrate and explain this. For the idea, the thought translated by man into living form in some outward work, was originally in immediate unity with his being, and bears unmistakably the impress of the personality and individuality of the particular human being. This thought in this particular form belongs only to *this* human being; and, were it to become conscious of itself in the form given to it, it could return to the totality of the thought of the man from whom it proceeds—i. e., it would give itself an account of its relation to the totality of thought of this man; in the consciousness of this relation it might develop and cultivate itself and thus raise itself to an apprehension of the totality of thought of this man; nay, it might even raise itself at least to a vague apprehension of the fundamental thought of the human being from whom it proceeds. For *every human being has*, indeed, *but one thought peculiarly and predominantly his own*, the fundamental thought, as it were, of his whole being, the key-note of his life-symphony, a thought which he simply seeks to express and render clear with the help of a thousand other thoughts, with the help of all he does. Yet, by the representation of that thought, and of all other thoughts in living outward form, man has not in any sense been diminished within himself; and, although this thought now appears only outside of man, yet he will always cheerfully recognize it as his own, and concern himself about its development and cultivation (see § 63).

The thinker and the thought—could the latter become conscious of itself—must ever be intensely mindful of the fact of their original unity; and yet the thought is not the thinker, although essentially one and united; such is the relation of the human spirit to God.

A father has one or many sons. Each one is an independent, self-conscious being. Yet who can fail to see that each son expresses, in a new individuality, the nature of the father?

The son, or each one of the sons, even in the most trivial thing and the most decided peculiarity, is again the father, only in a new individuality. Indeed, the sons of the same father, of the same parents, resemble one another in disposition, speech, tone of voice, and movements, so that, with the exception of a small new peculiarity, any one of them may, in many respects, be put in the place of another. Yet none of them is a part of another—each one is whole; not one of them is a particular part of the father. As they are whole and undivided, so, too, the father is still whole and undivided. Could we see human relationships clearly, we should apprehend and recognize the divine.

Similarly, unification does not imply a material union in time and space. Can not the thinking, feeling man be at one with his friends and beloved ones, and act in unison with them, although lands and seas separate them from him? Can not and does not man feel himself to be in spiritual union with human beings of whom he has only heard, whom he has never seen and never will see, and does he not act in unison with them? Can not man feel himself to be in spiritual union with human beings who lived and worked thousands of years ago, or who may appear upon the earth or elsewhere in space thousands of years later, and can he not act in unison with these?

Man spurns what might be to him a guide and a light in his material experiences. Therefore, he is apt to grope also without guide and light in the realms of the purely spiritual, of the divine, which is without time and space.

It is and remains forever true that, in purely and distinctly human relations, particularly in parental and spiritual human relations, there are mirrored the relations between the divine and the human, between God and man. Those pure relations of man to man reveal to us the relations of God to man and of man to God.

§ 61. If man consciously and clearly recognizes that his spiritual self proceeds from God, that it is born in God and from God, that it is originally one with God, and that consequently he is in a state of continuous dependence on God, as well as in a state of continuous and uninterrupted community with God; if he finds his salvation, his peace, his joy, his destiny, his life (which is the genuine and only true life as such), and the source of his being in this eternally necessary dependence of his self on God, in the clearness of this knowledge, in living and constant obedience to this knowledge in all he does, in a life, indeed, fully unified with this knowledge and conviction—he truly, and in the full sense of the words, recognizes in God his Father. *If he acknowledges himself to be a child of God, and lives in accordance with this, he has the Christian religion, the religion of Jesus.*

Therefore, a pure earthly, filial relation in thought and action is such as was told of Jesus—"and he was subject unto them" (his parents).

Therefore, a genuine parental relation in thought and action, honoring and acknowledging the as yet unrevealed and undeveloped divine spirit in the child, is such as was told of Mary: "But Mary kept all these sayings, pondering them in her heart."

Therefore, pure human, parental, and filial relations are the key, the first condition, of that heavenly, divine, fatherly, and filial relation and life, of a genuine Christian life in thought and action.

Therefore, the comprehension of the purely spiritual human relations, of the true parental and filial relations, furnishes the only key for the recognition and apprehension of the relations of God to man and of man to God.

Only in the measure in which we fully comprehend the purely spiritual, intrinsically human relations, and are faithful to them in life, even in the smallest details, can we attain a full knowledge and conception of the relations between God and man, apprehending them so deeply, vividly, and truly that every yearning of our whole being is thereby gratified, or at least clearly interpreted, and is transformed from an ever-ungratified longing into a steadily fruitful aspiration.

We do not yet know, we do not, indeed, apprehend in the least, that which is so near us, which is one with our life, with ourselves; we are not even loyal to the verbal knowledge and verbal apprehension of which we boast. This is daily shown by our behavior toward our parents, our children, our education.

We would be children of God, and are not yet children of our fathers, of our parents. God is to be our Father, and we are so far from being true fathers to our children. We would have an insight into the divine, and we leave unheeded the human relations that lead to such insight.

Insight into the relations between God and man, with full comprehension of these relations, blesses even to the thousandth generation through pure parental and filial relations, and a life in accordance with these.

We put outward limits to humanity eternally progressing in its development, we inclose it in external bounds, and we imagine that it has already reached these bounds, even in its earthly development. Humanity, which lives only in its continuous development and cultivation, seems to us dead and stationary, something to be modeled over again and again in accordance with its present type. We are ignorant of our own nature and of the nature of humanity, and yet would know God and Jesus. We imagine that we already know our own nature and the nature of humanity, and, therefore, fail to know God and Jesus.

We separate God and man, man and Jesus, and yet would come to God and Jesus. We fail to see that every external separation implies an original inner unity. However clearly and unequivocally this is taught in the word and in the idea of separation, we overlook it wholly.

The intimate unity of God and Jesus can not be expressed more comprehensively and exhaustively, more truly and adequately, than by the relation of father and son, the highest and most intimate relation that man can know and comprehend, but which generally is viewed only superficially, and not in its innermost spiritual, pervasive significance. The child, however, attains true sonship only by developing within himself the father's nature in full consciousness and clear insight, by making the father's views, the father's nature and aspirations, the motives for all his thoughts and actions; and by esteeming it his chief business, the source of peace and joy in his life, to be in all he does in harmony with his father whose high worth he has recognized. Such is the pure, genuine, and high, yet truly human, relation of the son to his father—the relation of the true, genuine son to the true, genuine father.

The relation of sonship always implies on the part of the son a conscious sharing of the father's views and aspirations—a complete, essential, intrinsic, spiritual accord between the son and father.

Of course, this relation is and should be established first with the oldest, first-born son. While all his younger brothers are still children, he is the only, the first-born son.

Jesus is the only-begotten Son of God—he is the beloved son of God; for among all human and earth-born, among all heaven-born children, he is the first who in his knowledge and insight, in his thoughts, views, and conduct, was equally filled and animated by his Sonship to God — by God's Fatherhood to him. Therefore, he is the first-born of God, the first-born of all created beings.

The oft-repeated saying of Jesus, " Believe in me —" If ye were to believe in me "—means this: " Could you but feel, know, see, that the highest thing that man,

as an earth-born creature of God, can see and understand—his divine origin and his constant dependence on
God—is expressed with equal clearness and vividness
in my life, my thoughts, and aspirations; could you be
brought by my life, my thoughts, my views, my conduct, my deeds and words, to feel, to know, and to see
that every human being should raise himself to this
knowledge and insight, and live accordingly—a knowledge and insight which can not be designated more adequately, purely, and worthily than by the relation of
father and son—you, too, would rise to the true life,
you would live as truly and eternally as God and I live
eternally, you would thus through me receive eternal
life, and I would give you truly eternal life."

To recognize this, and to apply it in a pure human
life, is *Christian religion.*

Christian religion is the eternal conviction of the
truth of the teachings of Jesus, and a firm, persistent
conduct in obedience to this conviction; it is the conviction that the truth of Christ's teaching confronts
every human being, wheresoever he may turn with his
spiritual eyes to seek, to test, to examine, to inquire;
that wheresoever he may turn he will be confronted by
this one truth, this one spirit; and that, as man's spiritual eye sees and discerns this one divine truth—this
one divine spirit everywhere in endless diversity—this
spirit would afford him the consolation and support
which he needs in representing that truth in a world
where the cultivation of the outer sensual eye is still so
far in advance of the cultivation of the inner spiritual
eye; where the knowledge and cultivation of the outer
man is still so far in advance of the knowledge and cul-

tivation of the inner man. Thus, with the aid of this spirit, he may rise to the highest knowledge, not alone of man, but of all created beings, to a knowledge of the truth that the infinite is revealed in the finite, the eternal in the temporal, the celestial in the terrestrial, the living in the dead, the divine in the human.

The Christian religion, therefore, is the clear insight and conviction, firmly and eternally self-grounded and free from all illusion—and a life and conduct in full harmony and perfect accord with such insight and conviction—that the manifestation and revelation of the one, eternal, living, self-existent Being—of God—must from its very nature be triune: that God manifests and reveals himself in his oneness as the Creator, Preserver, Ruler, the Father of all things; that he manifests and reveals himself, has manifested and revealed himself, in and through a man who absorbed his whole being in himself, in and through an only being of supreme perfection, who was therefore his Son, his only-begotten and first-born Son; that in all the diversity of created things, in all things that are and move, in the life and spirit of all things, he has manifested and revealed himself, and continues without interruption to manifest and reveal himself as the One Life and Spirit, the Spirit of God; and that he does all this ever as the One Living God.

Similarly we say, humanly speaking, but with a deep spiritual meaning, and with exhaustive fullness of spiritual truth: The spirit of the peace, of the order and purity of this family, is shown in every single thing as well as in the whole house. Or, again, with correct and true feeling: The spirit of the father is seen in all the children, and in the whole family. Or, in high creative truth: The spirit of the artist is manifest in all his works, as well as in each individual one. Or, with correct sense and feeling of truth: It is a *living* expression of himself.

The Christian religion carries with itself the eternal conviction that it is this knowledge which leads not man alone, but all created beings (i. e., all beings that have come from the unity of God into an individual existence), to a knowledge of their existence, to the fulfillment of their mission, to the attainment of their destiny ; and that every individual being—if it would attain its destiny—in necessary and indispensable obedience to its nature, must manifest and reveal itself in this triune way —*in and as unity, in and as individuality, in and as manifoldness in ever-continuing diversity* (see §§ 15, 18).

The truth of this conviction is the sole foundation of all insight and knowledge. It is the only test of our conduct. It is the foundation of all religious instruction. The knowledge and application of this truth enables us to recognize nature in its true character, as the writing and book of God, as the revelation of God.

The knowledge of this truth gives a language to things human as well as to things natural, and imparts true significance and true life to all teaching and learning, to all knowing and doing.

Only through this conviction life becomes in all its phases and manifestations a self-contained whole, a unit. This knowledge and conviction alone render genuine human education truly possible.

The knowledge of this truth, the insight into its nature brings light and life, and, if need be, consolation and support in all circumstances; it alone gives a meaning and a purpose to life.

Therefore, Jesus commanded his disciples: "Go ye into all the world and teach all nations"; purify and lead them to the knowledge of God the Father, of Jesus, the Son of God, and of the Holy Spirit of God, to a life in accordance with this knowledge and insight, and to all insight necessarily proceeding from this.

Therefore, the truth of the threefold manifestation and revelation of the One God is the corner-stone of the religion which suffices all men in all zones, and which they have felt, however vaguely, and sought, however unconsciously; for it leads man in the spirit and in truth, in insight and life, to God and in God.

Every human being, as a being proceeding from God, existing through God and living in God, should raise himself to the Christian religion—the religion of Jesus. Therefore, the school should first of all teach the religion of Christ; therefore, it should first of all, and above all, give instruction in the Christian religion; everywhere, and in all zones, the school should instruct for and in this religion.

B. *Natural Science and Mathematics.*

§ 62. What religion says and expresses, nature says and represents. What the contemplation of God teaches, nature confirms. What is deduced from the contemplation of the inner, is made manifest by the contemplation of the outer. What religion demands, nature fulfills. For nature, as well as all existing things, is a manifestation, a revelation, of God. The purpose of all existence is the revelation of God. All existing things are only through and because of the (divine) essence that is in them (see § 1).

Everything is of divine nature, of divine origin. Everything is, therefore, relatively a unity, as God is absolute unity. Everything, therefore, inasmuch as it is—though only relatively—a unity, manifests its nature only in and through a triune revelation and representation of itself, and these only in and through continuously progressive, hence relatively all-sided development (see § 61).

This truth is the foundation of all contemplation, knowledge, and comprehension of nature. Without it there can be no true, genuine, productive investigation and knowledge of nature. Without it there can be no true contemplation of nature, leading to insight into the essential being of nature.

Only the Christian, only the human being with Christian spirit, life, and aspiration, can possibly attain a true understanding and a living knowledge of nature; only such a one can be a genuine naturalist. True knowledge of nature is attainable by man only in the measure in which he is—consciously or unconsciously, vaguely or distinctly—a Christian, i. e., penetrated with the truth of the one divine power that lives and works in all things; only in the measure in which he is filled with the one living divine spirit that is in all things and to which he himself is subject, through which all nature has its being, and by which he is enabled to see this one spirit in its essential being and in its unity in the least phenomenon, as well as in the sum of all natural phenomena.

§ 63. The relation of nature to God may be truly and clearly perceived and recognized by man in the study and elucidation of the innermost spiritual relation of a genuine human work of art to the artist. In a secondary degree it may be perceived and recognized in every human work with reference to the human being to whom it owes its origin (see § 61).

All things that the living spirit creates, produces, and represents must have impressed and implanted in them the nature of this spirit, must bear the imprint of the seal of this spirit in every part of the product.

Absolutely nothing can appear, nothing visible and sensible can come forth, that does not hold within itself the living spirit; that does not bear upon its surface the imprint of the living spirit of the being by whom it has been produced, and to whom it owes its existence. And this is true of the work of every human being—from the highest artist to the meanest laborer, from the most material to the most spiritual human work, from the most permanent to the most transient human activity—as well as of the works of God which are nature, the creation, and all created things.

A keen, critical eye can discern in the work of art the artist's powers of thought and feeling, as well as their state of cultivation; thus, too, the creative spirit of God may be discerned in his works (see § 60).

We do not pay sufficient attention to this fact in human works, in works of art; therefore, it is so difficult for us to discern it in nature, in the work of God.

In the consideration of the human work of art we do not concern ourselves sufficiently with the innermost spiritual relation of the artist to the work; we judge its origin too mechanically and superficially. We do not consider sufficiently that these works, if they are works of high art, are not meant to be art-masks, but are always representations of the most individual, the most personal inner life of the artist; for this reason the genuine spirit of the art-work and the spirit of nature are equally foreign, equally dead to us.

Now, as the work of man, of the artist, carries within itself the *spirit* and *character*, the *life* and *essential being*, of this man, and—as we say in human metaphor exhaustively and most significantly—breathes out this spirit and life, and as the human being who produced it, who created it, as it were, out of himself, nevertheless remains the same undiminished and undivided being, and is even strengthened in his power by this work, thus, too, the spirit and being of God—although the cause and source of all existing things, and although all existing things carry within themselves and breathe the one spirit of God—remain nevertheless in themselves the one Being, the one Spirit, undiminished and undivided.

As in the human work of art there is no material part of the artist's spirit, and as nevertheless the work of art as such carries within itself the whole spirit of its artist in such a way that this spirit lives in this work, is expressed by it and exhaled by it, is even breathed by it into others, where it may live, be developed, and cultivated—as the spirit of man is thus related to the work produced by him, so is the spirit of God, so is God, related to nature and to all created things. The spirit of God rests in nature, lives and reigns in nature, is expressed in nature, is communicated by nature, is developed and cultivated in nature—yet nature is not the body of God.

The spirit of the work of art, the spirit to which the work of art owes its existence, is the one and undivided spirit of the artist; but, having as it were gone forth from the artist, it now lives and works on in the artist's work as an independent spirit, yet at one with the artist. Thus, the spirit of God, having gone forth from God, lives and works on in and through nature as an independent spirit, yet at one with God.

As nature is not the body of God, so, too, God himself does not dwell in nature as in a house; but the spirit of God dwells in nature, sustaining, preserving, fostering, and developing nature. For does not even the spirit of the artist, though but a human spirit, dwell in his work, sustaining, preserving, fostering, and keeping it? Does not even the spirit of the artist impart earthly immortality, as it were, to a block of marble, to a perishable piece of canvas—nay, even to a winged and fleeting word, which passes away at the moment of its birth—indeed, to all his works, be he musician, poet, painter, or sculptor? Does he not endow his work of art, as he puts it forth into life, with the choicest, most thoughtful care, the tenderest keeping, the high esteem of the most exalted human minds?

Who can fail to mark the lofty, mighty spirit of a true human work of art, the presence at once supplicating and commanding that goes forth from a lofty, pure work of art, as it does from the innocent look of a helpless child? And yet it is but the work of a human spirit; and this spirit preserves and keeps it, however long the time and wide the space that separate the work from the artist.

Toward a genuine work of art—though not, indeed, toward a merely mechanical piece of work with which thought had little or nothing to do—the artist feels as does a father who dismisses his son into life : he gives him words and thoughts to bless, guard, and keep him. To the true artist it is by no means a matter of indifference who buys his work, as a good father is by no means indifferent to the character of the companions of his son. Yet, full of trust and confidence, he dismisses his son into the world ; for his own spirit and aspirations rest upon and in his son. Thus, too, the artist's character lives and breathes wholly in his work, even in its least and smallest parts, in every line, and in the very mode of their connections. This spirit or character, whose lofty nature and aspirations the artist knows in his own being, fills him with the hope that it will keep his work of art, that it will bring his work to human beings who will receive the created spirit in their own lives, and will develop and cultivate it there.

The work of art is external to man—no material part, not a drop of life-blood, passes from him to his work—and yet man sustains, keeps, and preserves it ; he strives to keep away from it what may cause it the least injury now and in time to come. Man feels himself to be one with his work of art ; how much more, then, will God sustain, keep, and preserve his work, which is nature, and keep away from it all injury—for God is God, and man is only man !

Yet the artist, in whatever direction, remains ever unalterably and independently the same in himself

though all his works perish ; so, too, God remains unalterably the same, even though all nature perish.

Nay, the human work of art, as well as nature, the
divine work of God, may externally perish, and yet the
spirit expressed, revealed, living and moving in it, will
continue to be and to unfold itself evermore. Indeed,
it gains thereby true freedom, and, from this very fact,
is revealed more clearly and vividly.

Behold the ruins of perished human art-power ! be
they the mighty work of the giant strength of indi-
viduals or the colossal product of the omnipotence of
the intimate union of many for one purpose which is
common to all, and which each one of the workers,
on whatever stage of insight, holds and must hold as
his purpose — an omnipotence whose existence mankind have scarcely felt as yet, and in which they still
less believe. Those ruins admonish the succeeding
weaker generations ; and the generation that begins
to become conscious of its essential nature is lifted
in confidence and courage by those proofs of vanished,
though by no means only outer, human power and
greatness.

Thus the colossal remains of shattered mountains
and mountain-chains speak of the greatness of the spirit
of God, of the greatness of God ; and even man is encouraged, and lifts himself up by them, feeling within
himself the same spirit and power. Thus the slender
ivy climbs up on the mighty rock, and gathers from it
strength and food, not only for its life, but also for its
upward growth.

Thus we see everywhere the same living and deep,
inner and spiritual, pervading and sustaining relations

between man and the work of art, and between God and nature.

When barbarians—rough, unfeeling, thoughtless men —destroy the work of art, or even the slightest vestige of a human spirit that has lived and worked on earth, the noble, sensitive human being grieves perhaps even more than he would do if the life of an ordinary living being were destroyed.

For does not even the work of man imply the independent development of the spirit and thought it holds? May not the character expressed in a work of art influence entire generations, elevating or, on the other hand, degrading them? And yet they are but the works of man that may do this; what, then, may, will, and must the works of God do; what must nature, the work of God, be to man?

We study to acquaint ourselves with the life and aspirations, etc., of human works; we study the works of man, and justly so. The undeveloped, maturing human being should profit by the development of maturer men. How much more, then, should we endeavor to know nature, the work of God, to acquaint ourselves with the objects of nature in their life, their significance, in their relation to the spirit of God!

This is indicated to us, too, in the fact that genuine works of human art, human works that express the pure spirit of man, which is also the spirit of God, are not easily nor always readily accessible for every one, and under all circumstances; while, on the other hand, man finds himself everywhere surrounded by pure works of God, by works of nature that clearly express the spirit of God.

It is true, we can find and recognize God's spirit through and in the human spirit; but it is difficult to distinguish in each particular case that which belongs to humanity in general from that which belongs to the particular human being; it is difficult to distinguish which one of the two predominates, and which one, at any particular time, is acting. On the other hand, with pure works of nature, the natural as such preponderates very decidedly, the particular characteristics of the natural object are by far less prominent. Thus the pure spirit of God not only is seen more clearly and distinctly in nature than it is in human life, but in the clear disclosures of God's spirit in nature are seen the nature, dignity, and holiness of man reflected in all their pristine clearness and purity.

Again, man sees in nature not only general principles—as has been previously indicated—but he beholds therein his aspiration, his destiny, his mission, the necessary conditions, impediments, and phases of their attainment, as in a picture, in unmistakable and living characters, expressing not the notion, but the thing, the relation itself. Following these silent, absolutely reliable, outwardly intelligible, impersonal teachers, man may not only learn from them with certainty the thing to be done at every moment of life, but, acting accordingly, he will surely satisfy the demands made upon him.

Among all objects of nature, none seem in this respect truer, clearer, more complete, and yet simpler— because of their calm thoughtful aspect and the clear unfolding of their inner life—than plants, especially trees. They are, therefore, rightly distinguished among nat-

ural objects as trees of the knowledge of good and evil,
for they are such in reality ; indeed, they were so considered and named with touching, truthful, and deep
significance, on the very first appearance of self-consciousness in the human race.

The observation of the development of individual
man and its comparison with the general development
of the human race show plainly that, in the development of the inner life of the individual man, the history
of the spiritual development of the race is repeated,
and that the race in its totality may be viewed as ONE
human being, in whom there will be found the necessary steps in the development of individual man (see
§§ 15, 24).   Therefore, not only may we learn from the
trees, from the life of a tree, the phenomena of individual human life, but we may find therein the phenomena of the development of the race in their necessary
connection.   It is true, in their full distinctness, free
from all arbitrariness and triviality, this has as yet
scarcely been shown, yet the further development and
cultivation of the parables of Christ may lead to it
(see § 66).

A by far wider application might be given to this
contemplation of nature here only touched upon, were
it not out of place on account of the almost complete
ignorance that prevails concerning this subject, and
were it not founded on a now very rare mode of observation of external natural phenomena and of the development of inner life in ourselves.

If we seek the inner reason for this high symbolic
meaning of the different individual phenomena of nature, particularly in the phases of development of natu-

ral objects in relation to the stadia of human development, we find it in the fact that nature and man have
their origin in one and the same eternal Being, and that
their development takes place in accordance with the
same laws, only at different stages.

Thus the observation of nature and the observation
of man, in comparison and in connection with the facts
and phenomena of the general development of humanity, are mutually explanatory, and mutually lead to
deeper knowledge the one of the other. A clear insight
into the causative and creative relation of the human
spirit to its external work leads also to a clear insight
into the relation of the causative, creative spirit of God
to nature ; leads to a knowledge of the manner in which
the finite proceeds from the infinite, the material from
the spiritual, nature from God. Even man, although
externally a finite being, does not always need his arms
and hands for the production and outward representation of his work ; more frequently his will, his determining look, the breath of his word, create and bring
forth. Even man, although externally finite, can bring
forth material for his creations, without having recourse
to material existences.

Whoever wants further proof for this need only pass
in review the whole series of developments, conditions,
and phenomena, from the least material, innermost
thought to the most definitely formed, most material
word in writing.

Thus man may know and understand even the most
difficult process, the production of the external and material from the inner and spiritual ; may know and understand it—not as an idea, but as a fact—in the pro-

cesses of his own thinking as an effect and consequence of the transformation of his own innermost thought into an external work, an outer something.

Therefore, as the spirit of the artist is in the work of art, so is the spirit of God in nature. As the work of art lives and moves in accordance with its spirit and related to its maker, so nature, born from God, lives and moves in accordance with its spirit, as a work of God, living in and through God, and breathing the spirit of God, related to God, its Maker, and in inner spiritual relation to man.

As the world of art is the invisibly-visible * revelation and expression of the spirit of man, and thus becomes an invisibly-visible kingdom of the human spirit, so, too, nature is the invisibly-visible revelation of the spirit of God, and becomes an invisibly-visible kingdom of God.

§ 64. To feel the presence of this threefold kingdom of God (the visible, the invisible, and the invisibly-visible), to acknowledge it, and to let it influence life—this alone can give us the peace which we seek within and without, which from the first moment of self-consciousness we are driven to seek and to pursue, even at the expense of our own life, of our external possessions, of our external welfare, whatever its name.

For this reason alone, man—particularly in boyhood—should become intimate with nature, not so much with reference to the details and the outer forms of her phenomena as with reference to the spirit of God that

---

* *Unsichtbar-sichtbar* = invisibly-visible, i. e., visible to the mental, to the spiritual eye, though invisible to the physical eye.—*Tr.*

lives in her and rules over her. Indeed, the boy feels this deeply, and demands it; for this reason, where love of nature is still unimpaired, nothing, perhaps, unites teachers and pupils so intimately as the thoughtful study of nature, and of the objects of nature.

Parents and school-teachers should remember this, and the latter should, at least once a week, take a walk with each class—not driving them out like a flock of sheep, nor leading them out like a company of soldiers, but going with them as a father with his sons or a brother with his brothers, and acquainting them more fully with whatever the season or nature offers them (see § 98).

The schoolmaster who lives in a village or in the country should not object to this request, by saying, " My school-children are constantly out-doors anyhow, and running about in the fields and forests." They are, indeed, in the fields and forests, but they do not live there; they do not live in and with nature.

Not only children and boys, but indeed many adults, fare with nature and her character as ordinary men fare with the air. They live in it, and yet scarcely know it as something distinct, and much less with reference to its essential properties concerning the preservation of his life; for ordinarily the name air is given merely to the currents of wind or to their temperature.*

Therefore, these children and boys who spend all their time in the fields and forests see and feel nothing of the beauties of nature, and of their influence on the human heart. They are like the people who have grown

---

* This has reference to the German word *Luft* (air), which is popularly used for *Wind* (wind).—*Tr.*

up in a very beautiful country, and who have no idea of its beauty and its spirit.

Yet—and this is the essential point—the boy may possibly with his spiritual eye find, see, and apprehend the inner life of surrounding nature; but he fails to find the same feelings among adults who suppress that germinating inner life in its very beginning.

The boy seeks from adults the confirmation of his inner, spiritual anticipations, and justly so, from an intuitive sense of what the elder ought to be, from respect for the elder. If he fails to find it, a double effect follows—loss of respect for the elder, and a recoil of the original inner anticipation.

Therefore, it is so important that boys and adults should go into the fields and forests *together striving* to receive into their hearts and minds the life and spirit of nature, which would soon put an end to the idle, useless, and indolent loafing of so many boys.

The cruel treatment of insects and other animals in which, particularly, young boys engage good-naturedly and with no evil intention—though this does not apply to cruelty as such—originates in the little boy's desire to obtain an insight into the inner life of the animal, to get at its spirit. But failure to explain or to guide, as well as false interpretation or guidance, or the misunderstanding of this desire, may at a later period develop in such boys hardened intentional cruelty to animals.

§ 65. Such are the character and influence of nature as a whole, such are the character and influence of nature as the image and work of God, as the word of God, revealing, communicating, and awakening the spirit of

God in and by its integrity; as such, nature presents herself to inner contemplation.

Quite differently, however, she presents herself to ordinary outer contemplation. To this she appears as a diversity of many different and separate individualities without definite, inner, living connection; individualities each of which has its own peculiar form, peculiar development, peculiar absolute purpose; without any indication that these externally distinct and separate individualities are organically united members of one great living organism, of one great intrinsically and spiritually coherent whole; without any indication that nature is such a whole.

§ 66. This external view of nature, based on particular natural phenomena, on particular natural objects seen in their separation, is like the external view of a large tree, or of any complex plant, in which each leaf seems to be strictly separate from the others. Here, too, there seems to be no bridge, no inner connection among the leaves and twigs, nor in the little blossom between the calyx and corolla, and between this and the stamens and pistils. But here, too, when in thoughtful search the spiritual eye seeks and finds the common bond among the nearest particulars, and proceeds from every new-found unity to a higher and the highest unity, it is at last recognized as an external manifestation of an inner law acting deep in the very heart of the plant.

That external view of nature in her particulars resembles the external view of the starry sky, in which only by means of arbitrary lines particular stars are gathered into larger groups, and whose inner connection even the keenest, clearest, and most fully developed spiritual eye can apprehend only in the union of smaller world-groups into ever larger ones.

In this usual, merely external, view of nature, the particulars of the distinct and separate natural objects appear not so much as the products of one and the same existence, but rather as the products of different active forces. But this can not satisfy, even in boyhood, the mind and spirit of man, in itself one and undivided.

§ 67. Therefore at an early period, even in boyhood, man seeks unity and union for this externally separate diversity and individuality among objects; seeks unity and union in a separation which in obedience to a necessary law of inner development presents things outwardly in apparently confused heaps. His mind is contented when he begins to apprehend this unity and union, but only later on, when he has found it, is his spirit fully satisfied.

But a review of the diversities in the particulars of a plant leads to the recognition of deep-laid law discernible only for the spiritual eye. Similarly the patient following of this diversity itself leads to the recognition, too, of the external unity among the diversities and individualities of nature; for, however great the peculiarities, differences, and degrees of separation among natural objects, the peculiar nature and appearance, the structure and form of each thing, are always found to rest ultimately upon the nature of *force*, as the connecting unit from which all individuality and diversity proceed. Now force, from its very nature, is self-existent, proceeds from itself by its own activity as its own outward manifestation; therefore, active force is the ultimate cause of all things, of every phenomenon in nature.

The contemplation of the essence of force—in its manifestations as divine power as well as in its activity in our own minds and life—will enable us, too, to apprehend and understand nature in her numberless forms and structures, in her living inner affinities and developments, as well as in her external relations and deductions. Man is urged to contemplate the inner essence of force by the desire and hope of finding thereby the outer unity of the particular facts of nature, of the various forms and shapes of nature.

[Similarly Herbert Spencer declares force to be the ultimate of ultimates, and looks upon space, time, matter, and motion as "either built up of, or abstracted from, experiences of force."—*Tr.*]

§ 68. Force, as such, is a spontaneous energy equally active in all directions, proceeding either from absolute unity or from some relative unity, but always from a unity. At the same time, the nature of force necessarily implies the coexistence and simultaneousness of action and reaction.

Individual and varied existence as such, however, postulates necessarily a second, external condition or form and structure, viz., *matter*. It shows how all earthly and natural structure and form are born from matter which is the same everywhere, in every respect, even in the smallest details of cohesion and constitution, subject to the same laws, and therefore outwardly infinitely mobile in its minutest parts; and all this because of the everywhere equally diffused indwelling force, because of the external influence of the sun and of light and heat, in obedience to the all-pervading great law of nature, according to which the general gives rise to the particular.

All individuality and diversity of earthly and natural objects, as well as all inner contemplation of nature, show that force and matter are in themselves inseparably one.

Matter and spontaneous force proceeding from a point with equal activity in all directions mutually condition each other: neither exists without the other, neither can exist without the other; nay, strictly speaking, it is impossible to think one without the other.

The reason for the infinite mobility of matter in its minutest parts lies in the original spherical tendency of the indwelling force, in the original tendency of force, spontaneously proceeding from a point, to diffuse equally in all directions.

§ 69. Now, since force develops and diffuses itself in all directions equally, freely, and unimpeded, its outward manifestation, its material resultant, is a *sphere*. For this reason the spherical or, in general, the round form is most commonly the first and the last form of things in nature : e. g., the great heavenly bodies, such as the suns, planets, and moons, water and all liquids, the air and all gases, and even the dust.

In all the diversity and amid the apparently most incompatible differences of earthly and natural structures, the sphere seems to be the primitive form, the unity from which all earthly and natural forms and structures are derived. Hence, too, the sphere resembles none of the other natural forms, and yet essentially contains the possibility and the law of all of them ; it is, at the same time, formless and the most perfect form.

Neither point nor line, neither plane nor side, can be discerned on its surface ; yet it is all-pointed and all-sided, contains all the points and all the lines, etc., of all earthly structures and forms, not in their possibility alone, but even in their actuality.

Therefore, all structures of the living, active, effective objects of nature rest primarily on the law of sphericity, underlying the structure of the sphere ; rest primarily—starting from the conception of the inner essence of force, and viewing them as products of force —on the necessary tendency of force to represent in and through matter the spherical nature of force, the nature of the sphere in all possible forms and structures, varieties, and combinations. For in and with the spontaneous, spherical action of the force as a natural and earthly phenomenon, and as such united with matter, there is implied at the same time an inward swelling and surging, measuring and weighing tendency—causing differences in the effect and tension of the force in the different directions.

[How much Froebel was impressed with the significance of the sphere as a symbol of unity of life is shown in the following extract from " Aphorisms," written down in 1821 : " The spherical is the symbol of diversity in unity and of unity in diversity. The spherical is the representation of diversity developed from the unity on which it depends, as well as the representation of the reference of all diversity to its unity. The spherical is the general and the particular, the universal and the individual, unity and individuality at the same time. It is infinite development, and absolute limitation ; it connects perfection and imperfection. All things unfold their spherical nature perfectly only by representing their nature in their unity—in some individuality, and in some diversity. The law of the spherical is the fundamental law of all true and adequate human culture."—*Tr.*]

The differences in the quantity and intensity of the effect of the force in different directions—differences which in accordance with their nature must appear simultaneously in force and in matter—this fixed prevalence of the effect of the force in certain directions—this fixed, peculiar relation among the different directions of the force—this difference of tension in the different directions, and the corresponding and simultaneous difference in the individualization of matter—must, as a fundamental quality of the mass of matter as a whole, dwell in the same measure in each and every smallest particle of that mass.

This peculiar relation and inner law of the efficient force constitute, in every particular case, the essential cause of the form and structure in question.

The differences of direction and intensity in the action of the forces, these differences of tension and the resulting easy divisibility of matter, these planes and directions of tension, contain the fundamental law of all forms and structures. Their clear conception affords the possibility of seeing them in their nature, relations, and combinations.

Now, as each thing can manifest itself completely only by representing its being in unity, individuality, and diversity, or in the indispensable triune way (see § 61), the essential nature of force, too, is shown completely and perfectly only in such a triune representation of its being by and in form. This implies, at the same time, two other tendencies of nature: the tendency to represent the particular in the general, and the general in the particular; and the tendency to make the internal external, the external internal, and to represent the two in unity (to unify the two).

All individual forms in nature, in all their diversity,

have their origin in this triune representation by means of matter and through form, of force in union with those general tendencies of nature.

§ 70. Furthermore, however, one and the same force acts in one and the same material, either particularizing in many individual phenomena or undivided and in general; or within the limits of its formative law its action predominates in the direction of one of the dimensions—height, length, or breadth—producing a number of variations of crystalline form, such as the fibrous, the radiate, the granular, the laminate, the foliate, needle-shaped, etc. The former is due to the fact that as many particles of the material as possible in a relatively large mass tend to represent their formative law, but are reciprocally hindered by their very mass in the development and completion of their crystals. The latter is due to the fact that the representation of the law of formation is greater in certain dimensions than it is in the rest.

The pure and perfect crystal, which represents even in its outward form the relative intensity in the different directions of the inner force, is formed when all the individual particles and all the individual points of the active force subject themselves to the higher law of a *common* requirement and of the integral representation of the law of formation, a higher law which, though it may hamper and fetter individual particles or points, yet yields the greater, perfectly formed product.

The crystalline is the first phase of earthly formation. Action and reaction and their simultaneousness, which belong to the essential nature of force, give rise to a tendency toward predominance of the force in certain directions, and to a reciprocal hindrance and ten‧ sion even in the minutest parts, and consequently to the most sharply defined relations of tension in the material in all directions, and thereby to greater or smaller divisibility in these planes and lines of tension.

Therefore, the first crystals must of necessity have rectilinear outlines ; nay, in the first appearance of the crystalline, there must be evidence of resistance to the common subordination under the fixed law of a definite crystal—resistance to its perfect representation. Similarly, crystals in which the force acts unequally in different directions must appear earlier than those in which the force acts equally in different directions ; hence the external result will not be an all-sidedly equilateral crystal—as would be indicated by the essential nature of the force—but solid forms not in conformity with this all-sided equal activity of the force. Again, the development of the essential nature of force in its external manifestation of crystallization ascends from the unequilateral to the simplest equilateral forms ; while, at the same time, the essential nature of the force as such for the purpose of outward representation descends, from unity and all-sidedness, to individuality and one-sidedness.

If we now seek to recognize and represent this descent in the essential nature of the force from unity to individuality, we shall see nature at this stage, both in her inner tendency and her outer manifestations, in all her individuality and one-sidedness, but also in her unity and all-sidedness.

[Froebel's interest in crystallography was aroused by the lectures of Professor Weiss at Berlin in 1812. He saw in it the possibility of direct proof of the inner connection of all things. After the campaign of 1813 against Napoleon, he returned at once to this study, and was fortunate enough to secure the position of assistant to Professor Weiss in the Royal Museum of Natural History. He writes concerning this period : "What I had seen in so many ways in the great universe, in the life of men, in the development of humanity, I saw here again in the smallest crystal. I saw it clearly, that the divine is not only in the greatest, it is also in the most minute things ; in full abundance and power it is even in the least thing. Thus my earths and crystals became to me a mirror of the development and history of mankind." However, he was much disconcerted by the multiplicity of fundamental forms as taught in this science ; and he busied himself much with efforts to reduce all forms to one— probably the cube. The results of these efforts appear in the following paragraphs, and, although not accepted by the mineralogical science of the day, stand as a remarkable monument of Froebel's faith in the principle of life-unity.

In his letter to the Duke of Meiningen he exclaims, "The world of crystals proclaimed to me, in distinct and unequivocal terms, the laws of human life." His genius, however, urged and forced him away from stones to men, and, sacrificing everything, refusing even a professorship of mineralogy, he devoted himself to the work of education.—*Tr.*]

§ 71. In the entire process of the development of the crystal, as it is found in natural objects, there is a highly remarkable agreement with the development of the human mind and of the human heart. Man, too, in his external manifestation—like the crystal—bearing within himself the living unity, shows at first more one-sidedness, individuality, and incompleteness, and only at a later period rises to all-sidedness, harmony, and completeness.

Like all similar facts, this analogy in the development of nature and of man is very important for the purposes of self-knowledge and of the education of self and others ; it throws light and clearness upon human development and education, and gives firmness and sureness of action in their various requirements.

Like the world of the heart and mind, the world of crystals is a glorious, instructive world. What the spiritual eye there beholds inwardly, it here sees outwardly.

§ 72. Every crystallogenic force that manifests itself in and through formative and externalizing processes proceeds from a center, simultaneously tending in opposite directions. By its very nature, therefore, it imposes limits upon itself, is all-sided, radiating, rectilinear, and, hence, necessarily spherical in its operation.

Now, such a force, operating without hindrance, will necessarily act bilaterally in any one direction; and in the totality of all directions there will always be, starting in any direction from the center, *sets of three* such bilateral directions, perpendicular to one another, in the fullest equilibrium of independence and interdependence.

Again, on account of the limitations lying in the force itself, among all these sets of three bilateral directions, *three exclusively* predominate and appear wholly distinct from all others. Even the most abstract view of force will lead to this distinction and predominance, because they lie equally in the nature of force and in the law of human mental activity. The result of the predominance of these three bilateral, perpendicular directions, which equally control and determine all other directions, must be a crystal limited by straight lines and planes, revealing in every part the inner nature and action of the force; it can be only a *cube*, a regular hexahedron.

Each of the eight corners shows the perpendicularity

of the three bilateral directions at the center, and thus indicates externally the center of the cube. Similarly the three sets of four parallel edges show each of the inner directions fourfold. The six faces mark in their centers the six terminal points of the three bilateral directions, and determine the invisible center of the cube.

In the cube the tendency of the force toward spherical representation is in a state of highest tension. Instead of all-sidedness we have particular-sidedness of faces, corners, and edges; and these few points (corners), lines (edges), and planes (faces), subordinate and control all others. There appears, too, the tendency of the force to represent itself, not only in corporeal space, but also in each of the possible particular phases of space— as a point and in points, as a line and in lines, as a plane and in planes. This, again, necessarily reveals the tendency of the force *to derive the line and the plane from the point, to represent the point as a line and as a plane, the line as a point and as a plane, to contract the line into a point and to expand it into a plane,* etc.

We meet this effect of force, henceforth, at every step of the study of crystal forms; indeed, the operation of crystallogenic force seems to be limited to this, and all crystals seem to owe their characteristics exclusively to this tendency. Indeed, this must be so; it is the first general manifestation of the great natural laws and tendencies to represent each thing in unity, individuality, and diversity; to generalize the most particular, and to represent the most general in the most particular; and, lastly, to make the internal external, the external internal, and to represent both in harmony and union.

If, at the same time, we keep in mind that man, too, is almost wholly subject to these great laws, that almost all the phenomena and events of his life are based on them, these considerations will reveal to us also the nature of man, and teach us how to develop and educate him in accordance with the laws of nature and of his being.

Let us now pass from the study of the cube to the study and development of the remaining crystal forms. The corners of the cube will tend to become planes, the faces will tend to represent themselves as points ; more especially, the six directions lying about the center and, typically, in the six sides of the cube will tend to become externally visible as edges. The result of this is a crystal which has as many faces or sides as the cube has corners, as many corners as the cube has sides, and as many edges as the cube—viz., a regular *octahedron*. In this form, again, many things that lie invisibly in the interior appear outwardly, either directly or typically visible, but the explanations given in the study of the cube must suffice to indicate how these things may be found.

The three-times-two perpendicular principal directions (three bilateral directions) appear externally in the *cube* as three-times-two sides or *planes*, in the octahedron as three-times-two corners or *points :* there must be yet another crystal form in which they appear as three-times-two edges or *lines*. In the cube the six terminal points of the three perpendicular bilateral directions of the force appeared as six sides or *planes*, in the *octahedron* they appeared as corners or *points :* there must be another solid in which they appear as edges or *lines*, and this is the regular *tetrahedron*. Its nature is sufficiently determined by comparison with the cube and octahedron, and the interior phases expressed in its external appearance are easily found with the help of the hints given in the study of the cube.

[This is illustrated in the following figures: Fig. 1 indicates the three pairs of opposite directions (three bilateral directions) in which the force operates, constituting the three axes of the cube (Fig. 2),

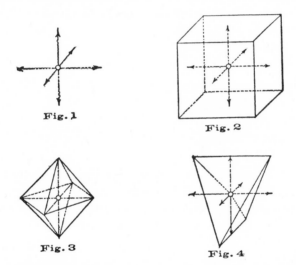

Fig. 1

Fig. 2

Fig. 3

Fig. 4

the octahedron (Fig. 3), and the tetrahedron (Fig. 4). In Fig. 2 the axes terminate in *faces;* in Fig. 3 they terminate in *points* (corners); and in Fig. 4 the terminal points of one axis lie in *edges.—Tr.*]

Thus the study of the necessary results of the force acting spherically, and manifesting itself in material crystallization, has revealed to us three bodies, bounded by straight lines and planes, of which the cube is the first, and, as it were, the central one, and the tetrahedron and octahedron the two derived bodies.

If, now, we survey the

CUBE, OCTAHEDRON, AND TETRAHEDRON

in their natural position, as shown in our deduction,
we again behold, in perfect harmony with the course of
our study, and as a necessary consequence of the oft-
repeated law of nature, that the *cube* rests on a *plane*,
the *octahedron* on a *point*, and the *tetrahedron* on a
line ; and in each of the three solids the *axis* of development coincides wholly with one of the three reciprocally perpendicular principal directions.

If, then, we consider each of these three solids as
wholly independent and fixed, each left to itself, seeking a point of rest and support, we find the cube
always symmetrically and permanently resting on one
of its faces, and the axis permanently coinciding with
one of its principal directions. On the other hand,
the octahedron and tetrahedron will *fall.* Thereby
one of the sides will become its base, and at the
same time both solids exhibit a new property quite
peculiar to them : the axis, the vertical or median line
of the solid, does not coincide with any of the three
principal directions, but stands at equal angles between
them.

Now, inasmuch as the nature of the octahedron
and tetrahedron lies in the nature of the cube, and inasmuch as the forms of the octahedron and tetrahedron
are deducible from that of the cube, the property which
permits the axis or vertical line to fall at equal angles
between the three perpendicular principal directions,
must lie already in the cube. Indeed, it is a direct result of the operation of the law of equilibrium ; for the

failing of the octahedron or tetrahedron, by which the axis or vertical line is brought at equal angles between the principal directions, when transferred to the cube, will necessarily cause the latter to *rise* correspondingly. This will make the cube seem to rest on one of its corners, so that the vertical line or axis passes now from one of these corners through the center to the opposite corner, no longer coinciding with one of the principal directions, but falling at equal angles between them. By this change in the position of the axis, the cube has been wholly changed *internally*, and presents *externally*, too, a wholly changed appearance, an entirely new form. In its former position the sides seemed grouped in sets of two, and the corners and edges in sets of two or four, everything seemed to be arranged in the order of the even numbers, two and four ; now everything seems grouped in sets of three—three sides, three edges, three corners.

Instead of the number *two*, we have now the number *three*, and a wholly new series of crystal forms seems thereby given and determined. However, the study and development of these must be postponed for the further study and development of the crystal forms with three among themselves wholly perpendicular principal directions.

In itself and in the crystal forms, force manifests the tendency to expand corners into edges or sides ; the tendency to contract edges into corners or to expand them into sides ; the tendency to represent sides as edges and corners ; the tendency to render externally visible inner concealed and invisible as well as outer typical directions, points, lines, and planes ; the tendency to represent externally in the crystal forms the inner, spherical nature of force on all sides equally energetic ; the tendency to reach again the spherical form in and through these crystal forms. Accordingly, starting from the cube, the octahedron, and the tetrahedron, three series of crystal forms are definitely given. These series variously overlap in several directions, but through a limited number of principal forms and a still measurable number of intermediate forms they again approximate sphericity.

In the formation of all the solids so far considered, there were always three equivalent principal directions, of relatively equal efficiency in determining the form. Now, the natural tendency of force to operate simultaneously in opposite directions, and the relations of tension necessarily induced thereby in the force as well as in the matter in which the force operates, necessarily lead in the further development of crystal forms to the development of differences among the three relatively wholly equal and equivalent principal directions : The principal direction coinciding with the axis of the crystal form will become either *greater* or *smaller* than the two others.

The series of crystal forms resulting from the first of these differences will yield chiefly *square prisms* and *elongated octahedrons ;* the series resulting from the second difference will yield chiefly flat, square prisms and flattened octahedrons. (Inasmuch as we are concerned here only with the necessary inner relations and effects of force, we necessarily leave out of consideration all differences in the forms of crystals depending on external conditions of matter.) The development of these two series of crystal forms proceeds always in forms yielding quadruple crystal forms.

Again, all three principal directions may differ in length. The forms resulting from this will be chiefly flattened, oblong, four-sided prisms and octahedrons, with three different sections. The development of this series proceeds by twos or multiples of two. Now, the development may proceed in such a way as to retain the equality of corresponding parts, or one part may develop more or less than its mate. The former yields the series just described; the latter gives series of crystals in which the parts appear grouped in sets of two-and-one or one-and-one.

The further development of these forms, too, ensues in accordance with the natural law and tendency of force to develop corners into edges and planes, and *vice versa*, and thus to represent externally the inner directions in spherical forms. Because of the peculiar fundamental conditions, all the solids resulting from these developments are, too, distinctly peculiar in their appearance and structure.

We have so far considered the principal conditions for the study and deduction of all crystal forms with three relatively equal principal directions, both in their individual characteristics and in their net-like inter-relationships. We now proceed to study the crystal forms whose structural axis falls symmetrically between the three principal directions, and whose fundamental form is the cube resting on one of its corners.

The first examination of the cube in this position revealed peculiarities determined by the grouping of its parts in sets of three. To these, further consideration

will add the following peculiar structural laws and
properties :

In the first place, even a superficial observation of
the cube in this position shows the peculiarity that the
six limiting planes appear no longer as six regular quad-
rilaterals with equal diagonals, but as symmetrical quad-
rilaterals with different diagonals, or as rhombs. At
the very next step in the development of this series of
crystal forms, this merely superficial appearance is confirmed by the actual external results of inner conditions.
Therefore, all the forms of this series limited by six
equal planes are always limited by six equal rhombs.
The fundamental form of this series of form, then, is
the rhombic hexahedron (rhombohedron) ; and the fundamental laws and limitations lying in the rhombohedron are the fundamental laws and limitations of all the
following formations.

The number of crystal forms derived from the
rhombohedron is large, almost incalculably large. Yet
they radiate right from the fundamental form in several
series, each of which is again headed by a principal
form determined by the character of the fundamental
form :

1. The three edges at the basal point and the three
edges at the vertex, in accordance with the law already
mentioned, are developed into faces until they mutually
limit one another. The result is a crystal form bounded
by twice six faces and twice six equal basal and vertical
edges, which unite respectively in the vertex and the
basal point—it is the *double-pointed, equal-edged dodecahedron* (double six-sided pyramid).

2. The lateral edges, in accordance with the inner

characteristics, form sloping double faces. The result is again a crystal form bounded by twice six faces, which unite in the vertex and basal point, but have only the alternate edges equal. It is the *double-pointed, three and-three-edged dodecahedron* (scalene dodecahedron).

3. The development of the lateral corners or edges of the rhombohedron or of one or the other dodecahedrons into faces parallel to the axis, and of the terminal corners into planes (perpendicular to the axis), yields two new crystal forms—two hexagonal prisms with perpendicular bases. They differ, however, in their inner nature and in their origin, inasmuch as one of the prisms is derived from the lateral edges and the other from the lateral corners of the fundamental solid ; they may be distinguished as the *hexagonal prism derived from the edges,* and *the hexagonal prism derived from the corners.*

In accordance with this inner connection, the principal forms are related as follows :

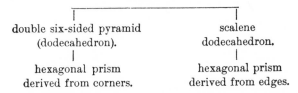

RHOMBOHEDRON.

double six-sided pyramid (dodecahedron).

scalene dodecahedron.

hexagonal prism derived from corners.

hexagonal prism derived from edges.

In accordance with the repeatedly enounced and applied law of crystallogenic force, and with other necessary conditions, the fundamental and principal forms derived above from the nature of the force give rise in strict progression to all possible forms of the rhombic and hexagonal system with constant approach to sphericity.

Thus, in the countless numbers of rhombic and hexagonal forms here implied, in connection with the cubic forms indicated above, all simple crystal forms are implied and determined. This does not exclude other still simple forms in which—in accordance with certain peculiar conditions in the operation of the crystallogenic force—the various forms may appear with variously modified dimensions, relatively greater length or breadth or thickness. On the other hand, by its very tendency toward ever-higher development of crystal forms, the crystallogenic force at last reaches so high a degree of tension, of inner and outer opposition, that at last even the external results show that the tendency to relieve this tension and antithesis has become the chief tendency of the force.

The first and simplest external manifestation of this tendency within the limits of crystallization is seen in the formation of crystals in precisely opposite directions. The result will be (compound) forms in which several simple crystals lying in opposite directions are united externally in a single form, appearing—when the law that unites them can not be unraveled—as capricious accumulations.

These latter formations give rise to a wholly new series of *compound* and cumulated crystals which appear to be imitations of higher forms of development, in a variety of clustered, protuberant, or globular forms. In the last-named accumulation, especially, it seems as if the component crystals *together* succeeded in attaining the original spherical form. which singly they could not reach. Thus, at this stage of crystallization, too, life appears as in a picture ; we see, in spite of all the rigid external separation, an inner living connection, the operation of one and the same law, as we see it more and more clearly at each successive stage of the development of nature.

Now, all these forms as external manifestations belong pre-eminently to the world of matter, to the world of simply energetic force. Their external *unit* is the sphere. They are all distinguished by the peculiarity that their parts are grouped in multiples of *two* and *three*. The operation of the force in directions grouped in multiples of *five* and *seven* seems to be wholly excluded, since these numbers appear either only subordinately and irregularly, or accidentally and transiently.

Furthermore, the material conditions of a crystal are the same at all points. There is no necessarily determined or determining permanent center. The center is only relative, and disappears with the related conditions. Hence, if the material remains the same, the continued operation of the force can increase only the mass of the crystal. The energetic force, therefore, appears as a simple and not as a complex unity.

So much for the development and manifestation of crystallogenic force within the limits of crystals. Now, the nature of force, as a self-active principle equally active in all directions, necessarily postulates in the crystal as its external manifestation a perceptible point in which the force has its seat, from which all its activities proceed, and to which they may be referred. But such a point is not found in solid crystals; indeed, it is excluded by the rigidity of the crystal, however peremptorily it may be demanded by the nature of the force that forms the crystal.

Again, the law of crystallization postulates a material whose crystalline character, whose state of inner tension, renders it impossible to develop a crystal corresponding with such a point; for the fact that the material is throughout uniform in its constitution excludes the predominance of one or several centers of force. For the same reason the establishment of such a center of force would destroy the crystalline character of the material.

Furthermore, force as such—in order to become an independent force—requires in its development a plurality of manifestations and activities within the law of unity and proceeding from unity.

The nature of force and its tendency toward complete development and representation is, therefore, not satisfied with mere many-sidedness in its operation; its fundamental tendency implies an organized community of forces, each of which operates self-actively, but toward a common end lying in unity.

A force thus organized in itself implies again a material similarly organized in itself. Now, material is so organized when, at any point assigned to it by the activity of the force, it adapts itself with equal readiness to the requirements of the force, be this in the representation of the general or the particular, of the inner or the outer, on any side or in any direction of the force.

Organized material obeys with perfect freedom and without friction in every direction. On the other hand, the inner tension of crystalline material excludes this. Therefore, organized force completely destroys all crystalline shape of the material and organizes it. Only by returning to a perfectly amorphous state, into a state of perfect incoherence and solution, can crystalline material become organized.

Here, too, we have a manifestation of life, we see the requirements and conditions of highest, most spiritual life as in a picture. Therefore, at this stage of the development of nature, it is so very necessary for the education of self and others to know and to understand the essential character of nature.

§ 73. We notice, at the same time, as an intrinsic condition of force, the tendency to exert itself in opposite directions. Now, we may consider force as proceeding from a definite demonstrable unity and unfolding a diversity related to that unity. This implies, necessarily, *alternation* in the opposite tendencies of the force ; and, as it destroys the crystallinity of the material, it destroys at the same time the *simultaneity* of the opposite tendencies, and in the state of the material reveals a surging, heaving, swelling of the force.

In the crystal the opposite tendencies of the force are simultaneous, in perfect equilibrium : hence the rigidity of the crystal. The disturbance of this simultaneity, with the slightest predominance of one or the other of the involved tendencies of the force, at once destroys the rigidity of the crystal, and hence the crystal itself, and renders the material earthy, liquid, or gaseous.

Now, the highest development of force implies its greatest exercise of freedom, together with the greatest possible simultaneity in opposite directions. It will, therefore, have attained this development at the stage where the pulsations of opposite tendencies alternate most rapidly. This continuity in the pulsations of force, together with the continuity of equilibrium in opposite

tendencies, we have in *life ;* and the definite demonstrable point whence these pulsations proceed, from which
all this self-active life is breathed out, is the *heart*, the
heart-point.

In perfect accordance with the nature of force, either
a great number of points, or only a limited number, or
only one, will tend to become heart-points. This is one
of the first grounds for the development of distinct living forms. The force tends more and more to render
itself independent of the material, so that the degree
of *life-expression* may no longer depend on the greater
or smaller mass of material. In accordance with this
fundamental law, all life-forms are grouped from the
very beginning in two series. In the first of these, the
material predominates ; in the second, life predominates.
The former is properly designated as *living* (vegetable) ;
the latter as *animate* (animal). From this point of
view, then, all natural objects may be grouped as follows:

Simply energetic
(crystalline).

| Living (*lebend*) | Animate (*lebendig*) |
| (vegetable). | (animal). |

Since life implies the ever-recurring return of the
activity to the center of force, or heart-point, and secures by this return ever again a new lease of external
existence, all living forms will necessarily *grow* from
within outward.

This necessary inner connection, here and previously
indicated, among crystalline, vegetable, and animal
forms, is demonstrated unmistakably also from another

point of view and in the general law of nature, according to which the particular implies the general.

Now, since the previously recognized attributes of force lie necessarily in its nature, they will continue with the continuance of the force, and will be unmistakably pronounced in the succeeding stages of development, although in different forms, combinations, or degrees of intensity. This requirement, lying in the very nature of the force, will necessarily be manifest in every form of the successive stages of development, and is the inner determining cause of each of these forms. While, therefore, in the crystals, circular and spherical forms seemed to be secondary and, as it were, accidental, they now appear to be essential; with this difference, however, that among the vegetable forms radiation and surface expansion predominate, whereas among the animal forms roundness and sphericity prevail.

Now, as organized force necessarily implies organized material, both imply an organized form. Hence the vegetable forms in which life still appears subordinate to the material will have a more radiate character, approximating the law of crystal forms, but in an enhanced, organized, living state. Therefore, we see in many plants the expression of the regularity of crystal forms, more particularly in the numerical relations of parts.

Zahl (number), as is indicated by many obsolete words and phrases, signifies originally the extremity, the end.* Therefore, the numerical relations in plants are so important, because they indicate, as it were, the

---

* *Zahl* is related to the English words *tale, tell*, but not to *tail* (*sagl*), as Froebel seems to assume.—*Tr.*

ends of the directions of force to which crystal forms, as well as successive higher forms, owe their peculiarities. As the binary crystal forms are characterized by great simplicity, so we find a similar simplicity among binary plant-forms, as compared with ternary plant-forms.

In binary plants this law is clearly manifest in the position of the leaves as well as in the form of the stem, etc. The peculiar numerical relations are also always accompanied by other constant peculiarities; and each particular numerical expression is constantly attended by certain particular inner properties. Thus, nearly all binary plants exhale very strongly aromatic odors, etc.

The life-forms, however, are by no means satisfied with ever more characteristic representation of the original directions, and the resulting numerical relations that yield crystal forms. By the removal of external tension the inner energy has been raised into life-energy, and higher activities must become manifest in the formations. Therefore, among vegetable as well as among animal life-forms, we observe soon the prevalence of numerical relations based on the number five, which play in crystals a very subordinate part, and appear only accidentally, as it were, and transiently.

Since, in all natural objects, the appearance of quinary relations marks very characteristic activities, it comes fraught with remarkable symbolism and significance.

In the vegetable kingdom these quinary relations rarely appear in perfect regularity—i. e., with all the units respectively equal or equivalent in position, form, and significance ; and, when they are regular externally, they are so variable that the regularity is perfectly maintained in a few cases only. This proves clearly its origin in the liberated energy of force—in the tendency of force, now lifted into life, to represent each relation independently.

Inasmuch as the representation of the numbers five and seven in independent and continuous development is excluded from the realm of simply energetic force, and inasmuch as every succeeding development of force-activity must be derived from simply energetic force, it follows that quinary and septenary relations can originate only from a subdivision or contraction of numerical relations lying within the realm of simply energetic force.

This is actually the fact. Quinary forms appear in the vegetable kingdom either in consequence of the subdivision of one of the principal directions of quaternary or binary forms, or in consequence of the combination of two principal directions of ternary forms. Nearly all quinary plant-forms show this to be the case.

It appears, then, that plants, which in their blossoms show scarcely any variation in the number five, are to be considered as truly quinary; that binary plants, which have the parts of their blossoms in fives, show the five as two, two, and one, inasmuch as this five results from the bisection of one of the four equivalent directions. Therefore, two of the parts will always belong together, and one will stand alone. Such plants, then, appear as representations of the law of two and two (binary law), passing into that of two, two, and one, etc.

In general, the quinary forms and combinations proceeding from the binary law are the most varied, as is shown in plants with alternate leaves. The lost equilibrium between the two twos is regained only with great difficulty.

It is different with the character of quinary forms appearing in ternary plants. Here it is not a bisection, but the union of two principal directions that yields the five; and the peace and calmness resulting from this union are manifest in the simplicity of the blossoms, as is seen in the rose, etc.

The number five, then, appears in nature and among life-forms as uniting the character of the numbers two and three; both in bisection and union, it appears as three and two. Hence, as developed under the influence of life-force, it is truly the number of analytic and synthetic life, representing reason, unceasing self-development, self-elevation; for, the higher the stage of development reached by the life-forms, the more persistent is this number.

Among vegetable forms, almost regular quinary arrangements of parts are found in plants that are capable of the greatest cultivation and variation, as is seen in the various fruit-plants that yield pomes and drupes (such as the apple, pear, cherry, etc.), as well as in the tropical fruits.

The former may be varied indefinitely. The same may be observed in roses, quinary plants derived from ternary relations; their varieties, too, may be increased indefinitely. Similarly, each locality yields its own variety of potatoes, although so many varieties have been developed in the few years of our acquaintance with this plant.

Again, the plants in whose flowers the parts appear almost regularly in quinary sets, are most easily propagated, improved, and induced to bear double flowers, as is seen in roses, pinks, primroses, and buttercup

Thus, wherever the number five appears, there is unmistakable evidence of a higher phase of life, which, through bisection or union of the parts implied by rigid law, calls forth this number.

Starting, not from the external features of the number, but rather from the innermost essential condition on which all variations and relations of numbers depend, the following additional considerations force themselves upon our notice:

The binary crystal forms, essentially simple and manifesting little variation of energy, resemble the different species of feelings; on the other hand, the ternary crystal forms, in their continuous external subdivision into ever-new forms, resemble forms of the understanding and of knowledge. As, in the ternary crystals, the structural axis is distinct from each of the three fundamental directions and placed independently at equal angles among them, their development through external subdivision and external union continues almost indefinitely. Therefore, the ternary form can subdivide the most subtile things; even light must submit to its analytic power, as in calcareous spar and in the three-sided prism—an artificial ternary form.

Therefore, the *falling* of the crystal from the binary into the ternary law of development resembles the *falling*, or—since the result is the same—the *ascent* of the mind of man from simple, uniform emotional development into the development of externally analytic and critical reason; for the ternary law, too, first introduces us to the external knowledge of crystal forms ascending in the scale of development.

Concerning the peculiar nature and effects of living force, the vegetable world shows the following facts: Throughout the various stages of upward development of the same living force in a plant, each part of the whole seems to possess the whole force only in a different degree of development; hence it is so frequently possible to produce the whole plant from a single part—from a shoot, a bud, a leaf, a fragment of the root. Hence, too, is derived the distinct fundamental law of vegetable life that each successive stage of development is a higher growth of the preceding one—e. g., the petals are transformed ordinary leaves, the stamens and pistils transformed petals. Each successive formation presents the essential nature of the plant in a more subtile garb, until at last it seems clothed only in a delicate perfume. The inner—having thus become almost wholly external —is taken up by the ovary, and again becomes internal. From the beginning to the time of blossoming, the life of the plant is an upward and outward unfolding; from this to the time of full maturity of the fruit, it is an exalted withdrawing.

Plant-forms, then, exhibit the (inner) force not only in multiplied diversity, but also in a state of progressive changes. Hence, too, when the (inner) force recedes, we notice quite frequently a retrogression of a later to an earlier form of development—e. g., the retrogression of petals to sepals, and of these to ordinary leaves; the retrogression of stamens and pistils to petals, so frequent in roses, poppies, mallows, tulips etc. As an instance of progressive transformation, we have the artificial change of the calyx to the corolla, with the aid of favorable position and food—e. g., in the garden primrose.

We see, then, that the essential nature of the whole plant lies in some peculiar manner in each individual part of the plant. Now, the first tendency of every thing and of every plant is toward the all-sided representation of its individuality. This tendency toward sphericity seems to be most fully restrained in the leaves. Therefore, it is frequently noticed, though not in the leaves alone, that after some injury the seemingly unfettered tendency toward spherical representation appears in the accessory formations; this is seen very beautifully in the rose-gall on injured rose-leaves.

Thus the plant seemingly represents the nature of life-force in external quiescence. Therefore, from this point of view, plants appear as the blossoms of nature; and as among plants, after the period of blossoming, the essential nature of the plant withdraws inwardly, thus, on the next stage of natural development—the stage of animal life—all external diversity is again gathered up in an inner unity, as it were in a kernel or seed, in spherical forms. Therefore, the lowest animals in their simple, spherical shapes resemble seeds endowed with animal life.

Thus, inasmuch as the law of the individual part is repeated in the whole, the totality of all mundane forms, although but a small part of the great universe, is nevertheless, relatively, a great, individual, organized, and organic whole. The animals, too, constitute again a great organic whole, seemingly one living form: this is manifest in the great general laws of nature that control the totality and apply distinctly in individual cases.

Thus, the quinary law, the necessary condition of higher life, one with the appearance of life on earth and inseparable from that life, is expressed with increased vitality in all animals; this is evident in the earliest forms, with the first appearance of animal life, as is shown by the remains of perished ages, and this fundamental law accompanies animal life in all its varied combinations and differentiations. Even in the human being, in whom life appears lifted into perfect spirituality, the number five is an essential attribute of his hand, man's principal member, his principal instrument in formative, creative activity, etc.

Another great, universally diffused law of nature, particularly well pronounced in the whole animal kingdom, and again representing the animal kingdom as a whole in relative individuality, is the law that makes the external internal, and *vice versa*. Thus we find the first animals having soft bodies, living in houses almost wholly composed of stone, almost wholly independent of the animals, and only externally inclosing their bodies as if they were foreign, separate things. Nevertheless, the existence of the animals depends on their fixed calcareous dwelling-place. Later on the animals appear detached, free, no longer like plants fixed in one point; they and their stony coverings are firmly united in growth, the solid covering incloses the body like a solid rind.

In succeeding (higher) animal forms, the half-gristly, half-stony covering unites more and more fully with the body of the animal, and at last disappears externally.

It sinks into the flesh, as it were; and, in the measure
in which it disappears outwardly, it becomes in fish
and amphibia an inner cartilaginous skeleton, with re-
siduary scales on the surface of the body.

In the still higher forms, this cartilaginous skeleton
is transformed more and more into a solid, bony skeleton, and the muscular mass, formerly inclosed in a stony
covering, now incloses the stony bones. What, in lower forms, was external is now internal; what was internal is now, in the perfected animal, external.

Again, the great law of equilibrium is manifested
with special distinctness in the animal world. By this
law a relatively determinate quantity of force dwells in
each life-form, and a relatively determinate quantity of
material is required for each body and for each kind of
its organs; consequently, if this material is used predominantly on one side in the formation of the body or
of its organs, the development of the body or similar
organs on the other side will suffer, and one organ or
side will grow at the expense of the other. Thus, in
fish, the trunk of the body is developed at the expense
of the limbs.

The operation of this law appears most clearly if the
human form in its symmetrical development is taken as
the criterion. If we compare, for instance, the arm and
hand of man with the wing of a bird, we see clearly
that certain parts or organs are developed at the expense of others.

§ 74. Thus, the forms of nature in all their diversity,
in all the stages of their development, result from the
operation of one and the same force. Primarily this
force appears as a unity, is clearly and fully pronounced

in completely individualized life, but is externally revealed in universal and all-sided application only in the
varied forms of nature, the possibility of whose representation is implied in the force. Here, too, is confirmed the great and universal truth that only in triune
representation, only in unity, individuality, and diversity
can each form of nature completely and perfectly express its inner being.

We have in this a new confirmation of the law of
development of crystals, the passing from special-sided-
ness to all-sidedness, from imperfection to perfection—
as the law of all development in nature. Man, then, appears as the last and most perfect earthly being, in whom
all that is corporeal appears in highest equilibrium and
symmetry, and in whom the primordial force is fully
spiritualized, so that man feels, understands, and knows
his own power. But, while man externally and cor-
poreally has attained equilibrium and symmetry of form,
there heave and surge in him—viewed as a spiritual being—appetites, desires, passions. As in the world of
crystals we noticed the heaving and surging of simple
energy, and in the vegetable and animal worlds the
heaving and surging of living forces, so here the heaving and surging of spiritual forces.

Therefore, man, with reference to spiritual development has returned to a first stage, as crystals are in the
first stage with reference to the development of life.
Therefore, again, a knowledge of the laws of crystal and
life forms is so highly important in the education of self
and others; it teaches and guides, gives light and peace.
For this reason, the boy—the learning human being—
should at an early period be taught to see nature in all

her diversity as a unit, as a great living whole, as one thought of God. The integrity of nature as a continuously self-developing whole must be shown him at an early period. Without a knowledge of this unity in the activities and forms of nature, it is impossible to attain or to impart a genuine knowledge of natural history.

This unity the boy's mind seeks at an early period; it alone satisfies him (see § 45). Go with a genuine boy into open nature, show the diverse natural objects, and he will soon ask you to indicate to him the higher, causal, living unity. While I write this, it is corroborated by constantly recurring questions from boys who have just entered upon this stage of development and who are interested in natural objects. All fragmentary study of nature, so different from the study of individual objects with reference to the unity that embraces all, deprives natural objects and nature of life and impairs the vigor of the human mind.

§ 75. These few hints for the study of nature as a whole must suffice here. They are simply intended to guide the father or teacher in leading the pupil to a knowledge of the universal application of the same law in all the various stages of natural development, to the apprehension of unity in diversity and of nature as a living organism. The inner connection among the activities and objects of nature has here been indicated only in general and only in one direction (that of form). Similarly, nature must be shown to the pupil as an organized and organic whole in all directions; for the various forces, materials, sounds, colors, etc., have—like the forms—their inner unity, their living inner con-

nection in and among themselves and with the whole.
Indeed, in their perfect development, all depend on the
influence of the same great, uniting, causal, natural objects, on the sun, which calls into being and sustains all
earthly life. It almost seems as if all earthly things
simply revealed the nature of sunlight; eagerly all turn
toward the sun, absorb the sunlight, hang upon his rays
as the children hang upon the words and looks of father
and mother—of the father who teaches in love, of the
mother who sustains and strengthens their development.
As the development and improvement of the children
are affected by the presence or absence of pure parental
love, of perfect parental spirit, so the development and
improvement of earthly things—the children of sun and
earth, as it were—depend on the presence or absence
of sunlight.   Thus, earthly things, as a whole, represent externally, visibly, and in manifold diversity the
nature of sunlight, which in the sun is seen as a unity;
and the knowledge of one leads to the knowledge of
the other.

Thus, father and son, teacher and pupil, parent and
child, walk together in one great living universe. Let
not teacher or parent object that he himself is as yet
ignorant of this. Not the communication of knowledge
already in their possession is the task, but the calling
forth of new knowledge. Let them observe, lead their
pupils to observe, and render themselves and their pupils
conscious of their observations.

An apprehension of the universality of law in
nature, of her unity, does not require special technical
terms for the objects or their attributes, but plain and
accurate observation and accurate naming of these things

in accordance with the character of language and of the thing named.

In rendering the boy familiar with natural objects we are by no means concerned with the teaching of names nor of preconceived views and opinions, but only with presenting the things themselves with their obvious attributes in such a way that the boy may view each object as the definite individual object it reveals itself to be in its form, etc.

Even the knowledge of a previously given or generally accepted name is unimportant ; only the clear and distinct apprehension and the correct naming of the general and particular attributes are important. We may give the object a wholly provincial name, or—if we have not this—we may give it a name suggested by the moment, or, better still, we may name it by circumlocution, until in some way we find out the generally accepted name. Through such endeavors we shall soon learn the generally accepted name, and thus be enabled to harmonize our knowledge with the general knowledge, and to correct and supplement it with the latter.

Let not the teacher of a country school object that he knows nothing about natural objects, not even their names. Even if he has had the scantiest education, by a diligent observation of nature he may gain a deeper and more thorough, more living, intrinsic, and extrinsic knowledge of natural objects in their diversity and individuality, than he can acquire from ordinary available books.

Besides, that so-called higher knowledge rests, ordinarily, on phenomena and observations within the reach of the plainest man, observations which frequently—if he know how to use his eyes—come to him with little or no expense, in greater beauty than the costliest experiment could yield them. But to this he must bring himself by continued observation; to this he must let himself be brought by the boys and youths around him.

Parents should not be timid, should not object that they know nothing themselves and do not know how to teach their children. If they desire to know something, their ignorance is not the greatest evil. Let them imitate the child's example; let them become children with the child, learners with the learner; let them go to father and mother, and with the child be taught by Mother Nature and by the fatherly spirit of God in nature. The spirit of God and nature will guide them.

One of the purposes of the college, indeed, is to open the inner eye for outer and inner truths; but it were sad for humanity if only those who go to college should learn to see. On the other hand, if parents and teachers teach children at an early period to see and think, colleges would again become what they ought to become, viz., *schools for the study of the highest and most spiritual truths; schools for the representation of these in the life of the students; schools of wisdom.*

From every point, from every object of nature and life, there is a way to God. Only hold fast the point, and keep steady on the way, gather strength from the conviction that nature must necessarily have not only an external, general cause, but an inner living cause, efficient in the most trivial detail; that it proceeds from one Being, one Creator, one God, in accordance with the self-evident, necessary law by which the temporal is an expression of the eternal, the corporeal a manifestation of the spiritual. You can not fail, then, to see the general in the particular, and the particular in the general.

The things of nature form a more beautiful ladder between heaven and earth than that seen by Jacob; not a one-sided ladder leading in one direction, but an all-sided one leading in all directions. Not in dreams is it seen; it is permanent; it surrounds us on all sides. It is decked with flowers, and angels with children's eyes beckon us toward it; it is solid, resting on a floor of crystals; the inspired singer, David, praises and glorifies it.

Would you have a fixed point, a reliable guide in all this diversity? It is given you in number (see §§ 38, 99). Number leads you on a reliable path; for it is determined by the external manifestations of the directions of inner energy. In the most direct way, it reveals the innermost nature of force, if you will but behold it with the keen eye of the boy, with the simple mind and heart of the child.

Let the boy's eye and mind be your guide, for you may know that a simple natural boy will not be satisfied with half-truths and false notions. Follow his questions thoughtfully—they will teach you and him. For they come from the mind of a child, and surely father and mother can answer a child's questions.

You object that children and boys ask more than parents and adults can answer. This is true. Either you stand at the limit of earthly things and at the threshold of divine things (if so, say so plainly; the child's or boy's spirit will be satisfied), or you stand at the limit of your knowledge and experience. Do not hesitate to say so; but beware of saying in this case that you stand at the limit of *human* knowledge in general—this would dwarf and stunt the human mind.

In such cases, examine the life within you, compare it with the life around you, lead your pupil to make the same comparison, and you and he will, in due time, find the answer to your question. You will see clearly, with the inner eye, the reliable and unequivocal answer which you seek. Thus you will clearly see God in his works; your earthly longings will be appeased; whatever of peace and good-cheer, whatever of consolation and help you may require in times of need, you will find in your own souls.

§ 76. Man needs a fixed point and a safe guide in the study of the inner connection of all this manifold diversity in nature. What can furnish a more reliable and uniting starting-point in this than that which ap pears as the source from which all diversity develops itself, the visible expression of all law and obedience to law, viz., mathematics, which, on account of this great exhaustive property, was from the very beginning so named—mathematics—i. e., the science of learning.

As a phenomenon of both the inner and outer world (of the macrocosm and microcosm), mathematics belongs equally to man and nature. Mathematics, as proceeding from *a priori* laws of thought, as the visible expression of thought and its laws, finds the phenomena, combinations, and forms logically deduced from these laws, again in the outer world independently established.

Similarly, man finds again in himself, in the laws of

his thought, the same diversity of forms which in nature are developed independent of him. Mathematics thus appears as a mediator between man and nature, between the inner and the outer world, between thought and perception.

This great mission, coexistent with the differentiation of inner and outer world, with the law of cause and effect, has secured for mathematics the high rank which it has enjoyed through all ages. Because of this, too, it could be seen in its true character and assigned its true place only by Christianity. Only the Christian who sees in all things the outgoings of the One Divine Spirit, can possibly appreciate its true character ; for only the Christian can understand the unity of the purely spiritual (*a priori*) forms with the forms of nature. Only he can solve the question whether mathematics has been deduced from natural phenomena, or whether natural objects were formed after laws of human thought, and have an existence only in these laws. For does not the same One Divine Spirit live and work in man and in nature ? Are not man and nature the creatures of the same one God ? Must we not, on this account, necessarily find unity and harmony and obedience to the same law in the spirit of nature and in the spirit of man, in external forms and forces, and in internal formation and thought ?

Therefore, it is possible to study nature in her forms and organisms, and with the help of the formulated laws of human thought, in mathematics.

For this reason mathematics mediates, unites, generates knowledge; it is not dead, self-limited, a certain sum of separate forms and truths found separately and accidentally and put on file, but it is a living whole, continually regenerating itself anew, strictly keeping pace in its development with the development of the human mind with reference to unity and diversity, and insight and contemplation; for it is the visible expression of thought, the expression of obedience to law in the spiritual as such, and therefore in this respect an organism, a product of necessity and freedom.

Mathematics is, then, neither foreign to actual life nor something deduced from life; it is the expression of life as such: therefore its nature may be studied in life, and life may be studied with its help.

Inasmuch as thought and its laws themselves pass from unity to diversity or all-sidedness, and, although apparently starting with a diversity (something external), yet always refer to some remote or obscure unity (something primarily internal), mathematics, too, passes necessarily from unity to diversity or all-sidedness; and, although externally and apparently it proceeds from individuality and diversity, yet a necessary inner unity underlies all its deductions.

All mathematical forms and figures should, therefore, be viewed as proceeding from the laws lying in the sphere and circle, and referred to these as their unity; the sphere itself, however, is to be regarded as proceeding from unity with its own self-active energy (see § 68).

Mathematical forms and figures should not, therefore, be considered as put together in accordance with external, arbitrary causes, but as the necessary outcome of a self-active, inner force, acting in all directions from a central point. They are not, in the very first instruction, to be considered as separate things, but in their necessary inner connection; even if we do start with individual and diverse forms and figures, we should always refer them to this ever-present and ever-active unity which may be likened to their soul.

Mathematics is the expression of the inner cause and of the outer limitations and properties of space. As it originates in unity, it is in itself a unity; and, as space implies diversity in direction, shape, and extension, it follows that number, form, and magnitude mutually imply one another, and are an inseparable three in unity.

Now, number is the expression of diversity as such, and, indeed, the expression of the inner cause of diversity, of the directions of energy; it does not result from dead, external addition, but from living inner laws that lie in the very nature of force. On the other hand, form and magnitude find their explanation only in diversity. It follows from this that a knowledge of number is first and most essential to a knowledge of the triune whole; that a knowledge of number is the foundation of a knowledge of form and magnitude—of a general knowledge of space.

Space itself, however, is by no means dead and stationary, but owes its existence to the *constant* operation of inner absolute energy. And, as space owes its existence to the cause and primordial law of all existing things, it follows that the universal laws of space underlie all that manifests itself in space and the laws of thought and knowledge themselves.

Mathematics should be treated more physically and dynamically, as the outcome of nature and energy.

This would make it even more instructive, more profitable than we even now anticipate, not only in the
study of nature, especially in her chemical (material)
structure, but also in the study of the nature and operation of the spiritual, of the laws of thought and feeling. This is especially true of the study of curves, of
the spherical, and the like.

Education without mathematics (at least without a
thorough knowledge of numbers, supplemented by occasional instruction in form and magnitude) is, therefore,
weak, imperfect patchwork; it interposes insuperable
limits to the normal culture and development of man.
Unable to free himself from his inner longing for progress, man attempts to leap over these, or, weary of his
fruitless endeavors, seeks to suppress the energy of his
powers; for the mind and mathematics are as inseparable as the soul and religion.

C. Language.

§ 77. What, now, is *language*, the third of the fulcra
of boy-life and of human life in general, and what relation does it hold to the other two?

Wherever there is true inner connection, true inner
and living reciprocity, there appears a relation similar
to that of unity, individuality, and diversity. This applies, too, to religion, nature, and language. In religion,
the aspiration of the soul which is directed toward unity
in man, prevails and seeks the fruition of its hopes. In
the contemplation of nature and mathematics, the aspiration of intelligence, which refers to individuality in
man, prevails and seeks certainty. In language, the de-

mand of reason which refers to diversity and unites all diversity, prevails and seeks satisfaction. *Religion* is a living in the soul that finds and feels the One in All; *nature* studies individualities in nature, in themselves and in their relations to one another and to the whole; and *language* represents the unity of all diversity, the inner living connection of all things. These three, therefore, form an inseparable unity, and the one-sided, fragmentary development of one or the other of them necessarily produces one-sidedness and, with this, finally, the annihilation, or at least destruction, of unity in man.

Religion strives to manifest and does manifest *being;* *nature* strives to manifest and does manifest *energy*, the cause of its action and this action itself; *language* strives to manifest and does manifest *life* as such and as a whole.

Religion, nature — (Mathematics represents, as it were, the tendency, laws, and causes of nature in man; mathematics represents nature as, in accordance with her necessary causes, she must lie in the mind of man; without mathematics man could obtain no knowledge of nature; with it he can see her more fully and harmoniously than her external phenomena would warrant) —religion, nature (mathematics), and language in all their diverse relations have the same one mission and purpose, to reveal the inner; to make the internal external, the external internal, and to show both the internal and external in their natural, primordial, necessary harmony and union.

Whatever, therefore, is true of one of the three will necessarily be relatively true also of the other two.

Whatever has been said heretofore of religion and nature (with mathematics), if it is only in itself true, must apply to language in the peculiar way determined by the character of language.

Therefore, unfortunately for humanity as a whole, we are confronted in life, as one of the greatest obstacles to the development of the three, by the illusion that each may have an independent existence and reach perfection in its development; that we may have *language* without religion and nature (mathematics), etc.

But as it was necessary that God, desiring to reveal himself unequivocally in the fullness and integrity of his being, should do so in the triune manner indicated (see § 61) ; so, too, religion, nature (mathematics), and language constitute an integral unity. A complete knowledge and firm confidence in the one necessarily implies complete knowledge and firm confidence in the other; a true study of the one necessarily implies also the true study of the other.

Now, since man is destined to know and to see clearly (see § 78), human education requires the knowledge and appreciation of religion, nature (mathematics), and language in their intimate living reciprocity and mutual causality. Without the knowledge and appreciation of the intimate unity of the three, the school and we ourselves are lost in the fallacies of bottomless, self-producing diversity

Such is the nature of language and its relation to man and his education. We shall now inquire how language itself manifests and corroborates this in its structure.

§ 78. In general, *language is the self-active outward*

expression of the inner. This is shown in the word *sprechen, s-prechen* *—i. e., to break one's self. As the breaking of a thing makes known its inner structure, as the opening (breaking-up) of a bud reveals the inner structure of the blossom, so the speaker self-actively reveals, expresses what is within him.

Now, the innermost (soul) of man is constantly moving *life,* therefore the attributes and phenomena of *life* must be revealed in human speech. Hence, perfect human language, as a continuous representative of the innermost soul of man, must manifest itself through the most mobile medium and by the slightest movements; it necessarily must be audible.

A man's speech should be, as it were, his self in its integrity, and that it may reveal him all-sidedly and continuously in greatest mobility. It will, then, inasmuch as man is a product of nature, reveal also the character of nature as a whole. It will become an image of man's inner and outer world.

Now, the soul of man, like the soul of nature, is law, necessity, spiritual, eternal—the Divine revealing itself in the external and through the external. Therefore, language must reveal this law in and through itself; it must be the expression of necessary conformity to law. All the laws of the inner and outer world, collectively and singly, must be revealed in language, must lie in language itself.

---

* In this case Froebel's play on the word comes nearer to truth. *Sprechen,* by the loss of *r* becomes in English *speak,* and is traceable to a root which signifies to *break,* to *split,* to *scatter,* etc. He looks here upon *s-prechen* as Sich BRECHEN, to *break* one's self which, however, belongs to another root.—*Tr.*

§ 79. Language, like mathematics, has two sides; it belongs both to the inner and to the outer world.

Language as evolved from man proceeds, therefore, directly from the human mind; it is the expression of the human mind, as nature is the expression of the divine mind.

The question whether language be a simple product of the mind or an imitation of nature is due to the adaptation of language to both views, an adaptation due to the fact that in all things the same Divine Spirit, the same spiritual, divine laws operate; to the fact that the spirit of nature and that of man are *one*, that they have the same source, which is God.

As language is an expression of man and nature, and therefore of the Spirit of God, it implies, too, a knowledge of nature and of man, and therefore a revelation of God.

Viewed in the light of the study of nature, language is an expression of energy lifted into life; viewed in the light of the study of man, it is the expression of the human mind lifted into consciousness. Language, therefore, must be born as the spirit of man enters consciousness, and is inseparably one with this spirit.

The mediatory character of language implies both physical and mathematical attributes, attributes of life and of motion. Hence, in its ultimate word-elements— in its vowels, semi-vowels, and consonants, and in the letters that represent these—language expresses the fundamental attributes and relations of the natural as well as the operations of the spiritual.

However imperfect and fragmentary our objective knowledge of language may be, it clearly reveals the ínner life that pervades language in its minutest fibers, and renders it a complete organism. In spite of this imperfection and fragmentariness of our experiments and knowledge, however, we can not repress the conviction, corroborated at every step, that in every language—primarily in our mother-tongue (German)—the sound and letters in their combinations express definite and fixed mathematical, physical, physio-psychical laws, resting on inner necessity; that the representation of an object, viewed from a certain standpoint, by a word, necessarily demands certain sounds and letters and no others, so that each word is the necessary product of certain word-elements, just as each material chemical product is the result of the combination of certain determinate elementary substances.

In other words, the word-elements in their various combinations represent, as in a picture, the natural objects, the forms of the mind and their relations in accordance with their innermost nature and the personal or national view of them.

Only a moderate attention to the conformity to law, manifest everywhere in the natural and spiritual, physical and psychical world, forces upon us this conformity to law in the formation of the words of our language. The inner conformity to law and, as it were, the vitality primarily of our German language admit of no doubt in him who is himself animated by its inner life and unity, although little can be definitely said about this, particularly in the dull forms of written language.

Well might this deter us from asserting this conformity to law in language, but we are here in the predicament of the musical amateur deficient in musical culture. Although he knows and can say but little concerning musical laws, and still less compose anything in accordance with these laws, he sees necessity and conformity to law at every step of a great musical production in spite of all its apparent freedom. Even one wholly without musical culture who may hear that music is rejoiced by it, although he has not the slightest notion of the law, and can hold fast only the coarse rhythmic phases, at best.

Similarly we may say of forms, colors, materials, and forces, that we are surrounded by their diversity and their various effects on us and others, without any notion or knowledge of their inner unity and conformity to law; but our inability to know and see them does not affect the existence of these laws.

The same is true of our mother-tongue and the more subtle laws of word-structure. It is true of our mother-tongue, because we speak it from the first dawn of self-consciousness. Therefore, it seems to us a mere heap of sounds, or, at best, with reference to its visible individual words and roots, a collection of motley stones and beautiful flowers from which we can make bouquets and a variety of jewels. The words, in their first beginnings, their so-called roots, seem to be adventitious material not subject to higher causes of production.

But as an organized musical whole proceeds from elementary sounds, as an organized material whole proceeds from elementary substances, and as shapes proceed from elementary directions of forces, so in language the words as images of objects and as expressions of ideas are organized wholes proceeding from simpler elements.

The elements of words (visibly, the letters) are, therefore, by no means without life, forming words by arbitrary or accidental contiguity; but they designate originally and necessarily elementary notions, having mathematical, physical, and psychical phases; they have a meaning, and in the formation of words they obey necessary laws of co-ordination. Every object, attribute, relation, etc., appears as an organized concept, the product of certain elementary notions by whose intimate mutual union the word is formed.

[*Translator's Synopsis.*—Here follow in Froebel's book a number of more or less fanciful illustrations of the operation of this law, all taken from the German language. Even in the German language, however, the operation of the law is nearly concealed or obliterated by other influences, and complicated by differences in "points of view" that may have prevailed among different tribes in the formation of different words for different ideas. In the English language these disturbing influences are notoriously much greater, so that it would be difficult to render Froebel's illustrations intelligible to the English reader in all their details. This is particularly true of illustrations in which vowel-sounds are concerned, whose mobility renders them peculiarly sensitive to every influence or change of condition, however minute.

For these reasons, I content myself with merely indicating Froebel's method of illustration, with the help of a few instances in which the Saxon forms of English are sufficiently like the German to render this possible. I feel that I am the more justified in this as Froebel, too, confines himself to a series of *illustrations*, and does not give a systematic presentation of the whole of this interesting study.

Collating words such as *fresh, free, frolic, freak, fruit, friend, fry,* and again, *flee, flight, flame, float, flow, flood, floor, flesh, fleet,* he finds in the first series the expression of spirituality manifested in a diversity of outward activities indicated by the sounds *fr,* and in the second series the expression of spirituality mani_ fested in continuous inner activity indicated by the sounds *fl.* In both series the sound *f* would point to the spirituality, *r* and *l* being due to its different manifestations.

Similarly, the sound of *c* or *k* in the words *crack, climb, creep, crab, cramp, cry, clear, clad; corn, kernel, cook, keep, keen, kick, kill, king; knell, knot, knock, know, knight, knoll,* etc., gives expression to the operation of self-active force prominent in the ideas covered by these words.

In general, he arrives at the law that *vowels* represent the *inner,* or unity; *consonants* (mutes), the *outer,* or individuality; and *semi-vowels* (continuants and sonants), the *mediations,* or diversity.]

It is by no means intended here to systematize these laws of language, but simply to insist that the boy's attention be directed to them at an early period; his unbiased observation will soon teach him more than has been indicated. What has been said must, therefore, suffice to direct attention to the mathematical, physical, and psychical attributes of language by which it becomes truly an image of the inner and outer world.

Of course, these attributes should be studied first in

our mother-tongue. However, they are by no means the exclusive property of the German, but are found also in Greek and Latin in a manner peculiar to these languages. Thus, this view of language reveals to us even an inner relationship among these languages, showing German, Greek, and Latin in the relationship of soul, life, and body.

In general, our children would reach a by far more thorough insight into language, if in our teaching we were to connect the words more with real ideas of the things and objects designated. Language would then cease to be for us merely a system of sounds and words, and would become a real living organism. Thus, it would lead more to the study of things, to the study of the essential nature of each thing and of the word itself. Thus, our language would again become truly a living language—i. e., born from life and generating life; whereas now it threatens by merely external study to sink more and more into death.

[Froebel devoted himself at different times with much zeal to the study of languages, particularly of the French, Latin, and Greek. In 1811 he became deeply interested in the Oriental languages, chiefly on account of their kinship with the German. The tendency to seek a definite absolute meaning in each sound and letter was a characteristic of the philology of his time. Froebel, in his great love of the German language, became deeply involved in this tendency. He became an enthusiastic follower of Rückert, who found in *eh* (pronounced with the long sound of the English ā) the root of all languages. *E* (ā) is the root of all vowels, *h* is the root of all consonants. This to him is shown in words like *eh* (*ante*, formerly), *ewig* (eternal), etc. Froebel finds corroboration, too, in the word *ehe* (matrimony). Later developments of philology have shown the futility of these deductions from a law of inner unity which still awaits formulation.—*Tr.*]

§ 80. Among the different things which, in addition to the things previously considered, language offers for consideration, the law of rhythm claims special attention. This law appears in the different parts of words, as well as in the combinations of words; it proves both the spiritual origin of language and its conformity to natural laws (see § 33).

The rhythmic law of language, its universal expression of life, belongs to it originally and inseparably as much as life belongs to the things represented in language. Hence, all primitive language expressions, as representations of active inner and outer life, are necessarily rhythmic; and the more so because man in his childhood and youth, as well as humanity as a whole in its childhood and youth, has a more living and keener perception of the inner life of things. Therefore, for early youth language representation should assume a rhythmic form, for this is its first form in the early youth of mankind; and, in general, man sees the whole in its rhythmic organization and in its connection with man before he sees its particulars in their respective individuality. Thus, a number of considerations point to rhythmic language as necessarily belonging to the early youth of man. The loss of this has deprived him and mankind as a whole of one of the foremost, most primitive, and most natural means of elevation.

If, then, we would restore our children to a true, higher, spiritual, and inner life, we must again awaken in them that inner life of language, of nature-contemplation, and of feeling. The way to this is so easy. We only need to let the child live in accordance with its own nature and to remove carefully whatever might

destroy or annihilate this natural life. Instead of this
we put an end to budding life with crude, dead, heart-
less words, and frighten back into rigid inactivity whatever of life strives to free itself.

Thus, we say, " Come, dear child, see the little
violet. Is it not nice? Break it off, and put it in some
water, but take good care of it. It would be a great
pity if you should lose it."

How different would be the impression and the
effect upon the same child's mind, if we should say
more rhythmically :

Come and see the

Blossoming violet ;

and then give expression to the child's feelings, thus :

Blossoming violet ! how

Much I do love thee (you) !

Let the skeptic who considers this above the capacity
of the child listen to children, simply, naturally, and
thoughtfully led. He will find how very early in the
simplest expressions of feeling and accounts of observations they express themselves unwittingly in more or
less rhythmic speech.

It is true there are few such children; but ther.

would be more, were we not ignorantly blunting so
many tendencies in our children or starving them into
inanition.

And, nevertheless, we expect our children, who have
grown up so barren and empty of feeling, to understand
poets and nature at a later period. Then, the drill-
master's art—even in our day and with the children of
cultured parents—is expected to impart its elocutionary
tricks. Behold the poor child, vain or trembling, con-
ceited or timid, reciting his piece, and say who is most
to be pitied, the child, his teacher, the poem, the poet, or
the audience.

[The instinctive tendency to rhythmic utterance in children is
quite manifest in the character of their first words—*pápa, máma,
tá-ta*, etc.; and in the delight they find in the rhythmic repetition of
seemingly meaningless syllables, which to many is mere senseless
jabbering. Preyer has recorded some of these utterances from the
"monologues" of his infant boy—e. g., *eda, didl-dadl, dldoh-dldah;
papa, mama, meme, mimi, momo; e—mama—mamemama—ma—
—me—ma—me—ma*. Perez records the following : "A little girl,
two years and two months old, went on repeating from morning to
night for a fortnight, *toro, toro, toro, rapapi, rapapi, rapapi*,
rhythmic monotone which caused her great delight. Another child,
nearly three years old, for three months went on repeating these
three syllables, articulated in a sonorous voice, *tabille', tabille',
tabille'*."

I am favored with clear remembrances from the time of my
babyhood, and can even now see myself lying in my crib keenly en-
joying the rhythmic spell of similar exercises.

I would here again refer the reader to Spencer. In "First
Principles," chapter x, he treats on "The Rhythm of Motion" quite
exhaustively.—*Tr.*]

§ 81. Religion, nature, and language place the child, the boy, and the man—developed in accordance with these principles—in the midst of all life. He finds himself unable to hold fast for himself and his memory the great number of facts, not even as such, and much less in their relations to time and place; and one experience seems to displace another. A still richer life is developed in his soul, so rich that the soul, unable to compass its abundance and wealth, overflows with it. This superabundance now meets him again from without as an independent, determinate, seemingly second life, and he can and does grasp it in its definiteness. And this is well, for this awakens in him the irresistible impulse and imperative need to snatch from oblivion for himself and others the blossoms and fruits of the rich but passing inner life, and to hold fast by means of external symbols the fleeting external life in shape, place, time, and other circumstances.

Thus, the *art of writing* is developed in each individual human being in the general historical way and in agreement with the general course of development of the human mind (see § 24). Indeed, we find ever again that the same laws which have guided mankind in its development, hold good, too, in the development of each individual human being; and we find at the same time that an externally richer life leads necessarily to *pictorial hieroglyphics*, and an internally richer life to *conventional letters* [alphabetic writing].

However, both the pictorial and alphabetic writing imply an exceedingly rich life—only out of this richness writing was born; and even now the true desire and need of it are thus developed in the child, in each human being.

Therefore, from this point of view, too, it is imperative that parents and teachers should be careful to render the inner life of their children as rich as possible, not so much in diversity as in inner significance and activity. Without this, the art of writing comes without a corresponding inner need, and the mother-tongue becomes—what it is now for so many in a very high degree—extraneous, meaningless, dead. Only if in each particular we choose again the great necessary highway of humanity as a whole, the great and vigorous early life of humanity comes to us again in and through our children; the enfeebled mental qualities and faculties, the weakened powers of intuition and insight will come back to us in their full vigor (see § 16).

And why, seeing that every boy endeavors to lead us on this way, should we not earnestly seek it? Here we see a boy making a sketch of the apple-teee on which he discovered a nest with young birds, there another busy over the picture of the kite he sent up high into the air. Before me a little six-year old child, in self-active endeavor, without external compulsion, draws, in a book kept for this purpose, representations of strange animals he saw the day before in a menagerie.

Who, having the charge of little children, has not been asked for some paper to write a letter to father or brother? The little boy is urged to this by the intensity of his inner life which he would communicate to these. It is not imitation, he has seen no one writing, but he knows how he can gratify his desire. To him his marks, resembling one another quite closely, mean different words which he intended to write to the person addressed ; and we see here a manifestation of the inner desire for symbolic writing, as in the former cases the inner desire for pictorial writing was shown.

There are, indeed, thoughtful boys endowed with great intuitive power for the spiritual with whom one might develop in the strictly historical manner the want and the invention of pictorial and symbolic writing. It is a well-known fact, too, that larger boys frequently invent their own alphabets. Certainly we should always proceed in some such way ; we should here, as in all instruction, start from a certain inner want of the boy. Indeed, to a certain extent such a want is indispensable if the boy is to be taught with profit and success.

There is in this a source of many of the errors in our schools. We teach our children without having aroused an inner want for the instruction and after repressing everything that was previously in the child. How can such instruction be profitable?

§ 82. It has been shown that the irresistible impulse of a soul overflowing with superabundance of life in some direction, and the desire to hold fast this wealth gave rise to writing; this art, therefore, appears as the fruit of thoughtful self-observation. Similarly, the written characters or letters can not have been chosen arbitrarily, and must have some connection with the idea designated and with the growth of this idea.

Although the laws to which letters owe their origin and development have become obscured, the little that is left of their first rudiments, seems to point unequivocally to an inner connection between the form and

the meaning—e. g., the letter *O* as symbol in the word
for the idea of absolute self-limitation, and the letter *S*
as symbol in the word for the idea of a return to
self.

An examination of the original Phœnician and later
Roman characters readily reveals in a number of them
a definite relation between the form of the letter and
the idea it stands for in the word. However, even if
the original definite connection between the letter and
the meaning of the word could no longer be proved,
some such connection should be assumed on the slightest foundation for the purposes of instruction. Nothing
should ever be brought to the notice of the human being in purely arbitrary connection—in a connection that
does not admit at least the possibility of discovering a
necessary inner reason. The neglect of this makes in-
straction in writing, at present, so mechanical, lifeless,
and dispiriting. [A sentence relating to the Gothic and
Latin styles of type is omitted here].

§ 83. I shall here add merely the suggestion that in
the same way *reading* again enters into its original and
natural relationship to the human being and to the
learner. Reading is the necessary outcome of the desire to render again audible to himself or others, to re-
suscitate, as it were, what has been written down.

Writing and reading, which necessarily imply a living knowledge of language to a certain extent, lift man
beyond every other known creature and bring him
nearer the realization of his destiny. Through the
practice of these arts he attains personality. The endeavor to learn these arts makes the scholar and the
school. The possession of the alphabet places the pos-

sibility of self-consciousness within his reach, for it alone renders true self-knowledge possible, by enabling him to place his own nature objectively before himself, as it were; it connects him clearly and definitely with the past and future, brings him into universal relationship with the nearest things, and gives him certainty concerning the most remote.

The alphabet thus places man within reach of the highest and fullest earthly perfection. Writing is the first chief act of free and self-active consciousness.

Now, since reading and writing are of such great importance to man, the boy (when he begins to practice them) should possess a sufficient amount of strength and insight. The possibility of self-consciousness must have been developed in him; the inner need and desire to know them must have manifested itself clearly and definitely, before he begins to learn these arts.

If he is to learn these arts in a truly profitable way, the boy must himself already have become something of which he can become self-conscious, instead of laboring to become conscious of what he has not yet come to be; otherwise, all his knowledge will be hollow, dead, empty, extraneous, mechanical. For, if the foundation is dead and mechanical, how could we expect later on to see developed therefrom life-activity and true life, which is the highest prize of all earnest endeavor; how could man truly attain his destiny, which is life?

D. Art and Objects of Art.

§ 84. If what has been said heretofore concerning the objective and central points, or axes, of human life is surveyed from a common point of view, human aims will present themselves under three aspects. There is either a tendency to inward repose and life, or a tendency to the study and comprehension of the external, or a tendency to direct representation of the internal.

The first is the prevailing tendency of religion; the second, of the contemplation of nature; the third, of self-development and self-contemplation.

Similarly, it will be found that *mathematics* is concerned more with the representation of the external in the internal, with the representation of inner conformity to universal law, with the representation of nature in inner (human) terms. For this reason mathematics mediates between nature and man; it has reference more to the understanding.

Language is concerned more with the outward representation of inner perception, has reference more to reason. There is still wanting for the complete representation of his nature as a whole the representation of inner life as such, of the mind. This representation of the internal, of the inner man as such, is accomplished in *art*.

§ 85. With one exception all human ideas are relative; mutual relations connect all ideas, and they are distinct only in their terminal points.

Therefore, there is in art, too, a side where it touches mathematics, the understanding; another where it touches the world of language, reason; a third where —although itself clearly a representation of the inner —it coincides with the representation of nature; and a fourth where it coincides with religion.

Yet all these relationships will have to be disregarded, when it is considered with reference to the education of man, in order to lead him to an appreciation of art. Here, art will be considered only in its ultimate unity as the pure representation of the inner. We notice at once that art, or the representation of inner life in art, must be differentiated in accordance with the material it uses.

Now, the material, as an earthly phenomenon, may be motion as such, but audible in sound, as tones which vanish while being produced; or it may be visible in lines, surfaces, and colors; or it may be corporeal, massive. Here, too, as in all actual things, there are, however, many transitions and combinations.

Art, as representation by tones, is music, particularly song. Art, as representation by color, is painting. Art, as representation by plastic material, is modeling. The last two are connected by drawing. This, however, may be considered simply as representation by lines, so that painting would appear as representation by surfaces, and modeling as representation by solids.

On account of the mediating quality of drawing, it appears very early as a phase in human development, and we noticed that even at an earlier stage children have the desire to draw (see § 36). Even the desire to express ideas by modeling and coloring is frequently found at this earlier stage of childhood, certainly at the very beginning of the stage of boyhood (see § 49).

This proves clearly that art and appreciation of art constitute a general capacity or talent of man, and should be cared for early, at the latest in boyhood.

This does not imply that the boy is to devote himself chiefly to art and is to become an artist; but that he should be enabled to understand and appreciate works of art. At the same time, a true scholastic education will be sure to guard him against the error of claiming to be an artist, unless there is in him the true artistic calling.

A universal and comprehensive plan of human education must, therefore, necessarily consider at an early period singing, drawing, painting, and modeling; it will not leave them to an arbitrary, frivolous whimsicalness, but treat them as serious objects of the school. Its intention will not be to make each pupil an artist in some one or all of the arts, but to secure to each human being full and all-sided development, to enable him to see man in the universality and all-sided energy of his nature, and, particularly, to enable him to understand and appreciate the products of true art.

Like drawing, but in a different respect, representation in rhythmic speech is mediatory. As representation of the ideal world in language, as the condensed representation, as it were, of the ethereal spiritual world of ideas, as the tranquil representation of absolute, eternally moving, and moved life, it belongs to art.

In everything, in life and religion, hence also in art, the ultimate and supreme aim is the clear representation of man as such. In its tendency, Christian art is the highest, for it aims to represent in everything, particularly in and through man, the eternally permanent, the divine. Man is the highest object of human art.

Thus, we have indicated in their totality the object, the aim, and the meaning of human life, as they are revealed even in the life of the boy as a scholar. It still remains to consider the sequences and connections in the development of successive phases of his nature at the scholastic stage, as well as the character, the order, and form of the instruction by which the school seeks to aid the boy in this development.

VI

CONNECTION BETWEEN THE SCHOOL AND THE FAMILY AND THE SUBJECTS OF INSTRUCTION IT IMPLIES.

A. General Considerations.

§ 86. In the family the child grows up to boyhood and pupilage; therefore, the school must link itself to the family. The union of the school and of life, of domestic and scholastic life, is the first and indispensable requisite of a perfect human education of this period. The union of family and school life is the indispensable requisite of the education of this period, if men, indeed, are ever to free themselves from the oppressive burden and emptiness of merely extraneously communicated knowledge, heaped up in memory; if they would ever rise to the joy and vigor of a knowledge of the inner nature and essence of things, to a living knowledge of things—a knowledge which, like a sound, vigorous tree, like a family or generation full of the joy and consciousness of life, is spontaneously developed from within; if they would cease at last to play in word and deed with the valueless shadows of things, and to go through life in a mask.

It would prove a boon to our children and a blessing

to coming generations if we could but come to see that we possess a great oppressive load of extraneous and merely external information and culture, that we foolishly seek to increase this from day to day, and that we are very poor in inner knowledge, in information evolved from our own soul and grown up with it.

We should at last cease making a vain display of the thoughts, the knowledge, and even the feelings of others. We should no longer seek the highest glory of our education and of our schools in efforts to garnish the minds of our children with foreign knowledge and skill.

This is, indeed, an old disease; for, if we inquire how the German people has obtained the first principles of its present knowledge, we discover unequivocally that those first principles always came from a distance, from foreign parts, or were even forced upon it from without. Therefore, we have not even a generally accepted term in our mother-tongue for these first principles, elements, or rudiments.

The strong German mind, it is true, digested this foreign acquisition and assimilated it, but it nevertheless continued to wear the character of its extraneous origin. For thousands of years we have worn these fetters. Shall we, therefore, never begin to plant in our own minds a tree of life and knowledge, and let it germinate and nurse it, that it may unfold in beauty, put out vigorous and sound blossoms, and ripen delicious fruit, which may fall from the tree in this world and yield a new harvest in the world beyond?

Shall we never cease stamping our children like coins and adorning them with foreign inscriptions and foreign portraits, instead of enabling them to walk among us as the images of God, as developments of the law and life implanted in them by God and graced with the expression of the divine?

Are we afraid that our children might excel us? What people and what time will be high-minded enough to deny itself for the sake of its children and in the interest of a pure humanity? Nay, what father and what family will allow its soul to be filled with this thought, and thus multiply and enhance its inner power manifold?

Only the quiet, secluded sanctuary of the family can give back to us the welfare of mankind. In the foundation of every new family, the Heavenly Father, eternally working the welfare of the human race, speaks to man through the heaven he has opened in the heart of its founders. With the foundation of every new family there is issued to mankind and to each individual human being the call to represent humanity in pure development, to represent man in his ideal purity (see § 48).

It is sufficiently clear, too, that the German mind can no longer be satisfied with the lifeless extraneous knowledge and insight of the time; that a culture of mere external polish can no longer suffice, if, indeed, we are to become self-centered, worthy children of God. Therefore, we need and seek knowledge and insight that have sprung into vigorous and healthy life in our own minds and grown strong in the sunshine and conditions of our own life.

Or would we ever again cover with rubbish the source of life which God has opened in the heart and

mind of every human being? Would we deprive our
children and pupils of the unspeakable joy of finding
in their souls the source of everlasting life? Would
you, parents and teachers, continue to compel your
children to stop up this source of life with valueless
waste and to hedge it with thorns?

You say: "Only thus can they get along in the
world. Children will soon be grown up. Who will
then take care of them? What will they eat? Where-
with will they be clothed?"

Ye fools! I shall not answer you by saying, "Seek
ye first the kingdom of God," etc.; for in your es-
trangement from God and from yourself you could not
understand this. But again and again I shall say unto
you, that we are not here concerned with a dull, brooding life, empty of knowledge and works (see § 23).

Mankind is meant to enjoy a degree of knowledge
and insight, of energy and efficiency of which at present
we have no conception; for who has fathomed the destiny of heaven-born mankind? But these things are to
be developed in each individual, growing forth in each
one in the vigor and might of youth, as newly created
self-productions.

The boy is to take up his future work, which now
has become his calling, not indolently, in sullen gloom,
but cheerfully and joyously, trusting God and nature,
rejoicing in the manifold prosperity of his work.
Peace, harmony, moderation, and all the high civil and
human virtues will dwell in his soul and in his house,
and he will secure through and in the circle of his
activity the contentment for which all strive.

Neither will he say that his son may take up any

business but his own, the most ungrateful of all; nor
will he insist that his son shall take up this business
which he himself carries on profitably and with satisfaction to himself.   He will see that the smallest business may be carried on in a great way, that every business may be ennobled and made worthy of man.   He
will see that the smallest power, cheerfully and rightly
applied to any work, will secure bread, clothing, and
shelter, as well as respect; he will, therefore, feel no
anxiety concerning the future welfare of his children,
whose soul-development has been his chief care.

§ 87. The various directions of this unified school
and family life, of this active educational life, are indicated by the degree of development man has attained
at this stage, by the inner and outer needs of the boy
entering upon this stage of pupilage.   They are, of
necessity, the following:

a. The arousing, strengthening, and cultivation of the
religious sense; the sense that brings the soul of man
into ever-more living unity with God; the sense that
feels and holds fast the unity in all the apparent di
versity of things, and by whose vigor and activity the
boy's life and actions are brought into harmony with
this unity.   For this purpose we have the memorizing
of religious utterances concerning nature, man, and
their relation to God, and particularly for prayer; furnishing him a mirror, as it were, in which the boy may
see, as in a picture, his feelings, intuitions, and tendencies in their original unity with God, and thus become
conscious of them and hold them fast in this aspect.

b. Consideration, knowledge, and cultivation of the
body as the servant of the mind and the medium for

the representation of its being, to be developed in orderly graded exercises.

c. Observation and study of nature and the external world, proceeding from the nearest surroundings to the more remote.

d. Memorizing of short poetical representations of nature and life, particularly of short poems that impart life to the objects of nature in the nearest surroundings, and significance to the incidents of home-life, showing them, as in a mirror, in their pure and deep meaning. This is to be done particularly for the purposes of song and in song.

e. Exercises in language starting with the study of nature and the external world and passing over to the inner world, but always with strict reference to language as the audible medium of representation.

f. Exercises in systematic outward corporeal representation, proceeding from the simple to the complex. Here are included representations by means of more or less prepared material (building, paper, card-board, wood-work, etc.), as well as modeling with plastic material.

g. Exercises in representation with lines on a plane, and in constant, visible relation to the vertical and horizontal direction, the media for the apprehension of all external shapes. These directions in their repetitions constitute a net-work of lines, which is to be the outer law for these drawing exercises.

h. Study of colors in their differences and resemblances, and representation of these in prescribed outlines, with special reference to the form of the outline (coloring of outline pictures) or to the color-relations (painting in the square net-work).

i. Play, or representations and exercises of all kinds in free activity.

j. Narration of stories and legends, fables and fairy-tales, with reference to the incidents of the day, of the seasons, of life, etc.

All this is interspersed in the ordinary school and family life, with the ordinary occupations of home and school.

For boys of this age should have some definite domestic duties to perform. They might even receive regular instruction from mechanics or farmers, such as has been frequently given by fathers inspired by vigorous and active natural insight. Especially should older boys frequently be set by parents and teachers to doing things independently and alone (i. e., errands), so that they may attain firmness and the art of self-examination in their actions. It is very desirable that such boys should devote daily at least one or two hours to some definite external pursuit, some externally productive work. It is surely one of the greatest faults of our current school arrangements, especially of the so-called Latin and high schools, that the pupils are wholly debarred from outwardly productive work. It is futile to object that the boy at this age, if he is to reach a certain degree of skill and insight, ought to direct his whole strength to the learning of words, to verbal instruction, to intellectual culture. On the contrary, genuine experience shows that external, physical, productive activity interspersed in intellectual work strengthens not only the body but in a very marked degree the mind in its various phases of development, so that the mind, after such a refreshing work-bath

(I can find no better name), enters upon its intellectual pursuits with new vigor and life (see § 23).

If we compare the just enumerated subjects of the educational life of home and school, they appear grouped in accordance with the inner needs of boyhood into subjects (a) of the more quiet, calm, inner life ; (b) of the more receptive, intro-active life ; (c) of the more expressive outwardly formative life.   They completely meet the needs, therefore, of man in general.

Furthermore, it will be noticed that they develop, exercise, and cultivate all the senses, all the inner and outer powers of man, and thus meet the requirements of human life in general.

Lastly, it will be seen that a simple, orderly home and school life can easily meet the requirements of all these subjects, and, consequently, the requirements of human development at this stage.

Let us now examine these subjects in their particulars.

B. Particular Consideration of the Different Subjects of Instruction.

A. AROUSING AND CULTIVATION OF THE RELIGIOUS SENSE.

§ 88. If the child has grown up in unity of life and soul with his parents, this unity will not only be maintained but strengthened and intensified during the period of boyhood, provided no disturbing and obstructing causes intervene.

The question here is not of that vague and indefinite unity of feeling which makes one body of two bodies, not uncommon between parents and child, but of that living soul-unity, that clear oneness of mind, which sees life as an unbroken whole in all its operations and phenomena.

This living unity of soul, this clear oneness of mind —which is not a mere external community of life—is the unshakable foundation of genuine religious feeling. For this spiritual unity between parent and child, the inner life, the pure outward representation of inner spiritual life of man is a common concern. What the father and mother because of the hindrances of life could not attain, they seek to accomplish in and through their child — the representation of pure humanity as such.

Dearly, and often painfully, the father has purchased clear and sure results from his experience in the development and cultivation of his own innermost life. His loss of strength prevents him from applying these results in his own life, but he communicates them to his son; and the son profits by this experience and applies it in his own life with the unbroken and full energy and vigor of his youth.

Where the life of parent and child has not been an unbroken whole from the earliest beginning, these communications have no effect; apparently the experiences of two different worlds are opposed to each other with different wants and different forces, and the connecting link is missing. Only he who has tried to secure them can appreciate the results of that spiritual unity between parent and child, which is based on the common purpose of cultivating and representing highest and purest humanity.

Such a spiritual union necessarily implies the obser-

vation of individual and common life in their inner
cause and purpose, in their inner and living connection.
From this the soul of man, even in boyhood, obtains the
most unequivocal proofs and conviction that, to speak
humanly, God continues uninterruptedly to guide mankind in its development and cultivation with fatherly
protection and care, and follows each individual as an
essential member of the whole in all the events of life
with fatherly aid and solicitude.

How could man better express the fact that the
events of life, truly seen and understood in their causes,
their nature and significance, are always for the best of
the individual and of the whole? Thus, we ever speak
of the divine most clearly and comprehensibly for ourselves in human terms.

The boy's mind thus steadily grows in clearness and
purity, his powers are ever enhanced and increased, his
courage and perseverance strengthened by thus finding
the confirmations of these truths in his own life and in
that of others, in individual and common life, in experience and revelation; by thus finding the harmony
and unity of revelation in scripture, nature, and life;
by thus seeing himself the member of a whole unfolding from the small domestic circle into ever wider and
higher realms, of a whole whose common purpose he
recognizes, amid the most positive evidences of divine
guidance and care, in the representation of the spiritual
in and by the corporeal, of the divine in and by the
human.

The life of such a family, of such a boy, will necessarily be a prayer of Jesus expressed in conduct and in
deeds, a living prayer of Jesus; a rich and efficient

Christian life, trusting in God, loving God and man spontaneously active in childlike obedience to God. Thus, the teachings of Jesus will be interpreted in their own life, and the application of these teachings in life will become possible.

Religious instruction, resting on such spiritual union between parent and child, stands on firm ground and is rich in blessings. It is fruitful and rich in blessings only in the measure in which fortunate circumstances of life have aroused in the boy at an early period a living sense, a quick and clear eye for inner spiritual life (see § 21).

There is no danger that any subject of inner spiritual life will prove in its nature too high and unintelligible for the boy's inner spiritual sense ; let him simply receive the facts, his inner power will soon find the inner meaning in forms accessible and intelligible to him.

We do not give early boyhood enough credit for religious power as well as for mental power generally. For this reason, in later boyhood, life and the soul are so empty, so wholly without experience, and, therefore, so callous and dull with reference to spiritual, ethical, and religious notions. Only a few threads, and these weak, are found there to which to fasten instruction concerning a truly religious life ; nevertheless, so much is asked in this respect of the boy in the succeeding period of youth.

Children and boys have their attention called at an early period to a great number of external matters, and receive instruction concerning these things which they can not understand, simply because they are extraneous. At the same time, they are left uninstructed concerning so many inner matters which they might understand, because these matters are within them. Thus, they are early introduced to outer life, and estranged from inner life ; for this reason, the latter is so hollow and dull.

If the human being is to understand many, particularly religious, truths, we must see to it that he have many experiences in this direction, that even in the more trivial events of his emotional and religious life he become conscious of the course and conditions of his spiritual development. Unless man ascends from the knowledge of the Fatherhood of God in his own life to a knowledge of His Fatherhood in the life of mankind, future religious instruction will be empty and barren in the same inverse ratio.

Very many religious errors and misinterpretations, many falsities and half-truths would be avoided through early attention to these matters, or through at least unhindered and undisturbed development of inner spiritual life in harmony with external life and with reference to it. Similarly, we could avoid the misunderstanding of certain prominent sayings of dogmatic religious instruction, which in this one-sided presentation effect in the life of man the exact opposite of what they are intended to effect. This is true, for instance, of the saying, " The good will be happy," so prominently emphasized in religious instruction, generally to the greatest detriment for the life, the happiness, the contentment, and the ever-progressive tendency of man.

The simple boy, still poor in outer experiences, feels and sees his life as an undivided whole ; to him inner and outer good, inner and outer happiness, inner and outer life are still undivided, without any differentiations or oppositions. Therefore, without any idea that it might be different, the inner pure soul-life is necessarily considered also as external; hence, the inner fruits of goodness are looked upon as identical with the external fruits.

The inner and the outer, the infinite and the finite, however, are two worlds, whose phenomena are necessarily and for ever different in form. Therefore, that general saying, if it does not at an early period disturb and weaken the inner peace and power of the boy, will at least fill his mind with false expectations and lead him to wholly false judgments, interpretations, and uses of his experiences—to serious errors in his life.

Dogmatic religious instruction should rather at an early period establish the truth, showing its application in individual and collective life, and tracing it in all development in nature and mankind, that whoever truly and earnestly, in singleness of purpose and self-sacrifice, seeks the good, the pure representation of humanity, must needs expose himself to a life of external oppression, pain and want, anxiety and care. For this very tendency implies that the inner, spiritual, true life be revealed and become manifest; and, if this is to be accomplished, the consequences indicated above are unavoidable.

In order to enable the boy to see this vividly, let him compare the requirements, conditions, and phenomena of the development of a tree with the requirements, conditions, and phenomena of the spiritual development of a human being. He will find that—

Every phase of development, however beautiful and proper in its place, must vanish and perish, whenever a higher phase is to appear. The sheltering bud-scales must fall when the young branch or the fragrant blossom is to unfold, however much these tender forms may thereby be exposed to the rough weather of spring. The fragrant blossom must make room for a fruit, at first sour, hard, and homely. The luscious, red-cheeked fruit must decay, that vigorous young plants and trees may sprout forth.

Thus, the psalms of David, and the hymns of many others who did battle for the lifting up of mankind, for the representation of pure humanity, resemble the fruits of their tree of life which could not appear without the sacrifice of many earlier phases of life development dear to them.

And do not the verses of those psalms and hymns resemble kernels which, sown in the fertile soil of human souls, bring forth shady trees filled with fragrant blossoms and strength-giving, eternal, immortal fruits?

Renunciation, the abandonment of the external for the sake of securing the internal, is the condition for attaining highest development.

This agrees with the saying, coming from another phase of contemplation: "The dearer the child, the more frequent the rod"; or, "Whom the Lord loveth he chasteneth." Every boy whose soul is not wholly estranged from himself will understand this truth. The human being who understands this truth and who is conscious of an honest purpose will not murmur and complain, like a stubborn child, about adverse occurrences in his life, saying: "Why is my lot so sad, so unhappy? I have done no harm, at least I am not conscious of any evil doing. Others are doing so well, although it is known how wicked they are, or, at least, that they act only from external points of view, and from transient and weak motives."

He will rather say to himself: "Just because you seek earnestly and steadily only the highest and best, only the absolute and permanent good, all merely relative and transient good must vanish, to make room for ever higher and more perfect developments and, at last, for abiding fruit."

No less detrimental to the attainment of human life is the predominance frequently given in religious instruction to the promise of a reward for good deeds in a future life, if they seem to go unrewarded in this life. Brutal minds who hold sensual pleasure highest are not affected by this; boys and human beings, generally with a normally good disposition, do not need it. For, if our life is pure, if our actions are right and good, no reward in a future world is needed, even though in this world all may be lacking that seems valuable to the sensual man.

It argues a low degree of insight into the nature and dignity of man, if the incentive of reward in a future world is needed, in order to insure a conduct worthy of his nature and destiny. If the human being is enabled at an early period to live in accordance with genuine humanity, he can and should at all times appreciate the dignity of his being; and at all times the consciousness of having lived worthily and in accordance with the requirements of his being should be his highest reward, needing no addition of external recompense.

Does the good child or boy, conscious of having acted in a manner worthy of the father, in his spirit and in obedience to his will, need more than the joy of this consciousness? Does the simple, normal child, conscious of having done right, think of any additional reward, were it only praise? Should not man be as pure and perfect in his actions toward God as the son is toward his earthly father? Jesus says: "My meat is to do the will of Him who sent me"—i. e., the consciousness of having done the Father's will gives sustenance, meaning, and joy to my life. He deems the poor already blessed—as they truly are—because their poverty enhances the efficiency of the soul and lifts conduct accordingly.

We ought to lift and strengthen human nature, but we degrade and weaken it when we seek to lead it to good conduct by means of a bait, even if this bait beckons to a future world, when we use even the most spiritual external incentive for a better life and leave undeveloped the inner self-active forces which in every human being prompt the representation of a pure humanity.

How very different are all these things if the boy's attention has been directed at an early period to the reactions of his conduct, not to the external pleasantness of his situation but to his inner condition, to his inner freedom, serenity, and contentment! Experience resting on this will necessarily arouse more and more man's inner sense, leading to genuine thoughtfulness, the most precious treasure of boyhood and youth.

Religious instruction should throw light upon such experiences, should bring them into clear consciousness, should harmonize and unite them, should deduce from them the self-evident and axiomatic truths, show their application in all conditions of life in which force, life, and spirit are active, should exhibit their agreement with the truths recognized and uttered by God-inspired men. This true religiousness will become the eternal heritage of man, and gradually of mankind as a whole, and all that is high and holy and has found utterance in humanity will again and again find utterance in man. Thus, the religious development of the individual will be brought more and more into harmony with the religious development of mankind, blessing all, dissipating superstition, doubt, and despotism, and fixing the glorious consciousness that in God we live and have our being.

§ 89. *Memorizing of Religious Sayings.*—It is natural that religious feelings, sentiments, and thoughts should spring up in the mind of man as such, as well as in the mind of the boy not estranged from himself and grown up in spiritual unity with his parents.

In the beginning these sentiments and feelings will manifest themselves in the mind of man or of the boy only as an effect, as an intuition, a fullness, without word or form, without any adequate expression of what they are, merely as something that uplifts our being and fills the soul. At this juncture it is most beneficial, strengthening, and uplifting for the young human being to receive words—a language for these sentiments and feelings—so that they may not be stifled in themselves, vanish in themselves for lack of expression.

There need be no fear that the words of others will force upon the child or boy an extraneous feeling. The religious element has the quality of pure air, of bright sunlight, and clear water; every earthly creature inhales them, and in each it assumes a different form and color, in the life of each it finds a different expression.

Take any simple religious maxim intelligible to every boy or child through and in his own life, let a number of boys memorize it, and it will produce in the life of each an effect peculiar to his individuality.

Of course, these words must find a response in the boy's life. The child must not be expected to give life and meaning to the words, but the words must give expression to what is already in the boy's soul and find their meaning in this.

Thus, a boy, scarcely six years old, asks every evening one of his parents taking him to bed: "Please, teach me a prayer." Then, after repeating it, he quietly goes to sleep. One day, he had done something that seemed to indicate that all was not right in his soul. The evening prayer opened with general terms; in a loud and strong voice he repeated the words as usual. Then a slight turn in the words pointed to the occurrence of the day, and suddenly his voice became scarcely audible, though, probably, his conscience spoke only the louder.

Yesterday, he said to me for the first time: "Please, repeat the prayer with me." I inferred that there was something that concerned him very much. I selected the prayer which seemed to me the right one, and he calmly went to sleep.

Not long ago, the same boy came to me and brought me a picture he had just found; he was pleased with it, for it was brilliantly painted. At the same moment a boy, about a year and a half older, very lively, and apparently little heeding inner life, came up. "How

cruel!" he exclaimed, looking at the picture, which represented an attack of Turks upon Greeks, particularly
upon Greek mothers and children.

I said to the boys that all ought to give thanks to
God for a life free from harm and sorrow. "Yes, indeed," exclaimed the older boy, "as we do in the morning and evening." Yet at no time had an explanatory
word been spoken to him.

Certainly it is neither necessary nor desirable that
with younger boys there should be frequent changes in
the sayings or utterances memorized for the purpose of
giving expression to their inner life.

B. RESPECT FOR THE BODY, KNOWLEDGE, AND CULTIVATION OF IT.

§ 90. Man respects what he not only knows in its
value, its meaning, and uses, but what he can apply and
use, the things on whose good qualities he knows the
attainment of his work and purpose to depend.

It does not follow that man, especially in boyhood,
knows his body, because it is so near to him, nor that he
can use his limbs because they are one with him. We
often hear boys admonished not to be so awkward, and
this particularly in walks of life that do not pay regular
attention to all-sided bodily activity in childhood and
early boyhood.

We see that men in whom the culture of mind and
body have not kept pace with each other, at certain
times and under certain circumstances, do not know
what to do with their body. Nay, many a one seems
to feel his body and his limbs to be a burden to himself.

The occasional cultivation of the body in domestic

occupations may do much to remedy this. But, in almost all cases, this is very subordinate, and generally exercises the body only one-sidedly. Besides, man is to know not only his power but also the means for applying it; and this can be attained only by means of an all-sided, equal cultivation of the body and its parts as the medium and expression of mental culture.

This appears already in the simplest cases of instruction, where the use and position of the body and its members are essential, *e. g.*, in writing, drawing, the playing of musical instruments, etc. If the pupil has not previously had the benefit of true all-sided cultivation and use of his body and its members, and has made this his permanent possession, only a mechanical training, equally blunting to teacher and pupil, can secure scanty success; the continual repetition of admonitions to sit straight, to hold the arm right, etc., drives all life and prosperity from instruction.

An active, vigorous body, in all conditions and pursuits of life, a dignified bearing and attitude of the body, can only result from all-sided cultivation of the body, as bearer of the mind. Surely, a great deal of rudeness, ill-mannerliness, and impropriety would disappear from boyhood, and corresponding admonitions would become less frequent, if we gave our boys regular, all-sided bodily training, proceeding from the simple to the complex, based on their mental culture, and keeping pace with it.

The will, as such, does not yet control the body at all times; therefore, the body should be enabled to obey the mind implicitly at all times, as in the case of a musical performer. Without such cultivation of the body, education can never attain its object, which is perfect human culture. Therefore, the body, like the mind, should in this respect pass through a true school, though not in a one-sided manner ; and regular physical exercises, proceeding from the simple to the complex, based on the mental development, are a proper subject of instruction in every school.

Thus alone is true discipline made possible. True discipline firmly places the boy, in all his actions, on the recognition and feeling of human worth, and on consequent respect for his own nature. This is the positive element of education at this period ; and the more vividly and distinctly the pupil apprehends the nature and dignity of man, and the more clearly and perfectly he sees and understands the necessary requirements of true humanity, the more positively and strictly the educator should insist upon the fulfillment of these requirements. Nay, if need be, he should not shun to descend from admonition to punishment and severity for the benefit of the pupil ; boyhood is the age of discipline. Only harmony of mental and bodily culture renders true discipline possible.

Furthermore, after severe mental activity, the body as well as the mind calls for strictly regulated, vigorous bodily activity, and this again reacts on the mind and strengthens it. Only where mental and bodily activity are thus in regular, living, mutual action and reaction, true life is possible.

But bodily exercises have yet another important side : they lead the human being (here the boy) subsequently to a vivid knowledge of the inner structure of his body ; for the boy feels with special vividness tha inner mutual connection in the activity of his members. These perceptions, aided by only tolerably good sketches of the inner structure of man, must lead to the vivid knowledge of this structure, and induce, at least, a living interest in the care and consideration of the body.

C. OBSERVATION OF NATURE AND SURROUNDINGS.

§ 91. The things considered under this head formerly—in the period of childhood—seemed isolated and without inner connection ; now they appear in an orderly arrangement and in their necessary inner connection, adapted to the development of man at this stage, and in the classifications and subdivisions indicated by the gradual differentiation of particulars from generals.

The knowledge of every thing, of its purpose and properties, is found most clearly and distinctly in its local conditions and in its relations to surrounding objects. Therefore, the pupil will get the clearest insight into the character of things, of nature and surroundings, if he sees and studies them in their natural connection.

Again, the boy will, of course, see most clearly and appreciate most fully the conditions and relations of objects that are in closest and most constant connection with him, that owe their being to him, or at least have in their being some reference to him. These are the things of his nearest surroundings—the things of the sitting-room, the house, the garden, the farm, the village (or city), the meadow, the field, the forest, the plain. The sitting-room, then, furnishes the starting-point for this orderly study of nature and surroundings

which thus proceeds from the near and known to the
less near and less known, and becomes for the purpose
of orderly classification and subdivision a real subject of
school instruction.

The course is as follows. Instruction begins again
with the necessary indication of the object. Thus, pointing to the table, " What is this ? " Then, pointing to
the chair, " What is this ? " etc. Then the question
comprehending all, " What do you see in the school-
room ? " " The table, the chair, the bench, the window,"
etc. The teacher writes on a slate the names of the
objects which one or several have named, and requests
the pupils to repeat the names in chorus. Again the
teacher asks : " Are the table and the chair in the same
relation to the school-room as the door and the window ? " " Yes—no." " Why yes — why no ? What
are the door and the window with regard to the room ? "
" They are *parts* of the room." " Name all the things
which you think are parts of the room." " Walls, ceiling, floor, etc.—all these are parts of the room."

" As the door, the window, etc., are parts of the
room, so the room is a part of some greater whole."
" Yes, of the house." " What other parts has the
house ? " " The hall-way, the sitting-room, the bed-
room, kitchen, etc., are parts of the house." It is quite
desirable, for the training of perception and language,
that the pupils should together repeat the answers in
proper form.

" Again, have all houses the same parts as this
house ? " " No." " What parts which other houses have
not do you find in this house ? What parts do you find
in other houses, but not in this house ? What deter-

mines the importance of the parts and rooms of a house?" "The use and purpose of the house." "What are the most important parts of a complete dwelling-house?"

"Besides the objects that are parts of this room, you named some that are not parts, but which you see in the room; name some of them again." "Chairs, tables, flower-pots, books, etc." "Do chairs, tables, etc., stand in the same relation to the room as flower-pots, books, etc.?" "No." "Why not?" "Chairs, tables, etc., are necessary to the room. Objects that are necessary to a room make up the furniture of the room." "Name all things which you know to belong to the furniture of a room. Has each of the other rooms of the house its particular kinds of furniture?" "Yes, the kitchen, the bed-room, etc." "What things belong to the kitchen, the bed-room, etc.?" "These things are called kitchen-utensils, etc."

"Are there in the house things that do not belong to a particular room?" "Yes" (naming some). "All things that belong to the house are the house-furniture. Name all things you know as house-furniture."

"The house has its definite parts, or rooms. Now, is the house again a part of a greater whole?" "Yes; the homestead (the premises)." "What things are parts of the homestead?" "The court-yard, the garden, the dwelling-house, the barn, the stable, etc." "The movable objects which belong in the court-yard are the furniture (implements) of the yard. All movable objects that belong in the garden are garden-implements," etc.

"As the house is a part of the homestead, so is the homestead a part of a greater whole?" "Yes; of the village." "What things make up the village?" "Houses, barns, gardens, homesteads, churches, schools, etc." "What kinds of houses do you find?" "Farm-houses, shops, stores, etc." "What belongs in a shop? What belongs in the church? What is around the village?" "The township." "What have you seen in the township?" "Mountains, valleys, roads, etc."

From this point the study of the earth's surface (geography) becomes an independent subject of instruction.

The study of surroundings has this peculiarity that all the studies of particular things or classes of things branch out from it at certain necessary places, like the buds on the boughs of a tree. This will be seen again and again in a natural and rational course of instruction. In general, the proper place for beginning with a new, distinct subject of instruction, is necessarily and regularly determined like the ramification of symmetrically organized plants.

It is true that the indications for this, like the beginnings of a new bud, are often very indistinct. Frequently they manifest themselves only in the mind and soul of the teacher who gives himself up thoughtfully to the requirements and relationships of the subject; or who is so full of the subject that he sees its requirements intuitively, as it were. If the moment of the natural budding of the new subject of instruction has been missed, every later effort arbitrarily to introduce the subject lacks life; and, although the subject may be necessary, it will always seem extraneous, dead, and will continue to behave as such.

Every teacher who in true love and fidelity seeks a truly natural and rational instruction must have felt this often and painfully when, in foolish subjection to rule and custom, or in ignorance or dullness, he has missed this moment of new budding. He will labor without success; the connections of his course of instruction will be like those of a limber-jack; his instruction will be empty and dull, like the noise of a toy mill.

Therefore, for the purposes of a living, life-giving, and life-stirring instruction, it is most important to note the moment, the proper place, for the introduction of a new branch of instruction. The distinctive character of a natural and rational life-stirring and developing system of instruction lies in the finding and fixing of this point. For, when it is truly found, the subject of instruction grows independently in accordance with its own living law, and truly teaches the teacher himself. Therefore, the whole attention of the teacher must be directed to these budding-points of new branches of instruction. To neglect this will, in its consequences, lead to an unnatural and incoherent course of instruction (see §§ 81, 82).

After this digression we return to the course to be pursued in the observation of the external world.

" In the surrounding country you see trees, steeples, rocks, springs, walls, forests, villages, etc. Consider again these and all other things you can see, and tell me if each one is the only thing of its kind, or if several may be classified together as being similar." " Several things may be classified together as being similar."

"Name several objects which you can thus classify together."

"If you go on comparing these things with each other, do you find an important difference between them?" "Yes; some things grow in nature (naturally); others are made by men. The former are *natural* objects, the work of nature; the latter, *artificial* objects, the works of man." "Name several natural objects that you know." "Trees, fields, grass, etc." "Name also several artificial objects that you know." "Walls, hedges, roads, etc." "Are fields and meadows purely artificial?" "Yes—no." "Why? Are hedges, vineyards, etc., purely artificial?" "No." "Why not?" "Such things we may call natural and artificial objects (works of nature and of man)." "Name several such objects in your surroundings." (To be followed by repetition in concert, as usual.)

"Name several natural objects in your surroundings, examine them more closely, compare them with one another, and see if you can find other great differences by which you can classify them—e. g., tree, rock, stone, river, bird, oak, stag, pine-tree, thunder, lightning, air, etc." "There are differences among them by which they can be classified." "What are they?" "The bird, the stag, etc., are animals; the oak, the pine, etc., are plants; the stone, air, etc., are minerals; thunder, lightning, etc., are natural phenomena." "Name all the animals you know; all the plants, etc."

Then follow observations of animals with reference to the locality they inhabit; yielding classes of domestic animals, animals of the field, of the woods; terrestrial, aquatic, amphibious, aërial animals.

Similarly, plants are considered and classified as house - plants, hot - house plants, garden - plants, marsh-plants, parasites, etc. ; then follow minerals, though these yield few points for comparison ; and, lastly, the various natural phenomena are arranged as terrestrial, aërial, aquatic, and igneous phenomena.

Subsequently it is found that, because of the locality they inhabit, natural objects are near or more or less remote with respect to man ; and the question is raised concerning the influence of this nearness or remoteness on their mode of life, their behavior, or their qualities. It is found that the nearer natural objects, exposed to the influence of man, are weaker, more sensitive, need-ing care, more docile, etc. ; indeed, more *tame*, and that the remoter objects are more crude, more *wild*.

Tame and wild animals are then named. The tame animals may be classified with reference to their uses as beasts of burden, of draught, etc. Wild animals, too, may be considered as useful or noxious. Similarly, plants are studied ; and even with minerals this may be done.

Again, natural objects may be considered with refer-ence to the time of their appearance ; yielding ideas of winter and summer fruit ; spring, summer, and fall flowers, etc. The swallow is recognized as a summer bird, the lark as a spring bird, etc.

With reference to time and place combined, we may consider the animals, particularly the birds, learning to distinguish these as migratory and resident birds.

Of great importance in the consideration of animals is their mode of life, yielding ideas of carnivorous, herbivorous, etc., animals.

Here follows directly, as a new, distinct branch of instruction, the study of *natural history*, first in its more descriptive, then in its anatomical and physiological features. Similarly, at an earlier period, the consideration of natural phenomena depending on the operation of physical forces pointed to *physics* as a new branch of instruction; this is indicated, too, in the study of minerals.

The consideration of the animals affecting man most nearly through use and injury furnishes the transition from the general observation of nature to physics and natural history. There follows now the distinction between viviparous and oviparous animals—between the oviparous that hatch their eggs, and those that leave the hatching of their eggs to the sun, etc.

Physics and natural history, subsequently, are concerned primarily with external differences and resemblances, their conditions and causes, their effects and consequences, and, particularly, with the consequent logical grouping of similar natural objects; with the study of those external properties in which the inner nature of the object finds its most unequivocal and characteristic external expression.

In thus ascending from the particular to the general, and then descending again from the general to the particular, in this fluctuation of the instruction—more particularly in the observation of the outer world—the course of instruction resembles life closely; and it becomes possible to exhaust the limits of knowledge with reference to each subject for each successive stage of mental development and power.

Up to this point natural objects have been studied with reference to all obvious, external characteristics of time, place, mode of life, etc. Now the works of man (artificial objects) are to be subjected to a similar external scrutiny.

[The pupil * is requested to enumerate the works of man in the surrounding district (the house, the village, the road, the bridge, the wall, the plow, etc.); he finds their differences in origin, material, use, and purpose; he finds those that give him shelter, those that serve as implements, those that facilitate intercourse, those that give pleasure, and those that are simply the products of human skill and thought.

He finds the characteristics of villages and cities; of the different private, industrial, and public buildings of a city; of workshops, factories, stores, and magazines; of the different kinds of workshops, etc. He studies each workshop and factory with reference to its particular tools and purposes.

He distinguishes among the various kinds of stores by their contents: those that keep food-products, sold chiefly by weight; those that keep artificial products (dry-goods), sold chiefly by measures of length, etc.

The public buildings, too, are distinguished and grouped by their purposes and uses, as educational, devotional, charitable, etc.

---

* The matter included in brackets [—] is a full synopsis of the subjects presented in quasi-catechetical style, as in the outset of this section. — *Tr.*

Subsequently, the pupil ascends in his study from the work to the workman, from the product to the producer, from the effect to the cause, therefore from human works to man (as from the study of nature he ascended to her creator, to God). He finds the names of the workmen in different kinds of workshops (carpenters, etc.), and classifies these workmen in accordance with the character of the place in which they work, the material on which they work, and the kind of work they do.

He then learns to classify the various products of human activity in accordance with certain internal characteristics, such as the material of which they are made (stone, earthenware, wood, etc.), the use to which they are put, etc.

Similarly the uses of public buildings are considered (of the court-house, the school-house, the church, etc.), as well as the official names of the persons who are occupied in these buildings. Cities are then classified. Other occupations of men (hunters, fishermen, etc.) are considered.

At last, questions are asked concerning the common features and the ultimate aim of all human work ; and it is found that all men live together, grouped in a common relationship, that of the family.]

" Since * all men live and have lived in families, and since the highest and ultimate aim of all men is the clearest consciousness of and purest representation of their God-given nature, where can all men be most

---

* On account of the great importance of the family in Froebel's view of education, I here give his complete catechism of this phase.— *Tr.*

surely and effectively prepared and developed for the attainment of this aim?" "In the family." "What are the external conditions of a family, and who are its most important members?" "Father, mother, children and servants." "What now must be the condition of a family, if it is to prepare and develop the human being for the attainment of the highest and ultimate purpose of life?" "They must know this ultimate purpose and the means for its attainment; they must be agreed concerning the ways and means to be adopted; they must aid and support each other in all they do, having only this purpose in view." "If a single family should fulfill these conditions, would it thereby be enabled to attain the purpose of man in and through itself?" "No." "Why not?" "Because a single family can not possess all the means for this purpose." "How, then, can the ultimate purpose of man be attained more easily and surely?" "When several families, who appreciate the highest purpose of man and who agree concerning the means for its attainment, unite for the sake of aiding and supporting one another in this work." "Only humanity as a whole, as a unit, can fully attain the highest and ultimate purpose of human striving, the representation of pure humanity."

Thus the pupil in a great meandering circuit has returned to the home from which he started on his explorings of nature and the outer world, has returned to the center of all earthly human endeavor; but with enlarged and keener powers of observation, although the objects of the outer world have been brought to his notice only in their external phases of being. He has found man in his various relations to the things of the outer world; he has found himself.

This subject of instruction, as the first one, has been presented in a detailed and suggestive manner, in order to emphasize how all instruction should start from the pupil and his nearest surroundings, and should again return to him.

It is scarcely necessary to say that the last of the above answers neither can nor should be given by the pupil in their completeness and connection, even though he may have grown in years; but the thoughts which they contain should be awakened in the pupil, and for this he is sufficiently developed even at a comparatively low stage of judgment.

Nor is it necessary to say that, because instruction is to be connected wholly with the boy's locality, in particular applications all things are to be excluded that lie beyond his circle of experience. It was the intention merely to show how the study of nature and the outer world, in accordance with a law and development of its own, embraces in one unbroken unity all that nature and the outer world may bring to the notice of the student. Yet these considerations will present themselves, for instance, in the study of commerce and of the higher mental activities of man, as well as of all the various pursuits of man; and the more obscure and the rarer they are, the more is it desirable to hold them fast in order to reach with their aid higher and more remote developments. For who can fail to see that the continual extension of, at least, external culture brings to the notice of the inhabitants of even the most secluded

spots ever new things, and that the knowledge and control of more remote and higher relations of life are
becoming more and more what they ought to be—a
task for mankind as a whole.

Again, it was not deemed necessary to indicate for
the thoughtful reader—and only thoughtful persons
ought to teach—the various budding-points for each
new branch of instruction : e. g., for physics, in the consideration of natural phenomena resulting from the obvious activity of inner forces ; and for chemistry, in the
consideration of other natural phenomena in which the
qualities of material were changed through the influence
of certain natural energies, such as light or heat, as in
the discoloring of leaves in fall, decay, etc.

In general, it is best that the teacher should find
these points himself ; his knowledge will then be more
vivid and his instruction will gain in interest.   And
why should not every thoughtful teacher find the
right way in himself, if only he gives himself up in
faithful obedience, and without conceit and distrust, to
the guidance of the spirit of his work.   In all human
beings there lives and acts the one divine spirit ;
therefore, even the most experienced teacher, when
he teaches again even the simplest thing, will learn
again—will, teaching, learn again—(at least, this is the
experience of the writer to this day).   How else could
the teacher maintain his energy and courage, which
are lost so easily through the hinderances and difficulties that arbitrary ignorance and prejudice oppose
to his work ?

Hence, it is well to meet at once the objection that
it is foolish to expect a boy—particularly between the

ages of six and eight, as here indicated—to have this detailed knowledge of things which even adults scarcely possess.

It is not the intention that he should possess it, but it should gradually come to him in the course of the instruction ; and it will surely so come to him, as repeated experience with the course here indicated has abundantly shown. At the same time, it arouses in the pupil such a keenness of observation that scarcely any thing of importance in the objects around will escape him, and he will readily find the proofs of the teachings of earlier lessons. Thus, the young human being learns at an early period *to observe* and *to think*. Besides, boys (human beings) know more than they are clearly conscious of.

It might yet be objected that such a course leads the boy too soon out of his naturally narrow limits, and might render him proud of his varied knowledge.

Varied knowledge in *necessary living connection* never makes one proud, but causes man to reflect, and teaches him how little he really knows ; thus he is lifted in his humanity and adorned with that most precious jewel, *modesty*.

But it is impossible to meet all the objections that have been or might be made. Therefore, we leave the course to the consideration of the reader, though much might yet be said of its importance. Rightly understood and handled, it may be used in the least favored schools ; for it places man at an early period in the center of all and in inner connection with all that is offered to man for his external study. Thus he is led to reflect and gains an insight into the character, origin, and purpose of all things. This, and the proper use of this, is the ultimate aim of all instruction, whatever its name

D. MEMORIZING OF SHORT POETICAL REPRESENTATIONS OF NATURE AND LIFE, PARTICULARLY FOR PURPOSES OF SONG.

§ 92. Nature and life, in their phenomena, speak to man at a very early period; but they speak in tones so low that the still undeveloped sense of the boy, the still untrained ear of man at this stage of development, while hearing these tones, can not interpret them and translate them into its own language. Yet, soon after the first dawn of the consciousness of self as distinct from the outer world, there are aroused in man the longing to understand life and language of the external world, particularly of nature, and the hope that he will one day receive into himself and make his own the life that confronts him on every side.

The seasons come and go as regularly as the times of the day: Spring, with its tide of new growth and wealth of blossoms, fills man (even in boyhood) with gladness and new life; the blood flows faster and the heart beats louder. Autumn, with its falling brilliant and fragrant leaves, fills man (even as boy) with a sense of longing and hope. And rigid but clear and steady winter awakens courage and vigor; and these feelings of courage, vigor, perseverance, and renunciation fill the boy's soul with a sense of freedom and joy. Therefore, the joy with which he greets the first flowers and birds of spring is scarcely as jubilant as that with which he hails the first snowflakes that promise to his vigor and courage a smooth, quick road on which to fly to the distant goal.*

All these things are presentiments of later life—hieroglyphics of a still-life slumbering as yet in the soul; rightly understood, they are angels that guide man through life. Therefore, man should not lose them; they should not vanish in empty vapor and mist.

What, indeed, is there in our life, if childhood and youth were poor and empty, void of vigorous, living forms, of the sense of longing, hope, and faith that lifts life, deprived of the sense and consciousness of our nobler self? Are not childhood and youth, are not the longings, the hope and faith of childhood and youth, the exhaustless fountains of strength, courage, and perseverance in later life? Do not the words, "The heavens declare the glory of God," etc., and "Blessed is he who fears the Lord," etc., express the fundamental thought of the psalmist's life, in spite of all his errors?

Even though this was not expressed in words in his earliest life, it yet appears from his later life that it moved and lived in him even in his earliest life. And did not the first of these psalms mirror his observation of nature, and the second his observation of life?

Was not this, too, the fundamental thought in the life of the Saviour? Witness his sayings: "Consider the lilies of the field and the birds of the air. God clothes and feeds them; how much more will he care for man, his child, in all the events of life?" and "I must be about my Father's business!" Are not both

---

* A reference to skating and coasting, the boy's delight in winter.—*Tr.*

of these based upon a thoughtful observation of nature and life?

However, not only do nature and life speak to man, but man, too, would express the thoughts and feelings that are awakened in him, and for which he can not find words; and these should be given him in accordance with the requirements of his soul-development.

The relation between man and man is neither as superficial as some people suppose nor as readily communicable in its inwardness as others think. It is, indeed, of deep meaning and high significance; but its soft chords must be early cared for in the boy, though rather more indirectly and by reflection than directly in argument and precept. The direct precept fetters, hinders, represses; it drills the child and makes a puppet of him. The indirect suggestion—e. g., in the mirror of a song without moralizing applications—gives to the soul and will of the boy inner freedom, which is so necessary for his development and growth; only, here again, the outer and inner life of the boy—and this is the first and indispensable requisite—must be in full accord with it.

The more rarely and vaguely this may appear in life, the more it should be fostered wherever it is possible to do so. Even instruction that scarcely touches life—even the school, generally quite distinct from life —should foster it.

Let us enter a school-room—a school-room where instruction in this sense and spirit has just begun. Twelve or more lively boys, six to nine years old, are assembled. They know that to-day again they are to have the pleasure of singing under the guidance of their teacher. In proper order they await the beginning of the instruction, of the *lesson*, as they call it. The teacher had been called away in the afternoon; it is evening. He enters, and greets them repeatedly in song:

Good   even - ing.

This song-greeting comes unexpectedly so near their inner life that it fills them with pleasure, joy, and merriment.

Then the teacher says: "Shall I have no answer?" and sings again the same greeting. Most of them answer in spoken words, "Good evening"; some say, "Thanks"; a few say, in a more singing tone, "Good evening."

These the teacher now addresses particularly, saying, "Sing the 'Good evening' to me." Softly one sings,

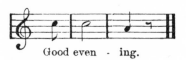

Good even - ing.

A second one, full of merriment,

Good   even - ing.

A third,

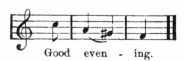

Good   even - ing.

Others whom the teacher addresses sing in about the same tone after him, " Good evening."

Then he sings to all as the first, second, etc., had answered, and has all to repeat these strains after him.

He then continues recitatively, as it were :

Bleak and win - try   is   the   sky.

"Is this true ?" he asks. "Well, then, let us sing it all together."

Again he continues :

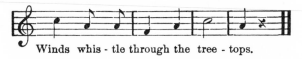

Winds whis - tle through the tree - tops.

"Is this, also, true ? Well, then, let us sing this together." Then one who feels and can express the truth of these words most fully, sings it alone.

Following the feelings awakened by the season, and expressing them in the description of the natural phenomena, the instruction proceeds in antiphonic song.

The instruction is to develop ear and voice simultaneously; it is to express the feeling in word and sound. If on the next day the external circumstances are similar to those of to-day, instruction again begins and continues similarly. At last, a lively boy, having sung the same thing again and again, asks: "May we not soon have a song about the sunshine?" This question expresses the boy's inner wish that the sun might shine again after the long-continued rain and fog and blustering wind. The teacher, responding to this feeling, sings to the boy:

Sunshine, laughing, sparkling, bright; Sunshine, laugh a-way the night.

Full of joy, all the boys repeat it together.

These first lessons have been selected here, because their topic is by no means the most favorable. Bleak, chilly fall-days, a wet and cold evening, do not call forth the inner life. The morning, the spring, a walk on a beautiful spring day, a cozy place on the slope of a hill, etc., would have been better fitted to arouse inner life. However, the boys whose expectation has been stimulated by this instruction surely will welcome only the more joyously the first clear day, revealing the fields clothed in their dress of snow, or the first clear, serene moonlit and starlit evening. Only the more fer-vently and feelingly will they sing to the new spring:

> Welcome to the warm blue sky,
> Welcome to the blossoms gay,
> Welcome grass and herbs and leaves,
> Decking fields and groves for May.

or some other suitable spring song. There are many well-known good collections of songs and small poems from which selections may be made by a teacher living in his work and filled with a sense of its worth. If these are not sufficiently simple and impressive in de-scription or representation of particular sentiments or thoughts, an attentive, thoughtful teacher can easily interpret the thoughts and feelings of the boys as well as the phases of nature in living, fitting words.

[Here follow a few quotations of songs referring to a number of varied relationships: songs in which the children view their own life (Oh, how great is our pleasure, When together we play, When alone without playmates, We are never so gay); songs in which individual life is pictured (Come, little dove, and get your food, The corn in my hand is sweet and good); songs that symbolize the life of animals (songs of birds and bees, illustrating affection and industry); songs concerning the relations of human beings to one another (songs of mother-love, of trades, of helpfulness and sympathy); etc.]

We should not forget, however, that this instruction —if, in view of its representing the child's own life, it may be called instruction—should start from the pupil's own life, and proceed from it like a bud or sprout. The boy should have the feeling, the inner life, before he receives the words or melodies. This is the essential difference between the instruction suggested here and that in which children learn mechanically small songs and poems coming wholly from without, neither arousing life nor representing it.

In general, indeed, all that was said concerning the memorizing of religious maxims—particularly at the outset—is true here.

[Like other material of instruction, songs should not at these early periods be learned for their own sake. They should come as the quasi-spontaneous expression of certain emotional conditions, as language expresses spontaneously certain intellectual states. The teacher should bring the song at the right time as her own way of expressing delight or some other feeling, should sing it to enliven the game or the work, or after a suitable story. In this way the interest of the majority of the children would be enlisted; they would get the spirit of the song, and would be able to repeat or use much, possibly all, of it after the very first time.

Of course, much depends on the character of the song and its adaptation to the child's wants. Much hinderance, too, comes from the excessive use of the piano. This instrument should not be used until the children thoroughly possess the song, so that the instrument may accompany them instead of teaching them. Because of the unavoidable inaccuracies of its intervals it is a poor teacher, but by good tempering it may be made a helpful accompanist.

The words of the song should be neither too puerile, as in " Little Bo Peep," nor beyond the child's comprehension; the pitch of the melodies should be neither too high nor, particularly, too low. The singing of scales and interval exercises should be relegated to later periods. Even, with the help of colors, these exercises are unsuitable for earlier periods, inasmuch as they give too much prominence to singing as a branch of instruction.—*Tr.*]

E. LANGUAGE-EXERCISES, BASED ON THE OBSERVATION OF NATURE AND SURROUNDINGS.

§ 93. The observation of nature and surroundings considers things merely as such with reference to their individual peculiarities and their general, more particularly local, relations. Language, as a means of observation, plays a subordinate part in this; for man observes things and forms ideas concerning them without speaking; but in instruction language comes in as an auxiliary in order to furnish tests of the extent and accuracy of the pupil's observations.

Now language-exercises, too, are connected with objects, but they consider objects with reference to their impressions on the senses, and are chiefly concerned with the designations of these things in words.

Observation of nature and surroundings is concerned with the objects themselves, language-exercises chiefly with their representation in audible speech, and particularly with practice and skill in language as a means of representation, though in intimate connection with the objects themselves. The observation of nature and surroundings asks: " What is ? " Language-exercise asks : " How does language designate that which is ? "

While the observation of nature and surroundings considers only the object as such, language-exercises consider its effect on the senses of man and the proper designation of these impressions by words. This implies at once a third field of observation, the observation of language as such and without reference to the object designated, but only as a result of the use of the organs of speech. These are *grammatical* exercises, and are based directly on the *language*-exercises.

Complete preparation for a thorough knowledge of language and thorough skill in its use implies, therefore, three things : First, the observation of the sensuous objects of language—the observation of the outer world ; secondly, the observation of language and objects in connection with one another, passing from the outer to the inner world—exercises in language ; lastly, observation of language as such, without reference to the objects designated—grammatical exercises.

The course of instruction in the observation of surroundings has already been indicated. The course of instruction in language-exercises, based on sense-observation and rising to inner perception, is the following :

The teacher begins: "We are in a room; many things are around us; name some of these things?" "Mirror, stove, book-case, etc." "Could we put other things into the room?" "Yes." "Could we put as many things into the room as we please?" "No." "Why not?" "Because there would not be room enough for them." "Why would there not be room enough?" "Because each thing takes up its own room." "Prove and illustrate that." "My hand can not be where my slate is. Where I write, my neighbor can not write at the same time. Where the stove stands, there is not room at the same time for the book-case." "What is meant, then, by saying that each thing takes up its own room?" "Where one thing is or acts, no other thing can be or act."

"In what manner and by what means do you perceive the presence and actions of things in their places?" "By my hands, ears, eyes, etc." "We call the organs by which we perceive things our eyes, ears, hands, etc., and the activities by which we do this—hearing, seeing, touching, etc.—our senses. We perceive things, then, by our senses." "How do we recognize and perceive things? Name the senses by which we recognize and perceive an object and its actions. Can we say of every object that it does something?" "Yes, and no." "Why? Name of every object around us something it does, and by which you notice it." "The mirror hangs, the sun shines, the scholar sits, etc."

[Froebel here continues in the same strain to develop successively a number of related ideas, as indicated in the subjoined translator's synopsis:

First, the fact is brought out that these things are perceived by different senses—some chiefly by sight, others by hearing, etc. Particular attention is then paid to the sense of touch as perceiving that the inkstand stands, the slate lies, etc.; and it is found that the same things may also be perceived by the sense of sight. Then objects are named which actually *stand*—the house stands, the pole stands, etc.; others of which it is said that they stand (still)—the water stands (still), the sun stands (still), etc. Then objects are named that *lie, lean, hang, sit*, etc., and others that are said to lie, lean, etc. It is found that all these activities have this in common, that they are only internal and without external motion. States of internal activity with external rest in man are then enumerated—man rests, sleeps, dreams, thinks, etc.; objects that actually *rest, sleep*, etc.; objects that show external and at the same time progressive motion—go, run, flow, fly, etc.; objects with externally visible motion without progression—heave, swell, boil, ripen, etc.; objects with external progressive motion communicated to other objects—draw, ride, lift, etc.; separating activities—cut, break, etc.; uniting activities—bind, weave, etc.; formative activities—paint, write, etc.; activities that can be seen only—shine, sparkle, etc.; activities that can be felt only—hurt, heat, etc.; that can be heard only; general activities of nature—storm, rain, etc.; objects with chiefly inner mental activity—love, hate, etc.; with reflexive activity—cut one's self, wash one's self, etc.; activities exclusively belonging to man; peculiarities of such activities.

It is then found that objects impress the senses not only by activities, but also by certain qualities; it is found that the inkstand is *round*, the pencil *long*, etc., many other actually *round* things are found; things that are said to be round—round number, round answer, etc.; the distinction between the roundness of the circle (circular) and that of the sphere (spherical) is made, and objects that have these shapes are named; from these he proceeds to cylindrical, oval, elliptical, triangular, etc., and all these impressions are united as impressions of *form* or *shape*. Similarly, broad, narrow, thick, etc., are classed as impressions of *size* or *extent;* others as impressions of *number, surface impressions, material* impressions (wooden, leaden, etc.), of *cohesion* (hard, solid, etc.), of *light* and *color*, of odor, etc.]

The observation of surroundings has already shown clearly the budding-points for the development of physics and chemistry as future distinct subjects of instruction (see § 91). Language-exercises, based on the observation of nature and surroundings, in considering the activities and impressions of objects, and their precise and accurate designation by words, must revert to physics and chemistry. They will do this the more directly, the more exhaustively the conditions and causes of those activities and impressions which result from the effects of inner forces and constituent material have been studied and the more suitably they have been designated by language. Surely the physical and chemical sides of nature-study, so important for man, will strike their roots the deeper in the pupil's interest the more this instruction has been exhaustive of essentials.

Unquestionably these sides of nature- and language-study receive too little attention in ordinary life; for this reason, and because they prepare for the study of

physics and chemistry, they should be specially considered in this instruction, otherwise the future instruction
in those sciences will have no basis; it will not be a
living branch sprouting forth spontaneously from the
tree of human knowledge, but, at best, an ingrafted
limb. Surely many whose senses and interest have not
been awakened in these directions in boyhood, but who,
nevertheless, at a later period took up these sciences,
can corroborate this.

On account of the importance of these studies, to
which these language-exercises revert again and again,
the subject is treated so much in its details. The boy
is thereby placed in the very center of the surrounding
external world, inasmuch as he studies things in the
most varied relations to one another, to man, and to
himself; thus he finds not only himself, but establishes
equilibrium and harmony between his inner mental culture and the outer world of things.

The study of number, form, and size—or mathematics—is a direct outcome of this instruction; the
budding-points (see § 91) for these are evident in what
has been indicated heretofore. For the knowledge of
number, form, and size—if at a later period they are to
be effective and fruitful in life—must needs be based on
the observation of actual space-relations.

[Froebel then continues his suggestions concerning
the course of language-lessons: "You said formerly,
'The bush is thorny,' etc." They are taught to render
the same thoughts in the form: "The bush has thorns,
the tree has leaves," etc. Then they name similar relations in which "one thing has the other thing. Man
has hands, the hands have fingers," etc.; they name

things that have a skin, scales, feathers, etc.; they are led to say where one thing has the other thing: "The tree has leaves on the branches," etc.; they name things that are at rest in some way on another thing: "The picture hangs on the wall," etc.; other relations of position (at, over, under, between, etc.) are named and variously illustrated; the name-relations of position in which one of the objects is in motion with reference to the other—the teacher comes to school, the bird flies on the tree, etc.; the two relations are compared—the picture hangs on the wall, the picture is hung on the wall, etc. He concludes the paragraph in the following words:]

The further presentation of this subject of instruction must here be interrupted for want of space. Let me merely add that, in designating these relations in language, we should proceed from the simple to the complex, and conclude with a comprehensive description or narrative exposition of actual phenomena.

F. EXERCISE IN SYSTEMATIC OUTWARD CORPOREAL REPRESENTATION, PROCEEDING FROM THE SIMPLE TO THE COMPLEX.

§ 94. Man is developed and cultured toward the fulfillment of his destiny and mission, and is to be valued, even in boyhood, not only by what he receives and absorbs from without, but much more by what he puts out and unfolds from himself.

Experience and history, too, teach that men truly and effectively promote human welfare much more by what they put forth from themselves than by what they may have acquired. Every one knows that those who truly teach, gain steadily in knowledge and insight;

similarly, every one knows, for nature herself teaches this, that the use of a force enhances and intensifies the force. Again, to learn a thing in life and through doing is much more developing, cultivating, and strengthening, than to learn it merely through the verbal communication of ideas. Similarly, plastic material representation in life and through doing, united with thought and speech, is by far more developing and cultivating than the merely verbal representation of ideas. Therefore, this subject of instruction necessarily follows the subjects just considered.

The life of the boy has, indeed, no purpose but that of the outer representation of his self; his life is, in truth, but an external representation of his inner being, of his power, particularly in and through (plastic) material (see § 23, 49).

In the forms he fashions he does not see outer forms which he is to take in and understand; but he sees in them the expression of his spirit, of the laws and activities of his own mind. For the purpose of teaching and instruction is

to bring ever more *out* of man rather than to put more and more *into* him; for that which can get *into* man we already know and possess as the property of mankind, and every one, simply because he is a human being, will unfold and develop it out of himself in accordance with the laws of mankind. On the other hand, what yet is to come *out* of mankind, what human nature is yet to develop, that we do not yet know, that is not yet the property of mankind; and, still, human nature, like the spirit of God, is ever unfolding its inner essence.

However clearly this might and should appear from the observation of our own and all other life, even the best among us, like plants near a calcareous spring, are so encrusted with extraneous prejudices and opinions, that only with greatest effort and self-constraint we give even limited heed to the better view. Let us confess at least that, when, with the best intentions toward our children, we speak of their development and education, we should rather say *en*velopment and *in*ducation; that we should not even speak of culture which implies the development of the mind, of the will of man, but rather of stamping and molding, however proudly we may claim to have passed beyond these mind-killing practices.

Those to whom we intrust our children for education may, therefore, well be full of anxiety. What shall they do?

Jesus, whom we all from innermost conviction consider our highest ideal, says: "Suffer the little children to come unto me, and forbid them not: for of such is the kingdom of God." Is not the meaning of this: Forbid them not, for the life given them by their heavenly Father still lives in them in its original wholeness—its free unfolding is still possible with them. Do we not in this, as in all that Jesus says, recognize the voice of God? Whom, now, shall the educator obey, God or man? And whom, if he could do so, shall he deceive, God or man?

God he can not deceive, and men he should not deceive. Therefore, he should obey God rather than men, and he should say distinctly that he means to obey God rather than men, and do so; he should rather not educate at all than to educate badly and in wrong directions. For God, and not prejudiced man, gives the true educator his calling; for only in all-sided, natural, and rational development of himself and his spiritual power man finds his welfare and the welfare of mankind, and every other course hinders the true development of mankind.

But just with respect to natural and rational all-sided development and representation of ourselves in external visible works, in external productive activity, our domestic education is most superficial and unsystematic; therefore, domestic education is particularly in need of schooling—i. e., induction into a natural and rational system of procedure.

The outer material representation of the spiritual in man must begin with efforts on his part to spiritualize the corporeal about him by giving it life and a spiritual relation and significance.

This is indicated in the course of development of mankind itself: the corporeal material with which the representation of the spiritual is to begin must present and distinctly declare even in its external form the laws and conditions of inner development—it must be rectangular, cubical, beam-shaped, and brick-shaped.

The formations made with this material are either external aggregations—*constructive*—or developments from within—*formative*.

Building, aggregation, is first with the child, as it is first in the development of mankind, and in crystallization.

The importance of the vertical, the horizontal, and the rectangular is the first experience which the boy gathers from his building; then follow equilibrium and symmetry. Thus he ascends from the construction of the simplest wall with or without cement to the more complex and even to the invention of every architectural structure lying within the possibilities of the given material.

Laying or arranging tablets beside one another on a plane has much less charm for the boy than placing or piling them on one another—a clear proof of the tendency of the mind for all-sided development, manifested in all his activities.

The joining of lines seems to come still later. Thus, the course of human development and culture seems to free itself more and more from corporeality, to become more and more spiritualized; drawing takes the place of the joining of concrete lines or splints; painting, the place of tablet-work; true modeling, the corporeal development from cubical forms, the place of corporeal building.

In spite of this obvious, living, progressive development from the external and corporeal to the inner and spiritual, in spite of this continuous progression in the growth of human culture, some nevertheless are inclined to doubt the utility of these exercises for children.

And yet even these could not have reached the degree of general culture they enjoy, if Providence—ruling in secret—had not led them on this very way, either without their knowledge or through their own perseverance against the opposition of their surroundings.

Man should, at least mentally, repeat the achievements of mankind, that they may not be to him empty, dead masses, that his judgment of them may not be external and spiritless; he should mentally go over the ways of mankind, that he may learn to understand them. Nevertheless some are inclined to consider these things useless in the boyhood of their children (see § 15).

Perhaps, however, it is not necessary to go so far; but you do know that your sons need energy, judgment, perseverance, prudence, etc., and that these things are indispensable to them; and all these things they are sure to get (in the course indicated), and by far more, for idleness, ennui, ignorance, brooding, are the most terrible of poisons to growing childhood and boyhood, and their opposites a panacea of mental and physical health, of domestic and civil welfare.

The course of instruction here, too, determines itself, as it does, indeed, in all cases when we have found the true starting-point, when we have apprehended the subject of instruction and grasped its purpose.

The material for building in the beginning should consist of a number of wooden blocks, whose base is always one square inch and whose length varies from one to twelve inches. If, then, we take twelve pieces of each length, two sets—e. g., the pieces one and eleven, the pieces two and ten inches long, etc.—will always make up a layer an inch thick and covering one square foot of surface; so that all the pieces, together with a few larger pieces, occupy a space of somewhat more than half a cubic foot. It is best to keep these in a box that has exactly these dimensions; such a box may be used in many other ways in instruction, as will appear in the progress of the boy's development.

The material next to this will consist of building-bricks of such dimensions that eight of them will form a cube of two inches to the side. In the former set of blocks there was the same number of each kind and length. In this set, the greatest number of blocks—at least five hundred—are of the described brick-shape and size ; in addition there are successively smaller numbers of twice, thrice, to six times the length indicated, as well as some of half the length.

The first thing the boy should learn is to distinguish, name, and classify the material according to size. During the progress of building, too, it should always be carefully arranged according to size. In the next place, all that has been produced should be carefully and accurately described by the boy—e. g., I have built a vertical wall with vertical ends, a door, and two windows at equal distances ; the bricks are placed alternately, or so that in each upper row each brick rests on and covers the ends of two bricks below.

Subsequently, a simple building with only one door may be put up ; then, the number of doors and windows is increased ; at last, partitions, another story, etc., are added.

Similar considerations control the work with tablets, although the forms are more complicated. Still greater diversity is attainable with linear splints one half to five inches long, with special reference to writing, drawing, and building.

Modeling with paper and paste-board has its peculiar progressive course.

Still more profitable, but only for those who have attained a certain degree of mental power, is the modeling of plastic soft material in accordance with the laws indicated by the cubical form. However, this, as well as the free modeling of the same material, belongs to a later part of the period of boyhood.

[In this and the succeeding paragraphs we have the first indications of the sytem of *gifts and occupations* subsequently developed in Froebel's kindergarten. Even at the date of the publication of "Education of Man," Froebel appreciated the value of simple playthings, but, as the paragraphs here translated show, his ideas on the subject were still crude. Not before 1835, he gained from some children playing ball in a meadow near Burgdorf the inspiration that *the ball* is the simplest and as such should be made the first plaything of the little child. In 1836 he had reached the first five gifts, and even among these the *second gift* lacked the cylinder, and the *fifth gift* consisted of twenty-seven entire cubes. The cylinder was added to the *second gift*, probably not before 1844, when the idea of the *external mediation of contrasts* in educational work was first clearly seen and formulated by him. In a weekly journal which Froebel began to publish in 1850, a *System of Gifts and Occupations*, similar to the one now used in kindergartens, is described. These are arranged by Hanschmann in thirty-six gifts, by Marenholtz-Bülow in eleven gifts and eight occupations, with the promise of more for advanced work. A few modifications and additions have been made since Froebel's death. So far as they seem to be in accordance with Froebel's thought, they have been embodied with the *Synoptical Table* given below. This table gives a concise description of each gift where this appeared desirable; and, in the first six gifts, a few words are added in brackets, [ ], designating in order the chief external (1) and internal (2) characteristic of the gift, and the essential lesson (3) which the gift, could it speak, is meant to teach the child.

SYNOPTICAL TABLE OF GIFTS AND OCCUPATIONS.

Gifts.

A. BODIES (Solids).

    I. [Color (1);—Individuality (2);—" We are here ! " (3).] Six colored worsted balls, about an inch and a half in diameter.—*First Gift.*

    II. [Shape (1); — Personality (2); — " We live ! " (3).] Wooden ball, cylinder. and cube, one inch and a half in diameter. —*Second Gift*

III. [Number (divisibility) (1):—Self-activity (2);—"Come, play with us (3)."] Eight one-inch cubes, forming a two-inch cube (2 × 2 × 2).—*Third Gift.*

IV. [Extent (1); — Obedience (2); — "Study us!" (3).] Eight brick-shaped blocks (2 × 1 × ½), forming a two-inch cube. —*Fourth Gift.*

V. [Symmetry (1);—Unity (2);—"How beautiful!" (3).] Twenty-seven one-inch cubes, three bisected and three quadrisected diagonally, forming a three-inch cube (3 × 3 × 3).—*Fifth Gift.*

VI. [Proportion (1);—Free obedience (2);—"Be our master!" (3).] Twenty-seven brick-shaped blocks, three bisected longitudinally and six bisected transversely, forming a three-inch cube.—*Sixth Gift.*

B. SURFACES.—Wooden tablets.—*Seventh Gift.*

I. *Squares* (derived from the faces of the second or third gift cubes).

   1. *Entire* squares (one-and-a-half in. square or one-inch square).

   2. *Half* squares (squares cut diagonally).

II. *Equilateral triangles* (length of side, one inch, or one inch and a half).

   1. *Entire* triangles.

   2. *Half* triangles (the equilateral triangle is cut in the direction of the altitude, yielding right scalene triangles, acute angles of 60° and 30°).

   3. *Thirds* of triangles (the equilateral triangle is cut from the center to the vertices, yielding obtuse isosceles triangles, angles 30° and 120°).

C. LINES.—*Eighth Gift.*

I. Straight. (Splints of various lengths.)

II. Circular. (Metal or paper rings of various sizes; whole circles, half circles, and quadrants are used.)

D. POINTS.—Beans, lentils, or other seeds, leaves, pebbles, pieces of card-board or paper, etc.—*Ninth Gift.*

E. RECONSTRUCTION.—(By analysis the "system" has descended from the solid to the point. This last gift enables the child to *reconstruct* the surface and solid synthetically from the point. It consists of softened pease or wax pellets and sharpened sticks or straws.)—*Tenth Gift.*

Occupations.

A. SOLIDS. (Plastic clay, card-board work, wood-carving, etc.)

B. SURFACES. (Paper-folding, paper-cutting, parquetry, painting, etc.)

C. LINES. (Interlacing, intertwining, weaving, thread games, embroidery, drawing, etc.)

D. POINTS. (Stringing beads, buttons, etc.; perforating, etc.)

The distinction between the *gifts* and *occupations*, though never clearly formulated by Froebel, is very important. The *gifts* are intended to give the child from time to time new universal aspects of the external world, suited to a child's development. The *occupations*, on the other hand, furnish material for practice in certain phases of skill. Anything will do for an occupation, provided it is sufficiently plastic and within the child's powers of control; but the gift in form and material is determined by the cosmic phase to be brought to the child's apprehension, and by the condition of the child's development at the period for which the gift is intended. Thus, nothing but the *First Gift* can so effectively arouse in the child's mind the feeling and consciousness of a world of individual things; but there are numberless occupations that will enable the child to become skillful in the manipulation of surfaces.

The gift gives the child a new cosmos, the occupation fixes the impressions made by the gift. The gift invites only arranging activities; the occupation invites also controlling, modifying, transforming, creating activities. The gift leads to discovery; the occupation, to invention. The gift gives insight; the occupation, power.

The occupations are one-sided ; the gifts, many-sided, universal. The occupations touch only certain phases of being; the gifts enlist the whole being of the child.

Froebel has formulated four conditions which true *gifts* should satisfy :

1. They should, each in its time, fully represent the child's outer world, his macrocosm.

2. They should, each in its time, enable the child to give satisfactory expression in play to his inner world, his microcosm.

3. Each gift should, therefore, in itself represent a complete, orderly whole or unit.

4. Each gift should contain all the preceding, and foreshadow all the succeeding gifts.

In short, each gift should, in due time and in the widest sense, aid the child " to make the external internal, the internal external, and to find the unity between the two."—*Tr.*]

G. DRAWING IN THE NET-WORK, OR IN ACCORDANCE WITH OUTWARD LAW.

§ 95. However little we may appreciate the fact or be able to account for it, the horizontal and vertical directions mediate our apprehension of all forms. We refer, however unconsciously, all forms to these directions. In our imagination we constantly draw these lines across our field of vision; we see and think according to these; and thus there grows in our consciousness a net-work of lines keeping pace in clearness and distinctness with our consideration of the forms of things.

Now form, and whatever may depend on form, reveals in various ways inner spiritual energy. To recognize this inner energy is a part of man's destiny; for thereby he learns to know himself, his relation to his surroundings, and, consequently, absolute being. It is, therefore, an essential part of human education to teach the human being, not only how to apprehend but also how to represent form; and, inasmuch as the perpendicular relations (of the vertical and horizontal) aid the development of form-consciousness, the external representation of these relations as a means for the study and representation of form is based on the very nature of man and of the subject of instruction.

Now, if the representation of the vertical and hor)

zontal directions is repeated at regular intervals, the result is a network of equal squares.

As an auxiliary form, the square very much facilitates representations in the field of vision, particularly in enlarged and reduced scales. By this fact its use is still further justified.

The use of the triangle as a help in the study and representation of form is derived, as will be seen in the course of the instruction, from the use of the square.

In the use of the square, the amount of inclination (of a line) is determined by measurable relations to the sides, but in the use of the triangle it is determined directly by its measurable relation to the perpendicular. Both find their application, and should be practiced in instruction, the latter, however, at a higher stage of development.

Another necessary requisite of instruction is not only that the form should be represented with ease, but also that the representation should be easily erased. This is met by the slate and slate-pencil. This, then, implies as the first requisite in this instruction a slate ruled in a network of equal squares.

The size of the squares, too, as will appear in the course of instruction, is by no means indifferent. If the distances between the lines are too small, the representations will appear trivial; if the distances are too great, the representations will be too large for the pupil's power of simultaneous survey; the distance of one-fourth inch is the best.

The first business of this branch of instruction is to exercise the pupil with the help of this ruled slate in the clear representation and, consequently, perception of

the chief fundamental relations of form and extent.
The course of instruction itself is connected with former
corporeal perceptions; where the boy—as was shown
particularly in the previous paragraph—learned to distinguish different lengths.

Thus, this branch of instruction, too, as will be
shown in the course of instruction to be sketched directly, is connected with those previously considered;
for, as has been said before, there should be no break
anywhere in the instruction, nothing should stand detached and isolated; but, like life itself, all things together, in the living union of cause and effect, should
constitute an inwardly connected whole.

The course of instruction is as follows:
In one of the grooved sides of one of the squares
the teacher draws a line of the length of this side (one-
fourth inch), and says as he draws the line: "I draw a
vertical line." Then he asks the pupil: "What did
I do?" The pupil answers: "You have drawn a
vertical line." "Draw now a row of such vertical lines
across the slate." When this has been done to the
teacher's satisfaction, he continues: "What have you
done?" "I have drawn many vertical lines," the pupil
answers. When several pupils are instructed simultaneously, the teacher, after examining the work of
each, may ask them in common: "What have you
done?" "We have," etc.

On account of their varied usefulness, these questions
and answers should never be omitted in this branch of
instruction; for man is to translate the representation
into word and thought, and interpret word and thought

in the representation—this essentially constitutes his humanity.

[Froebel now continues similarly—drawing and asking questions—with lines of two, three, four, and five times the length of the first, and then goes on:]

By drawing the lines themselves in the network, the pupil strengthens and liberates his hand, as well as his powers of perception and representation.

Since, for the purposes of perception and memory, the *comparison* of dissimilars is more profitable than that of similars, vertical lines of the different lengths are then drawn side by side with the customary comments and exercises.

The instruction does not here pass beyond the five-fold length, because with the number *five* all subsequent numerical differences are at least indicated. In fact, these differences are indicated already in the numbers one, two, and three, inasmuch as these contain odd, even, square, and cubic numbers; and nearly all these relations are repeated in the series one to five, and thus become sufficiently clear for the purposes of representation. Besides, six is only three doubled or two trebled, and seven in this respect is similar to five; so that these and all subsequent exercises do not go beyond five.

In these comparative arrangements of lines, a num ber of variations may be made to suit the needs particu· larly of weaker pupils. Thus, the lines may have their upper or lower ends lying in the same horizontal line; in either case, the shortest or the longest line may be drawn first on the right or on the left. Such variations are quite useful, particularly where it is desirable to avoid ennui by presenting the same exercise under different forms; yet their use should be left to the teacher.

[*Translator's Synopsis.*—In a similar way the horizontal lines are worked through. Then vertical and horizontal lines are combined and compared; for this purpose it is thought best to have the two kinds of lines meet in a point. These combinations may be made in different directions, as shown in these figures: ⌊ ⌋ ⌈ ⌉. It is suggested that, in order to facilitate comparison, the longer lines should always include the shorter ones, thus:

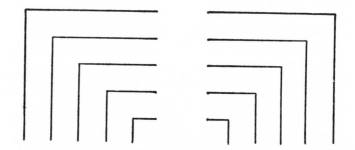

Subsequently, the vertical and horizontal lines differ in length, one being made two, three, etc., times the length of the other; or one half, one third, etc., of the other. Considerable stress is laid on this genetic difference: when the shorter line is drawn first, the longer line appears as a multiple of the shorter; when the longer line is drawn first, the shorter appears as a part of the longer.

These exercises are followed by the drawing of *squares* and *oblongs*. In the latter, the distinction between "long" and "high" oblongs is emphasized; in the former, the horizontal dimension is greater, in the latter, the vertical dimension is greater.

Then follow exercises in the drawing of diagonals, the chief purpose of which is "the clear perception and accurate representation of the inclination." In the combinations, a number of characteristic terms help these developments. The diagonal of a square has the *full slant;* that of an oblong, in which one side is one half the other, has the *half slant,* etc. Slanting lines that are nearer the horizontal side of the oblong are said to be *falling;* others that approach more the vertical side are said to be *rising.* In the exercises, he begins with lines of full slant drawn outward from a common center in all directions, then inward toward a common center; then follow lines of half-slant, etc., and combinations of these, exercises with the falling slant preceding those with the rising slant. At first the outlines of the corresponding squares and oblongs may be drawn, but gradually these are omitted. Another important differentiation lies in the radiation of the slanting lines from a common center, and their symmetrical grouping around a common center, which is the center of a *figure* inclosed by the slanting lines.]

At this point we reach an entirely new stage of drawing, which indicates at the same time a new stage of development in the pupil—the stage of *invention,* of the spontaneous representation of linear wholes with the help of all the lines lying within the law of the network.

Invention is every spontaneous representation of the inner in and by the outer, adapting itself to given external conditions, yet obeying an inner necessity easily recognized by the pupil himself.

The presentation of a course of study for the invention of figures is reserved for the next scholastic stage. Similarly, the presentation of the variously developing influence of this instruction on true human culture must be reserved for the latter part of a presentation of instruction in drawing as a whole.

Only he who has used this course of instruction, not only with others but also with himself, can truly appreciate its nature and effect. Indeed, this is the case with every kind of instruction which aims deliberately to awaken energy and life and to give skill and dexterity of representation.

For the purposes of self-development and of the development of others, at least in essentials, these indications will, however, suffice, especially for him who follows the course step by step, applying it to himself, and who thus finds within himself its simple law.

The use of this instruction would supply one of the greatest wants of our schools in town and country, and should be introduced in them all. Every intelligent person who looks into the matter will clearly see this; for this instruction addresses itself equally to the senses, and through them to the power of thought, and to external manual activity. Thus, it avoids ennui and lack of occupation so pernicious to those from whom the teacher's attention is called away for a time. So much for the school; but in addition to this it teaches the eye a knowledge of form and symmetry, and trains the hand in representing them; and these find much to do in all relations and activities of practical life. Indeed, we have heard of late many impressive complaints concerning the great disadvantages resulting to our citizens, more particularly to the artisan and farmer, from the lack of development in the perception and representation of form and symmetry.

H. STUDY OF COLORS; COLORING OF OUTLINE-PICTURES; PAINTING IN THE NET-WORK.

§ 96. Every one who is not a total stranger to boy-life will concede that children, particularly in early boyhood, feel the need of a knowledge of colors and of some degree of occupation with pigments.

This must be so. It is implied even in the general cause of all activity in the child, in the tendency to develop and exercise all his powers in all possible particular phases. This is strengthened by a second reason, even weightier, so far as the inner spiritual development as such is concerned—by the intimate connection between color and light, by the fact that all colors are determined by greater or smaller degrees of light.

Color and light again are most intimately connected with life-activity, with all that lifts and varies life. Even mere earthly light points to the heavenly light to which it owes its being and existence.

Thus, the boy seems to notice or feel the high significance of color (as he did in another respect of form in nature) as an embodiment, as it were of earthly light, of sunlight, as a visible revelation of its nature. The hope of thus obtaining with the aid of the colors an insight into the nature of earthly light, of sunlight, is possibly the true, innermost, though sub-conscious, motive of the boy in his eager occupation with colors; indeed, the experience of boys positively corroborates this.

It is said, indeed, that colors are variegated, and that it is this variegation that attracts children and gives them pleasure.

Very well; but what is variegation of color? Is it not the effect of one cause (light) in various phases of appearance (colors)?

It is by no means external variegation that attracts the boy and gives him pleasure, for the possession of external variegation does not satisfy him, as, indeed, mere quantity never satisfies him; the pleasure lies in the finding of the inner connection, in the power to spiritualize it. If it were otherwise, the boy would be satisfied when he is surrounded with an abundance, and a variety of things, and we should not so often hear the reproof addressed to him: "What in the world do you still want; you have this and this and this, and yet you are not satisfied."

The boy seeks unity of life, expression of life, connection of life—life, indeed. Therefore, variegation of color interests the child; he is looking for unity in diversity, for inner connection. For this reason he likes to see colors in their combinations, in order to find the inner unity that makes them one.

Yet, in spite of the high significance of this tendency in boyhood, we leave its development toward the knowledge and use of colors to merest chance.

We give the boys, among many other things, also, paints and brushes, as one gives food to beasts, inconsiderately or good-naturedly; and they throw them about like their other playthings, as the beasts do unsuitable food.

What, indeed, should they do with them? They

do not know how to give them life and unity; and we do not help them.

However distinct and different form and color may be, to the young boy they are undivided, united, like the body and its life. Indeed, the idea of color seems to come to the boy, as it did possibly to mankind generally, through form; and, conversely, the forms are brought out and nearer through colors. Therefore, the notions of color and form should at first be united and undivided.

Now, since form and color at first appear to the boy as an undivided whole—but mutually enhance and reveal each other—it is necessary in the development of the color-sense in man by means of observation and representation to consider three things:

1. That the forms should be simple and definite, wholly adequate to the things to be designated and represented.

2. That the colors be as pure and distinct as possible, and corresponding with those of the object, particularly if it be a natural object.

3. That the colors should be studied as nearly as possible in their actually natural relations, in their differences and resemblances.

As the colors themselves should be studied as definitely as possible in their impressions, they should, too, be designated with equal definiteness in language: first, the color as such—e. g., red, green, etc.; then its intensity—e. g., dark, bright, etc.; then the variety of color according to kind and mixture. In the last, two phases are noticed: first, a comparison with objects that show the color most frequently—e. g., rose-red (*rosenroth*), sky-blue, etc.; secondly, a comparison of colors among themselves—e. g., green-yellow (*grün-gelb*), or, approximately, greenish yellow, etc.

Generally, all color distinctions should be based on natural objects in which these colors prevail most constantly; if they have been understood, they may be transferred to the colors of other objects.

Colors, whose names are derived from objects, should have been observed frequently in the objects themselves —e. g., violet-blue.

In the beginning, only a few distinctions are made, but these should be adhered to strictly and constantly. Similarly the boy should receive for use only a few, but clearly defined, colors. The secondary colors should, later, as far as possible, be made by the pupil himself from the primary colors.

The figures to be painted should, particularly in the beginning, not be too small, and if possible point to natural objects, as indeed all instruction should start from objects in the pupil's surroundings—e. g., leaves, large flowers, wings of butterflies, even birds. The colors of quadrupeds and of fish are too indefinite.

However, the effort to represent natural objects in their peculiar colors will direct the pupil's attention more and more to their actual colors, as is indicated by questions like these: "How shall I paint the trunk of this tree, this flower," etc.?

The more the notions of colors are separated from objects, the more it will become desirable to represent the colors for their own sake, but still in definite forms.

When colors come to be viewed wholly independent from form, form steps wholly into the background. The form of representation, for a number of practical reasons, is based on the square network.

The coloring material is best chosen from the vegetable pigments.

The instruction itself is easily connected with the boy's life; a hundred opportunities present themselves; every circle offers its own peculiar starting-points. Properly conducted, the instruction will take root in the children's life, and will itself live.

I shall write down what I saw and see. The more favorable the circumstances, the better the beginning; however, circumstances may not be made but only used.

About a dozen boys of suitable age are gathered around their teacher like sheep around their shepherd. As the shepherd leads his sheep to green pastures, so the teacher is to lead the boys to joyous activity. It is Wednesday afternoon, when there is no ordinary school instruction; but to-day there is no call for other activity. It is fall, and the desire to paint has often been expressed by each one of these active boys. Perhaps fall invites the boys most urgently to paint, because the colors in nature are most varied and massive in the latter part of fall; and each one has probably tried in his own way to obey the summons.

" Come, let us paint," the teacher says. " It is true, you have painted a great deal; but painting itself and the things you painted did not seem to please you long, for you did not paint in distinct and pure colors. Come, let us see if we can not do better together." " Now, what shall we paint? What is easy enough for us?

For we are to learn, and what we paint should be simple, and of one color if possible."

Teacher and pupils decide quickly that it is easiest to paint leaves, flowers, or fruits. Leaves are chosen; for the beautiful, bright red, yellow, etc., trees, and the gorgeous leaves which in perfect fall days float with a gentle rustle from the branches, and deck the ground with a brilliant carpet, have been keenly noticed by the boys, and often they have bound them in wreaths and brought them home.

"Here are outlines of leaves" (the teacher had prepared them for the purpose); "how will you paint them?" "Green." "Red." "Yellow." "Brown." "Which leaves will you paint green, red, etc.?" "Why?"

The teacher then distributes the paints, properly prepared. First, the colors are correctly designated. It need, however, scarcely be mentioned that—inasmuch as the representation of the object is the secondary, and the knowledge and treatment of the colors the primary consideration—we can not expect to do more than to give the leaves approximately exact coloring. For the present, even distribution of the color, keeping within the lines, etc., are as yet the most important concerns; the proper position of the body, in order to insure free movement of arm, hand, and finger, is a matter to be attended to, of course.

Inasmuch as each pigment requires its own treatment, we do not pass from one color to the next until the pupil has attained some proficiency in the use of the former.

From leaves we proceed to flowers. We choose flowers with large monopetalous corollas of only one or a few very distinct colors—e. g., blue campanulas, yellow primroses, etc. Simple flowers are preferred to double ones, and they are first painted in full front view or full profile.

We should constantly keep in view conscious efforts to distinguish colors as accurately as possible, to represent them in the greatest possible purity, and to name them as clearly as possible; although at this stage of development these things will still be done quite imperfectly. The pupil's feelings are awakened, and he aspires to understand the relation of one color to another. Thus color is more and more abstracted from form, and may be observed more and more independently. The pupil, too, begins to take more interest in each color, and seeks to enter fully into its character; for he wants to control it, and feels the inadequacy of his present knowledge and skill.

This calls for the representation of colors as such, without essential reference to form, in figures derived from the network.

The first consideration in these exercises is to paint the surfaces evenly and sharply, progressing from smaller to larger surfaces. Therefore, we first paint with each color surfaces of one square, then of two to five squares, either continuous (i. e., in rows touching each other edge to edge) or interrupted (i. e., in rows touching each other corner to corner). By this procedure, the pupil becomes thoroughly familiar with the peculiarities and treatment of each color.

These exercises begin with pure red, blue, and yellow; they conclude with the pure secondary colors, pure green, orange, and violet.

The series begins with red and green, because experience teaches that these two colors are most interesting to boys.

Similarly, in the subsequent exercises, two, three, and finally all the six colors are used in continuous (edge to edge) or interrupted (corner to corner) series—in two principal arrangements—so that either the long sides of the colored forms or their short sides touch. The order of the colors most fully in accordance with nature at large is now from blue to green, yellow, orange, red, and violet.

The last phases at this stage of development are four color-groups, similar to the two line-groups in the drawing of lines. These are derived in accordance with one law from the thing itself, and present the series of colors in all directions implied by the network with reference to some given center.

These four color-groups appear again in two sets. Either the various equal-colored rectangles touch one another at their long sides, appearing in horizontal or vertical position sharply defined, or the various colored series, lying in the direction of the diagonals of the squares, the component squares touching only in the corners, fit into one another (like the teeth of two saws).

In each of these sets there are two members. In one of these, the various series proceed from a visible center; in the other, they are arranged around an invisible center, or, rather, inclose it.

These four groups close the course at this stage. The next stage would comprise—as in the case of the invention of figures in drawing—the free invention of color-groups, the study of colors in their various degrees of intensity and tint, and the study and representation of natural forms in the square network.

However limited the preceding course in this subject, experience proves that it has quite an influence on the scholar. Like song, it lifts man into a nobler moral atmosphere, quickens the color-sense, and enhances interest in nature and life. Its further connection with other subjects, as well as with practical life, will be clear to him who appreciates the requisites of these things.

I. PLAY, OR SPONTANEOUS REPRESENTATIONS AND EXERCISES OF ALL KINDS.

§ 97. To the many things said about play, I would add the following: The plays or spontaneous occupations of this period of boyhood differ in three ways. They are either imitations of life and of the phenomena of actual life, or they are spontaneous applications of what has been learned at school, or they are perfectly spontaneous products of the mind, of any description, and with all kinds of material. The last either seek the laws lying in the material of the play, and adapt themselves to these, or they obey laws lying in the thought and feelings of the human being. In every case, however, the normal plays of this period are the pure outcome of vital energy and buoyancy (see § 49).

The plays of this period, therefore, imply inner life and vigor—an actual external life. Where this is lacking, there can not be true play which, itself full of genuine life, can arouse, feed, and elevate life.

This explains the remark of a young man who had been zealous and inventive in these plays of boyhood.

He said, concerning some boys that seemed to have lost all zest for such plays: "It is strange to me that these boys can not play; how vigorously we played at this age!"

This shows clearly that even the plays of this age should be under special guidance, and the boy made fit for them—i. e., his life at school and out of it should be rendered so rich that, like a swelling bud, it will burst forth from within for joy and in joy. Joy is the soul of every activity of boyhood at this period.

The plays themselves are physical plays, either as exercises of strength and dexterity, or as the mere expressions of buoyancy of spirits; sense plays, exercising hearing, sight, etc.; or intellectual plays, exercising reflection and judgment.

[In the hands of thoughtful kindergartners, the social game has become a powerful aid in the guidance of social development. The children learn to use the several games as it were like common playthings, with the help of which they may, as a social body, give expression to their collective ideas on matters of social concern.

The teacher, for this purpose, does not teach the game in a certain fixed way, *using the children,* as it were, to carry out the intentions of the game. Indeed, were she to do this, each child would in an individual way, and without reference to others, learn to play the game as he would a lesson, and then lose active interest in it. She plays the games at first quite simply, sometimes at the table, sometimes in the ring, teaching the children how to represent the simplest things she may find in their minds concerning the subject involved. Subsequently she progresses quite gradually, adding from time to time new facts and relations, gained by observation or instruction, frequently modifying the games in order to represent the various facts from new standpoints or in more complex relationships.

This will induce and encourage the children in due time to bring to bear in their plays the results of their own observations, and to suggest modifications and additions in accordance with their growing knowledge and interest. Thus the game will grow with

their growth in social insight and power, and will become an adequate expression of their inner development in this direction.—*Tr.*]

J. NARRATION OF STORIES AND LEGENDS, FABLES AND FAIRY TALES, ETC.

§ 98. Man understands other things, the life of
others, and the effects of other powers only in so far as
he understands himself, his own power, and his own
life. Therefore, the highest and most important experiences of a boy of this age (as well, perhaps, as of
man generally) are, the sensation and feeling of his
own life in his own breast, his own thinking and willing, though they manifest themselves ever so vaguely
and almost as a mere instinct.

But knowledge of a thing can never be attained by
comparing it with itself. Therefore, too, the boy can
not attain any knowledge of the nature, cause, and
effect of the meaning of his own life, by comparing his
own transient individual life with itself. He needs
for clearness concerning this, comparison with something else and with some one else; and surely every-
body knows that comparisons with somewhat remote
objects are more effective than those with very near
objects.

Only the study of the life of others can furnish such
points of comparison with the life he himself has experienced. In these the boy, endowed with an active
life of his own, can view the latter as in a mirror, and
learn to appreciate its value.

It is the innermost desire and need of a vigorous,
genuine boy to understand his own life, to get a knowledge of its nature, its origin, and outcome. If he fails
in this, the sensation of his own life either crushes him

or carries him on headlong, without purpose and irresistibly.

This is the chief reason why boys are so fond of
stories, legends, and tales; the more so when these are
told as having actually occurred at some time, or as
lying within the reach of probability for which, however, there are scarcely any limits for a boy.

The power that has scarcely germinated in the boy's
mind is seen by him in the legend or tale, a perfect
plant filled with the most delicious blossoms and fruits.
The very remoteness of the comparison with his own
vague hopes expands heart and soul, strengthens the
mind, unfolds life in freedom and power.

As in color, it is not variegated hues that charm the
boy, but their deeper, invisible, spiritual meaning; so he
is attracted to the legend and fairy tale, not by the
varied and gay shapes that move about in them, but by
their spiritual life, which furnishes him with a measure
for his own life and spirit, by the fact that they furnish
him direct intuitions of free life, of a force spontaneously active in accordance with its own law.

The story concerns other men, other circumstances,
other times and places, nay, wholly different forms; yet
the hearer seeks his own image, he beholds it, and no
one knows that he sees it.

Are there not many persons who have seen and
heard how children at an earlier period asked their
mother again and again to tell them the simplest story,
which they had heard half a dozen times—e. g., the
story of a singing and fluttering bird, building its nest
and feeding its young?

Even boys do the same. "Tell us a story," is the

request of a crowd of eager listeners to some companion who has proved his art. "I do not know any more; I have told you all I know." "Well, then, tell us this or that story." "I have told it two or three times." "That makes no difference; tell it again." He obeys; see how eagerly his hearers note every word, as if they had never before heard it.

It is not the desire for mental indolence that leads the vigorous boy to the telling of stories and makes him a pleased listener. You can see how eager he is, how a genuine story-teller stirs the inner life of his hearer, to try its strength, as it were. This proves that a higher spiritual life lies in the story, that it is not its gay and changing shapes that attract the boy, that through them mind speaks directly to mind.

Therefore, ear and heart open to the genuine story-teller, as the blossoms open to the sun of spring and to the vernal rain. Mind breathes mind; power feels power and absorbs it, as it were. The telling of stories refreshes the mind as a bath refreshes the body; it gives exercise to the intellect and its powers; it tests the judgment and the feelings.

Hence, too, genuine, effective story-telling is not easy; for the story-teller must wholly take into himself the life of which he speaks, must let it live and operate in himself freely. He must reproduce it whole and undiminished, and yet stand superior to life as it actually is.

It is this that makes the genuine story-teller. Therefore, only early youth and old age furnish good story-tellers. The mother knows how to tell stories—she who lives only in and with the child, and has no care beyond that of fostering his life.

The husband and father, fettered by life, compelled to face the cares and wants of daily life, will rarely be a good story-teller, pleasing to the children, influencing, strengthening, and lifting their lives.

The brother or sister, only a few years older, both still unacquainted with life in its stern realities, not yet fettered or hardened by it, still standing outside of it, as it were; the grandfather, with his wide experience, raised superior to life, having rid himself of its hard exterior; or the old tried servant, whose heart is full of contentment in the consciousness of duty well done— these are the favorites with an audience of boys.

No practical application need be added, no moral brought out; the related incident of life, in itself, in whatever form it may appear, in its causes and consequences, makes a deeper impression than any added words could do; for who can know the needs of the wholly opened soul, of stimulated, wholly self-conscious life.

We do not tell our children enough stories; at best, little stories whose heroes are mechanical contrivances, puppets which we have whittled or stuffed ourselves.

A good story-teller is a precious boon. Blessed is the circle of boys that can enjoy him; his influence is great and ennobling; the more so, the less he seems to aim at this. With high esteem and full of respect I greet a genuine story-teller; with intense gratitude I grasp him by the hand. However, better greeting than mine is his lot; behold the joyful faces, the sparkling eyes, the merry shouts that welcome him; see the blooming circle of delighted boys crowd around him, like a wreath of fresh flowers and branches around the bard of joy and delight.

However, boys of this age are benefited by mental ctivity, especially in connection with physical action. Therefore, the roused and stimulated inner life should at once find an external object on which it can manifest and, as it were, perpetuate itself.

Therefore, with boys of this age, the hearing of stories should always be connected with some activity for the production of some external work on their part.

Again the story, in order to be especially effective and impressive, should be connected with the events and occurrences of life. One of the least significant occurrences in the neighbor's life is developed to-day into an event of such importance that it determines not only his inner peace, as well as his external prosperity, but influences also the life of many others.

Whatever similar experience lies in the scope of the life of each individual, or may have happened to his friends, is connected with this event of the day. Behold how the attention of each boy, under the influence of inner excitement, is wholly given to the event in question. Every story seems to him a new conquest, a fresh treasure; and whatever it shows and teaches he adds to his own life for his advancement and instruction.

K. SHORT EXCURSIONS AND WALKS.

§ 99. Out-door life, in open nature, is particularly desirable for young people; it develops, strengthens, elevates, and ennobles. It imparts life and a higher significance to all things. For this reason, short excursions and walks are excellent educational means, to be highly esteemed even in the beginning of boy- and school-life (see § 64).

If man is fully to attain his destiny, so far as earthly development will permit this, if he is to become truly an unbroken living unit, he must feel and know himself to be one, not only with God and humanity, but also with nature.

The feeling of oneness, in order to become a unit in himself, must be developed early in man. He must feel the connection between the development of nature and of man, between the phenomena of nature and of humanity in their mutual relations—e. g., the different impressions made on the same human being, by external natural causes and by internal human causes, so that man may appreciate as fully as possible the character and phenomena of nature, and that she may ever more become to him a guide to higher perfection.

All shorter and longer excursions and all observations they involve should be made in this spirit of harmony, unity, and living oneness of all natural phenomena, and in the conviction how necessarily, because of the nature of life and force as such, unity comes from multiplicity, simplicity from complexity, that which in its impression is great from the apparently small.

Therefore, all boys are in such a hurry to get forward on their excursions; they desire quickly to take in a great unit. The search for details is the more interesting the more fully a relatively greater unit has been previously grasped, though this need by no means be the greatest possible whole.

These excursions should enable the boy to see as a whole the district in which he lives, and to feel that nature herself is a constant whole.

Without this, excursions would yield no direct spiritual benefit. They would repress instead of quickening; they would waste instead of enriching life.

Man considers the surrounding atmosphere as a part of himself, and gains bodily health by inhaling the pure air. Similarly he should look upon surrounding nature as a part of himself, and breathe in the Divine Spirit that dwells therein.

Therefore, the boy should early see the objects of nature in their actual relations and original combinations. His excursions are to show him his valley in its whole extent; he should explore its ramifications; he should follow his brook or rivulet from its source to its mouth, and study its local peculiarities in their causes; he should explore the elevated ridges, so that he may see the ranges and spurs of the mountains; he should climb the highest summits, so that he may know and understand the entire region in its unity.

Actual inspection should reveal to him the mutual relations of mountain and valley and river in their form and formation. He should see in their native places the products of mountain, valley, and plain, of the earth and of the water; he should in the higher regions seek the former homes of the stones he found in the fields and river-beds of the lowlands.

In these excursions the boys should see the animals and plants in their life, as it were; they should observe them in their natural abodes, some basking in the sun and drinking in light and warmth, others hiding in darkness and shade, seeking coolness and moisture. They should seek to determine to what extent the abode and food of living things affect their color and even their form ; how, for instance, the caterpillar, the butterfly, and other insects, in form and color, are connected with the plants to which they seem to belong. He should not fail to notice how this external resemblance serves to protect the animals, and how higher animals almost intentionally make use of such resemblances ; how, for instance, certain birds build their nests on trees whose color is scarcely to be distinguished from that of the nests ; how, indeed, the color-expression of animals harmonizes with the character of the time of day when they are most active, or with the activity of the sun—e. g., the brilliant colors of butterflies, the dull colors of moths, etc.

This direct and independent observation of the things themselves, and of their actual living connection in nature, and not the mere explanation of words and ideas which are of no interest to the boy, should awaken in him, vaguely at first but ever more and more clearly, the great thought of the inner, constant, living unity of all things and phenomena in nature.

In these excursions he should see man, too, in his unity with nature—first, in his daily life, his occupations and callings, later in his social circumstances, his character, his mode of thought and action, his manners, customs, and language.

However, this should be left in actual life, as well as in our hints on the subject, to later stages of development in boyhood and youth.

In considering the means of instruction, directly implied in man's tendency of development, as well as the method of instruction thereby conditioned, we were confronted clearly and distinctly, as necessarily proceeding from the observation of the external world and from language-exercises, by the demands for the study of number, of forms of speaking (grammatical exercises), of writing and of reading; we found, too, indications of the points from which these particular subjects proceed naturally.

Inasmuch as these subjects of instruction, according to their nature, have to be taken up later than those which we have treated, and not before the subjects on which they depend have been carried to a certain point, their special consideration has been postponed, so that all the others might first be fully presented.

But the subjects named belong to the second half of the period of boyhood under consideration. Therefore, their special treatment must now be taken up.

L. ARITHMETIC.

§ 100. The development of number, the abstraction of number ideas from objects, and the growth of skill in counting, at least up to ten or twenty—these things have been clearly presented and often employed in the previous considerations (see §§ 38, 75).

This varied use of number soon presents to the pupil the necessity of a more thorough, more comprehensive and varied knowledge of number, and he welcomes arithmetic as a special subject of instruction with pleasure as a needed help.

This is right. No new subject of instruction should be brought to the pupil unless he at least feels vaguely that it is based and how it is based on previous work, how it is applied in this, and that it satisfies a mental need.

Number, in its forms of multiplicity and size, reveals to the first glance the property it shares with many things, particularly with things of nature, the property of a double origin—from without by accumulation, and from within by growth or development.

But, as it shares with objects of nature their mode of origin, so it shares with them also the property of transiency, of annihilation; and this, too, shows itself in two phases, that of destruction from without, and that of dissolution from within.

Wherever there is a beginning and a ceasing, increase and decrease, there is also comparison; and, of course, again, a merely external and a more internal comparison, a comparison according to an externally visible law, and another according to an internally perceptible law.

Thus arithmetic will have to consider the increase, diminution (annihilation), and comparison of numbers each according to an outer and an inner law.

The intimate connection between number and nature and their laws, as just indicated, is so prominent in our time, which is entering so thoroughly into the study of nature, that a natural and rational study and treatment of number forced men even fifteen years ago to accept the terms inorganic and organic formation, diminution and comparison of numbers (*vide* Joseph Schmid's "Number," 1810).

Arithmetic, as well as all instruction, should meet not only the feeling, early aroused in the boyhood of man, that natural laws prevail in many ways in human life, thought, and action, but also the feeling that there is a living and necessary conformity to law in all things; therefore, it should constantly direct the attention to the laws of number, render them prominent, and enable the pupil to see them clearly.

The prominence and the vivid and varied perception of numerical laws on the one hand, and practice in the quick comprehension and understanding of numerical relations on the other, are both equally important and should receive equal attention. The pupil at this stage should not only be quick in numbers, but should readily see and understand numerical relations. Therefore, it is most desirable in this as in all similar instruction to secure clear comprehension by means of self-active representation of the quantities; practice and repeated application; surveys of the whole subject; the prominent bringing out and discussion of particular points.

The course of instruction is indicated in these words, and can be easily prepared. For this reason, and because Joseph Schmid's arithmetical method is quite widely known and followed, I limit myself to only a few hints in the following :

[*Translator's Synopsis.*—Froebel first (1) bases the work on previous knowledge; for this purpose he suggests exercises in counting forward or backward, continuously or with omissions from one to twenty. He next (2) presents the numbers from one to ten as a con-

tinuous whole. The pupils count from one to ten,
making at each number as many vertical lines as the
number indicates, in vertical arrangement, thus:

I

II

III, etc.

This is followed by general exercises, fixing the relation between the word and the number. Pointing to
the marks they have made, they say, starting with the
word or numeral: One is one one, two is two ones,
three is three ones, etc. Starting next with the number,
they say: One one is one, two ones are two, three ones
are three, etc. Considering, at last, the number ab-
stractly, they say: One is one, two is two, three is
three, etc.

In the third place (3) are exercises distinguishing the
odd and even numbers. Reading through the column, all
say: One is neither odd nor even; two is an even number; three is an odd number, etc. Froebel adds here
by way of parenthesis: "It is well to direct the pupil's
attention here at once to a great far-reaching law of
nature and of thought. It is this, that between two
relatively different things or ideas there stands always
a third, in a sort of balance, seeming to unite the
two. Thus, there is here between odd and even numbers one number (one) which is neither of the two.
Similarly, in form, the right angle stands between the
acute and obtuse angles; and in language, the semi-
vowels or aspirants between the mutes and vowels.
A thoughtful teacher and a pupil taught to think
for himself can scarcely help noticing this and other
important laws."

He then has the pupils to represent with lines all the even numbers from two to ten, again in vertical arrangement, and has this learned as the natural order of even numbers in ten. The same is done with the odd numbers. As soon as some pupils have represented the series on their slates, the teacher represents it on the blackboard, and fixes it by pointing to certain numbers, and having the children designate their places in the series, etc.

This is followed (4) by exercises in addition. In the first exercise, the pupils add I to each number of the first ten (I and I are II), by which they obtain the series from two to eleven; in the second exercise, they add I to each even number in the first ten, obtaining a series of odd numbers; in the third exercise I is added to each odd number. Then follow similar exercises with the addition of II, III, etc., and an exercise in which to each number is added the succeeding number in the series, yielding a table in vertical arrangement: I and II are III, II and III are IIIII, etc., up to nineteen.

Then follow exercises in the addition of three and more numbers, proceeding in every case deliberately and thoroughly, and not exceeding thirty in the sums; and at last the consideration of special questions, such as: What is the sum of all numbers from 1 to 10? What is the sum of all even numbers between 1 and 10? What is the sum of the first and last numbers in the series 1 to 10? Of the second and last but one? etc.

In the fifth place (5), he presents exercises for the study of compound numbers. The pupils are taught to look upon each number of the series 1 to 10 as a unit, a whole. Teacher and pupils read their table: One (I) is a

simple unit, two (II) is a compound unit, etc. They
represent a number of twos, threes, etc., on the slate.
They make a series of all the twos from one two [1 (2)]
to ten twos [10 (2)], and read this in a variety of
ways—e. g., one two (II) is neither an odd nor an even
number of twos; two twos (II II) is an even number of twos; three twos (II II II) is an odd number of
twos, etc.

Then follow (6) exercises to represent numbers in
all possible forms—e. g.: Two as two ones (I I) or as one
two (II); three as one three (III), one two and one one
(II I), three ones (I I I), etc. Froebel lays stress upon
the foreshadowing of an important law, which is, however, merely to guide the teacher at this stage of the
work, and whose development with the pupils is left to
a subsequent stage. He formulates this law as follows:
"Every number always gives twice as many combinations (including those differing merely in the arrangement of component numbers) as its predecessor in the
series; or, the number of combinations of the component parts of any number is obtained if two (2) is
raised to the power indicated by the number in question less one—e. g.: 4 yields 2^{4-1} or $2^3 = 8$ combinations."

Subtraction (7), or the diminution of the number
from without, is carried on similarly.

For multiplication (8), or the development of the
number from within, Froebel starts again with the
series of numbers from 1 to 10. The pupil is then required to take each number once, or "as often as one
has units," obtaining a vertical arrangement like the
following:

I , I , I
II , I , II
III , I , III etc.

This is read in a variety of ways, as : II taken as often as I has units gives II ; or, II repeated in the law of I gives II ; or, two increased by the law of I gives II ; or, II taken I time (once) gives II ; or, II I time (once) gives II ; or, II times I is II. In this way, a variety of multiplication tables are made and read, and a number of arithmetical laws developed.

Similarly (9), the squares of the numbers and their roots are found and fixed; then (10) all possible combinations in which a number may be obtained through multiplication are studied—10 is 10 (1), 1 (10), 2 (5), 5 (2) ; this is followed by division (11) and measurement, and the comparison of numbers (12 and 13) in accordance with their outer and inner law.]

M. FORM-LESSONS (GEOMETRY).

§ 101. As formerly indicated, the observation of the outer world and language-exercises already led to the consideration and study of form. Yet the objects of the outer world usually exhibit form in such variety and complication, and their forms are so difficult to analyze and define, that the study of form itself always leads to the consideration of objects with simple forms, to objects bounded by simple planes with equal and right angles.

A knowledge of any form always implies ultimately a knowledge of lines, and forms are examined and determined through the mediation of straight lines. Therefore, in the study of objects with reference to their form, curvilinear objects are soon laid aside, and rectilinear objects at first chosen—e. g., *curved* are the surface of a cylindrical stove, a watch-glass, the rim of an inkstand; plane and *straight* are the jambs of the doors and windows, the window-sash, the frame of the looking-glass.

Again, objects as well as their parts and outlines are considered with reference to their position and direction—e. g., the two long and the two short pieces of the window-frame are respectively *parallel;* a long and a short piece of the window-frame are respectively *perpendicular*, etc.

[*Translator's Synopsis.*—Similar material for study is afforded by the table-legs and other parts of the table, the sides, floor, and ceiling of the room, etc. The consideration of these complex rectilinear objects is followed by the consideration of simple rectilinear objects —cubes, prisms, pyramids, etc. When, through these exercises, linear outlines have been made clear, the pupil feels the need of studying the linear relations as such. This study begins with the consideration of single lines with reference to their relative directions; it then proceeds to combinations of lines as to number of points in which they meet, and to their direction with reference to the points of union. This is followed successively by the study of angles, of polygons, and at last of the circle. For lack of room and of cuts, Froebel does not present the details of the course, but promises to do so in the discussion of a later stage of development, a promise that was never realized. He insists, however, that at the present stage attention is to be given to frequent representation of figures, and the actual examina tion of forms, rather than to the formulation of general truths; that complicated relations and complex inferences should be avoided; and that each form-relation should be studied independently, but in as many figures as possible, and in quite simple and familiar combinations. In conclusion, he points to the fact that the study of lines of equal inclination leads from form to free-hand drawing.]

N. GRAMMATICAL EXERCISES.

§ 102. We turn now again to a wholly different side of instruction. The subject of form-instruction is visible, permanent; the subject of language is audible, transient. Thus the two objects are direct opposites, complementing each other, and therefore belong together. The form represents the object; language, too, tends to represent and picture the object.

It was the purpose of the language-exercises to secure correct and clear ideas of the things of the outer world, and to have them represented precisely and definitely by language. The grammatical exercises are concerned with language as material of representation, with exercises leading to the knowledge and correct use of this audible material, and with the study and practice of the manner in which man with the aid of his organs of speech seems to create and form this material.

Therefore, grammatical exercises consider the *word* as such irrespective of the thing it designates; their purpose is to give the pupil a knowledge of language considered as material.

This leads necessarily to the formerly indicated connection of language, particularly of the original word and its parts with the objects and their qualities, to the study of the contrasts and resemblances between language and object: it leads to *etymology* as a new subject of instruction.

[*Translator's Synopsis.*—Froebel here maps out the following succession of points for the course of study. The first consideration is the size of the word, which is determined by the number of its *syllables;* this is followed by the consideration of vowels, which form the constant element of syllables. The vowels are simple or complex, and the former again are primitive or derivative. This leads to the observation of the use of the organs of speech in producing the various vowel-sounds, and shows that the purity and distinctness of the sound depend on the proper position and shape of the cavity of the mouth, etc. Then follows the study of the *consonants*, which are first classed as *mutes* and *sonants;* and then grouped as *nasals, labials, linguals, dentals, palatals, gutturals*, etc. Lastly, the different degrees of intensity of force required in the production of the various consonants are noted. Thus the pupil gradually finds that clear pronunciation and speech imply the proper use of the organs of speech, and gains conscious control of these.] There is, too, developed in him the feeling of an inner living connection that unites the activities of the mind, of the body, and of nature, for language as a mental product through the activity of the body furnishes him satisfactory representations of his inner and outer worlds.

[*Translator's Synopsis.*—The next section of this paragraph contains a few suggestions for carrying out this course. Teacher and pupil first speak words of one, then of two syllables, etc., slowly, deliberately separating the syllables, accompanying each syllable with a clap of the hands, and then following up the pronunciation of each word with the number of claps of the hand indicated by the number of syllables—e. g. :

Teacher or { says: foot . . . one } or { win-dow . . . one, two } etc.
pupil { claps: (—) . . . (—) } { (— —) . . . (—) (—) }

Froebel attaches importance to the clapping with the hands, which makes the *audible* separation of the word *visible* in the clapping on the teacher's part, and *sensible* in the clapping on the pupil's part.

In order to direct the pupil's attention to the vowels, Froebel would have the teacher and pupil pronounce successively and together monosyllabic words ending in vowel-sounds, and after each word speak the vowel-sound separately—e. g. : *me — e, he — e,* etc. Then words are found that begin with this sound (eel, each, east, etc.) ; then words that contain the vowels (bead, read, etc.). Subsequently the fact is brought out that there are no monosyllabic words that do not contain some vowel ; polysyllabic words are similarly examined ; the prevalence of certain vowels in certain syllables is found ; the succession of certain vowels in the same word is observed ; the sonants and mutes are similarly studied, etc. Finally, tables of the various classes and groups of sounds are prepared, and a number of exercises are made giving ready control of these tables in the formation of words.

The next requirement that forces itself upon our attention in this instruction is the art of *writing,* by

which the "audible and transient sounds are made
visible and permanent."]

§ 103. [*Translator's Synopsis.* — By this Froebel
does not mean penmanship as an art, but merely the
skill to write legibly. For the beginning he suggests as
most suitable the capital Roman letters, because their
forms please children, and because they can be readily
made with the help of the horizontal, vertical, and slanting lines with which the child is already familiar.

In the course of instruction he begins with the letter
I (sounded E in German), carefully analyzing its form
and lines; then follow N, M, E, U, O, A, etc. The intro
duction of each new letter is followed by the writing of
as many combinations with previous letters as will yield
true words. "The most important point is that at every
step the pupil should apply the newly learned letter and
combine it with formerly learned letters in as many
ways as possible."

From monosyllables he proceeds to polysyllables;
then the children are taught to write words and short
sentences by dictation or otherwise. At this point he
recommends that all that has been written on the slate
should subsequently be copied on paper. This enables
the teacher to correct the work; to let pupils whose
work has been corrected correct that of others; and
leads to considerations of orthography. He concludes
the paragraph in the following words:

When the pupil has reached the skill to represent in
this way all the notions and ideas he possesses, and thus

to represent his inner life, as it were, the purpose of this branch of instruction is accomplished; for the *center*, the universal *fulcrum*, the *human* being has been found, and the possibility of the representation of his innermost soul at this period of development has been secured, as by means of lines in drawing, by means of colors in painting, by means of plastic material in modeling, so here by means of words—transient in speech and permanent in writing. Thus, every stage of instruction should in a certain sense form a complete whole, a complete representation of the human mind; it should render possible the representation of some complete (external) whole with reference to man and in its relation to his mind.

The fact that the pupil is required to copy on paper the corrected representation of his own thoughts or observations printed by him on his slate soon leads him to see the use and feel the need of a more rapid mode of writing. At this point, the writing in script appears as the new subject of instruction, meeting a want which the pupil himself feels. It is the business of every form of instruction in its respective stage to arouse in the pupil a keen and definite feeling of the need of the next stage. The business of instruction in this succeeding stage is then to meet this need as promptly and as fully as possible according to the requirements of sound mental development.

In these two simple and important points, current methods of instruction are still quite deficient, as well as in other matters indicated in what has been said. It is the business of pedagogics to reveal these deficiencies beyond all doubt, and at the same time to indicate a course of instruction which avoids these faults and shows a better way.

P. READING.

§ 104. [*Translator's Synopsis.*—Reading is the converse of writing. They are opposites, like giving and taking; and as taking implies giving, as, strictly speaking, one neither should nor can truly take who has not before given, so also in this case reading should follow writing. The course of instruction is implied in the nature of things. In fact, the boy can already read; the writing of every word was followed by its reading, and in the copying exercises this was specially practiced; so that reading in the ordinary sense now becomes quite easy, and the task of a year may be accomplished in a few days.

The first thing to be done is to show the equivalence of the small Roman letters to the capital letters heretofore employed; and to do this in such a way that the resemblances between the two kinds of letters may be seen even in their details. As a connecting exercise, Froebel recommends that the pupil copy passages from the reader in his usual capital letters, thus comparing the two styles of letters.

The point to be reached at this stage is correct reading in pronunciation and punctuation, so that he may be able to understand the writing of others, and test the thoughts and feelings of others by what he himself has thought and felt. Higher, more expressive reading is relegated to the next stage of development.]

VII.

CONCLUSION.

§ 105. Thus we have sketched the growth and development of man in all their phases and conditions from the first origin of his being and existence to the first years of boyhood. We have, too, surveyed in a general way in their living inner connection, their necessary mutual dependence and natural ramifications, the important means by which man may be and should be developed in this period in accordance with the requirements of this period and of his being, if his goal is perfection.

If we now survey all that has been determined and said so far in this connection, we see that many phases in the life of boyhood have as yet no specific, definite direction. Thus, the work with colors does not in any way mean to develop a future painter, neither is the work in singing intended to train a future musician. These occupations simply have the purpose to secure in the young human being all-sided development and unfolding of his nature; they furnish in a general way the food so necessary for mental growth; they are the ether in which his spirit breathes and lives in order to gain strength and scope, inasmuch as the mental tend-

encies which God has given him, and which irresistibly
unfold from his mind in all directions, will necessarily
appear in great variety, and must be met and fostered
in a corresponding variety of ways.

Therefore, we ought at last to understand that we
do great violence to boy-nature when we repress and
supplant these normal many-sided mental tendencies in
the growing human being; when, in the belief of doing a service to God and man, and of promoting the
future earthly prosperity, inner peace, and heavenly
salvation of the boy, we cut off one or the other of
these tendencies and graft others in their places.

God neither ingrafts nor inoculates. He *develops*
the most trivial and imperfect things in continuously
ascending series and in accordance with eternal self-
grounded and self-developing laws. And God-likeness
is and ought to be man's highest aim in thought and
deed, especially when he stands in the fatherly relation
to his children, as God does to man.

We should consider, at least with reference to the
education of our children, that the kingdom of God is
the realm of the spiritual, and that consequently the
spiritual in man, and therefore in our children, is at
least a part of the kingdom of God. For this reason
we should give our attention to the *universal* cultivation
of the spiritual in our children, to the pure cultivation
of the specifically human, which is the divine in individual manifestation; for we may well be convinced
that whoever has been cultivated to genuine humanity
is also educated for every particular requirement and
need in civil and social life.

Many will say: "This is all very well for earlier

periods, but our sons are too old for this—they are
already in the last quarter of boyhood. What can they
do with this general and rudimentary instruction?
They need something definite, something that bears
directly on their future vocation; for the time is near
when they will enter practical life, when they will have
to earn their own living or help us in our business."

It is true, our sons are rather old for what they are
still to learn. But why did we not, when they were
children and in early boyhood, supply the needs of
their minds? Are the boys now to lose this development and cultivation for their whole lives?

We may console ourselves with the illusion that
when our boys have reached adult life they will have
enough leisure to make up their losses.

Fools that we are! Our own soul refutes this, if
we will but listen to what it says and study its meaning.
Here and there a few things may indeed be retrieved;
but, in general, whatever of human education and development has been neglected in boyhood will never be
retrieved.

Shall we, men and fathers, and perhaps mothers, too,
not at last be frank, and cease to conceal from ourselves
the never-healing wounds and the permanently callous
places in our disposition, the dark spots left in our souls
by the ruthless extirpation of noble and elevating
thoughts and feelings in the days of our misguided
youth and boyhood? Shall we never see that noble
germs were at that time broken and withered, nay,
killed in our souls? And shall we not heed this for our
children's sake?

We may fill an important office, we may have an

extensive professional practice, we may have a lucrative business, we may be expert and energetic, we may possess a high degree of social refinement ; but can all this keep us, when we are alone, from seeing the flaws and faults of our inner culture? Can it destroy in us the feeling of incompleteness and imperfection chiefly due to our early education?

Therefore, even though our sons have reached the third or fourth stage of boyhood, if we would have them become competent, full men, and if they have not yet learned and unfolded what their age implies, they must necessarily return to the work of childhood and early boyhood, in order that they may yet do what can be done and retrieve what can be retrieved.

Possibly our sons may thereby finish school-life a year or two later ; but is it not better that they should thereby attain a worthy aim rather than (by a more expeditious course) an illusory one?

We claim to be practical men, and we fail to understand the requirements of genuine, true, practical life. We claim to be business men, and we vaunt our prudence and foresight, yet we do not comprehend the business that concerns us most, and prudence and foresight fail us where they are of so much impor tance.

We boast of our wealth of experience of life, and yet where it would yield delicious fruit we seem to possess so little.

We disdain altogether to examine our own youth from which we might learn so much that would benefit our children. Yet this admonition, too, to turn back and observe our own youth and to keep our soul fresh and warm in eternal youth, lies in the words of Jesus: " Become as little children."

Indeed, much that Jesus said to his time and contemporaries, our inner spirit now says to us and to our time. What was said at the time of Jesus, and more particularly with reference to the beginning of a wholly new view of life, is now again spoken, as it were, to all mankind, and finds its application in all human relations with reference to the endeavors of man to attain a higher stage of human perfection. Thus, we are now told: " If you will not fulfill in yourselves and in your children the spiritual requirements of childhood and boyhood, if you will not secure this for yourselves and your children, you will not attain what in the happiest, most blissful periods of your life caused your soul to swell with hope, what your heart yearned for in the noblest hours of your life, what lifts and ever lifted the souls, what fills and ever filled the hearts of the noblest human beings."

When we concentrate in one point the elevation of culture which the human being has attained by the developing education so far discussed, we find quite definitely the following: The boy has reached the point of divining his independent spiritual self ; he feels and knows himself as a spiritual whole. There has been aroused in him the ability to grasp a whole in its unity and in its diversity, as well as the ability to represent outwardly a whole as such and in its necessary parts, to represent in and through outward diversity his own self in the unity and diversity of his being.

Thus, we find the human being even at the earlier stages of boyhood fitted for the highest and most important concern of mankind, for the fulfillment of his destiny and mission, which is the representation of the divine nature within him.

To secure for this ability skill and directness, to lift it into full consciousness, to give it insight and clearness, and to exalt it into a life of creative freedom, is the business of the subsequent life of man in successive stages of development and cultivation. To discuss ways and means for this, and to introduce these in the practice of life, is the purpose of a continuation of this work and of the author's life.

SYLLABUS OF
FROEBEL'S EDUCATION OF MAN.

Pages 1 to 39.

1. EDUCATION defined by the law of divine unity.
2. The knowledge to which education should lead man.
3. Free self-activity the essential method in education.
4. The relations existing between teacher and pupil conditioned upon the law of right, not upon despotic authority.
5. Unity, individuality, and diversity the phases of human development.
6. Self-control to be fostered from infancy, and willfulness to be guarded against.
7. The earliest religious influence in the development of child nature.
8. The several stages of childhood, boyhood, and manhood to be duly respected in their order.
9. The various powers of the human being to be developed by means of suitable external work.

Pages 40 to 93.

10. A parallelism between the development of the individual and that of the race.
11. Process and order of the development of the senses.
12. Line of separation between infancy and childhood.
13. Nature and value of the child's play.
14. Importance of due attention to matters of food and clothing.
15. The aim of parental care is to arouse to full activity all the child's physical and mental powers.

16. The child's early efforts at investigation of proper-ties.
17. Value of the early attempts at drawing.
18. Early knowledge gained from association with the older members of the family.
19. Line of separation between childhood and boyhood.

Pages 94 to 127.

20. Boyhood is the period for learning on the child's part; for training on the part of parent and teacher.
21. To strengthen and direct the will is the essential work of the school.
22. The true basis of right will culture lies in the proper activity and firmness of the feelings and of the heart.
23. The family is the type of true life and the source of active interest in all surroundings.
24. Importance of wisely nurturing the formative in-stinct as manifested in the child's efforts to assist in work.
25. The early adventures of the boy are in quest of knowledge, and they result in parallel develop-ment of power.
26. The games of boyhood educate for life by awaken-ing and cultivating many civil and moral virtues.
27. The love of story and of song are further manifes-tations of right mental activity, and should be utilized to the child's development in knowledge and power.
28. The evil characteristics so often manifested in boy-life have been developed by neglect of right tend-encies and by arbitrary and willful interference with right activities.

29. The true remedy for any evil is to find the original good quality that has been repressed or misled, and then to foster and guide it aright.

30. Much harm is done by attributing wrong motives to deeds that were mere results of impulse without any due appreciation of consequences.

Pages 128 to 139.

31. The purpose of the school and of its work is to give to the child the inner relations and meanings of what was before merely external and unrelated.

32. However inefficient the teacher may be, the child naturally comes to him with a spirit of faith and hope.

33. The *intensive* power decreases and the *extensive* power increases in passing from youth to old age.

34. Errors in dealing with these powers result in serious and permanent harm.

35. The essential work of the school is to associate facts into principles, not to teach isolated facts.

36. The personality and the surroundings of the child constitute the essential subjects of school instruction.

Pages 140 to 187.

37. Religion defined in respect to three distinct and harmonious phases.

38. Religious instruction must assume the pre-existence of some degree of religion as its basis of reception and influence.

39. The unity of God and man is illustrated and demonstrated in the observation and experience of man in his personal relations.

40. Only so far as we comprehend the spiritual in human relations, and live in accord therewith, can we attain to full conception of the relations between God and man.

41. The purpose of all existence in the world of nature is the revelation of God.

42. In the development of the inner life of the individual man the history of the spiritual development of the race is repeated.

43. Parents and teachers should lead children into familiarity with nature and into recognition of God in nature.

44. Active force is the ultimate cause of every phenomenon in nature.

45. Matter and force mutually condition each other, so that it is impossible to think of one without the other.

46. The sphere is the outward manifestation of unimpeded force, diffusing itself freely and equally in all directions.

47. The crystal represents the action of force unequally or in different directions.

48. The various crystalline forms may be traced in necessary order of development from the simplest to the most complex.

Pages 187 to 229.

49. The relations of life forms to crystalline forms.

50. Relations of the number five in plant forms to the numbers two and three.

51. Manifestations in the diversity and progressive changes of plant forms of the peculiar nature of the inner living force.

52. Illustration in progressive animal forms of the mutual interrelation of the external and the internal.

53. The law of unity, traced through all manifestations of force, from the simple crystal formation to the spiritual life of man.

54. The essential matter in the study of nature is the observation of objects and their attributes irrespective of any ability to give accepted names.

55. The contemplation of nature leads necessarily to the recognition of God.

56. Mathematics constitutes the needed starting-point and guide in the study of the diversity of nature.

57. Mathematics should be treated physically, and mathematical forms and figures should be considered as the necessary outcome of an inner force acting from a center.

58. Language, the third element of education in correspondence with religion and nature.

59. Language, considered as primarily a complete organism, with its word elements bearing necessary relations to objects and attributes named.

60. The rhythmic law of language should be regarded in the early speech training of the child.

61. Writing and reading grow out of the self-active desire for expression, and should be taught with special reference to this fact.

62. Art and the appreciation of art constitute a general talent, and should be provided for in the education of all youth.

Pages 230 to 250.

63. The union of school and family influences essential to right education.

64. By the co-operation of home and school the right development of inner life should accompany the acquirement of external knowledge.

65. The unity of thought and purpose between parent and child may be maintained and strengthened during the school period.

66. The inner experiences and forces of mind and heart should be specifically cared for and developed.

67. Religious instruction should appeal to the immediate inner life rather than to hope of reward or fear of punishment hereafter.

68. Religious maxims should be memorized as expressing common experiences.

69. Direct training as to care of the body and use of the limbs is essential.

70. Physical training should involve in due time a knowledge of the bodily structure and a high regard for its true welfare.

Pages 251 to 265.

71. The knowledge of things found in their local conditions and in their relations.

72. The first objects to be presented in the right course of instruction are the ones that are near and known as directly related to the child.

73. Every particular branch of instruction has its proper place of development from the earlier subjects of instruction.

74. In the study of plants, animals, etc., the work proceeds from particulars to generals, and again from generals to particulars in varied succession.

75. After the study of natural objects the works of man are to be presented.

76. From natural objects and the products of man's effort the study should proceed to include the relations of mankind.

77. The prime purpose throughout is not to impart knowledge to the child, but to lead the child to observe and to think.

Pages 265 to 332.

78. The relations of nature and of life are to be interpreted largely through the medium of song and poetry.

79. So far as may be, the exercises of this class should grow out of immediate conditions and circumstances.

80. Observation lessons and language work, as pertaining to the affairs of ordinary life and as a basis of systematic science studies.

81. Development and culture come from work done rather than from ideas acquired.

82. By means of the several kindergarten gifts and occupations the constructive and formative faculties are to find expression.

83. Instruction in drawing begins with representation and comparison, and proceeds into invention.

84. Color work should deal with simple forms in pure and distinct colors.

85. Colors should be studied in their natural relations, in their differences and resemblances.

86. The right development of the color sense lifts man into a nobler moral atmosphere and adds interest to nature and life.

87. Spontaneous play is the outcome of vital energy and buoyancy, and, under the guidance of the teacher, may be utilized in social development.

88. Stories and fables are necessary as furnishing a basis for the comparison of transient experiences.

89. The several ordinary branches of school study belong to a later period of education than do those modes of instruction already considered.

90. The general purpose of family and school instruction is to advance the all-sided development of the child and the complete unfolding of his nature.

THE END.